DATE DUE			

AMERICAN

FEDERALISM

RICHARD H. LEACH

Department of Political Science, Duke University

W · W · NORTON & COMPANY

New York · London

ISBN 0 393 05402 0   *cloth*
ISBN 0 393 09881 8   *paper*

Printed in the United States of America

6 7 8 9 0

To Christopher Alan Leach

PRINCETON CLASS OF 1973

CONTENTS

PREFACE

NOT LONG AGO, the Canadian political scientist J. Murray Beck addressed himself to recent developments in Canada, entitling his remarks "Canadian Federalism in Ferment." He suggested that federalism in Canada was at a point of crisis. Although there is no single focal point of crisis in the United States such as Quebec provides in Canada, the same title and conclusion are appropriate to American federalism. The American federal system is currently beset with problems, and much of the future of the United States depends upon how and what solutions are adopted for them.

Federalism is a vast and complicated subject, yet it comprises only one aspect of American government. To master it completely and to understand its linkage with the other strands of the American political fabric are projects for a lifetime, if that long would be enough. But some grasp of the major characteristics of federalism is essential for even a rudimentary understanding of the American political and governmental process.

In the first three chapters of this book, attention is centered on theoretical aspects of federalism, on the impact of federalism on the use of power in the United States, and on focal points of power in the federal system. The fourth chapter describes one field of extensive governmental activity—education—and suggests some of the difficulties the federal system poses for operation at the program level there.

In succeeding chapters four critical areas in American federalism are examined in some detail: weaknesses at the state and local level, the problem of governing metropolitan areas, the problem of administration, and the problem of finances. It is in these areas that most efforts to improve the federal system are now being concentrated.

The final chapter deals with federalism in the future. If there is anything sure in the world of politics, it would appear to be the certainty that the American federal system will continue to be used as the basic container for American government. Federalism does not always work smoothly, but it has pleased Americans and served them well. What form will American federalism take in the future? What forces might cause it to change and in what direction? Can something wholly new be expected or will whatever evolves be an adaptation of what has gone before? These are some of the questions considered in the closing chapter.

The main point to make at the outset is a simple one: a thorough understanding of the phenomenon of federalism is not a promised outcome of the reading you are about to begin—nor, in all honesty, can it be promised by any single source. At best, the reader will leave these pages more aware of the complexity of federalism and more concerned to continue to read and learn about it than he otherwise might have been.

The literature on federalism in general and American federalism in particular is voluminous and rapidly increasing. Fortunately, W. Brooke Graves, formerly of the Library of Congress, is now preparing for publication a definitive bibliography of that literature. No attempt has been made here to duplicate Graves's work. Nor in fact can the author claim to have read all the entries therein. Some of what he has read appears in the footnotes of the book, and they must satisfy as a bibliography until Graves's book appears.

Despite the voluminous literature of federalism, there still is a crying need for more research into all aspects of intergovernmental relations. State and local government has too long been relegated to the chimney corner of American political science. Too little careful and selective attention has been paid to intergovernmental cooperation in the United States to make possible reliable predictions about the future. Solid data on many aspects of the subject are simply not available. Certainly the increasing pattern of federal-private relationships in such enterprises as COMSAT, nuclear research and production, and defense bear close study and assessment, and not by case study alone. Likewise the literature on federal-local and inter-local relations needs to be enriched. The gap between popular understanding of federalism and the actual intergovernmental facts of life is especially wide and must be bridged.

I want to thank Dr. Graves for his willingness to let me see his bibliography in draft and for the many times he has given me help and information. I should also like to thank Reverend Francis Canavan for his incisive and corrective ideas. I am indebted to Bruce E. Langdon for his help in preparing the material for part of Chapter IV and to Charles Hoffman for his assistance in getting some of the data together for Chapter V.

RICHARD H. LEACH

Villa Serbelloni, Bellagio, Italy, April 1968
Durham, N.C., May 1969

AMERICAN

FEDERALISM

I

FEDERALISM AND THEORY

FEDERALISM has been a subject of controversy in American government and politics since the beginning of the Republic. It continues so today. For it is at the center of American governmental action. It is, as the late Morton Grodzins wrote, "a device for dividing decisions and functions of government . . . It is a means, not an end." [1] It ordinarily involves two major levels of government, each, at least in democratic societies, assumed to derive its powers directly from the people and therefore to be supreme in the areas of power assigned to it. Each level of government in a federal system insists upon its right to act directly upon the people. Each is protected constitutionally from undue encroachment or destruction by the other. To this end, federalism entails a point of final reference, usually a judiciary. The people in federal systems are held to possess what amounts to dual citizenship. Sovereignty, in the classic sense, has no meaning; divided as power is, the element of absoluteness which is essential to the concept of sovereignty is not present. Federalism is concerned with process and by its very nature is a dynamic, not a static, concept. In operation, it requires a willingness both to cooperate across governmental lines and to exercise

1. Morton Grodzins, "The Federal System," Ch. 12 in *Goals for Americans. The Report of the President's Commission on National Goals* (Englewood Cliffs, N.J., Prentice-Hall, 1965), p. 265.

restraint and forebearance in the interests of the entire nation.
Although federalism is used in other nations, the United States
is regarded by many students as the archetype of a federal system. Thus when Australia set about to federate in 1901, it turned
to the United States for a model. Even general definitions of the
term seem to derive from the American model. That model, however, was not purposely constructed but evolved out of circumstances peculiar to the emerging American nation. First of all, had
we been settled by other than English colonists, had we been subjects of other than English kings, it is unlikely that federalism as
we know it now would have developed. A strong feeling of local
autonomy prevailed in seventeenth-century England. At the level
of the town and shire, the English people had since Saxon days
been accustomed to self-government locally, and by the 1600's,
when American colonial settlement began, both the feeling for
local autonomy and its practice were carried over intact to the
colonies. The colonists from the outset were thus practicing for
federalism.

Federalism took root as well in the working relationship that
evolved between the English Crown and government and the colonies during the colonial period. Isolated geographically from
England, the colonies were tied governmentally to the mother
country only loosely, and the nature of the ties varied from time
to time and from colony to colony. Nor was a successful attempt
ever made to rationalize and formalize the relationship. A system
of divided power inevitably evolved under the circumstances, and
its practice for a period of over one hundred and fifty years set it
too deeply in the habits of the people to be overturned upon independence.

In the second place, the development of federalism was at
least suggested in the several different sets of relationships which
grew between the units of government in the colonies themselves.
Although difficulty of transportation and communication made
these relationships hard to develop, there were a number of issues
—defense against the Indians and against foreign powers (the
New England colonies feared expansion by the Dutch, for example), and, later, offense against Great Britain itself—which lent
themselves to intercolonial action and solution. The New Eng-

land Confederation, formed in 1643 and dissolved in 1684, is the best-known example of cooperation among colonies, but it was very likely not the only one. (There is no definitive history of intergovernmental relations in colonial times.) There were, of course, a number of disputes over boundaries, which resulted in a certain amount of intercolonial conflict.

At first, colonial towns and the colonies were virtually synonymous, but as population grew, other centers were established outside the main villages, so a set of relations began to develop between each colonial capital and other local centers. For practical reasons, a good deal of local autonomy continued to be allowed town government; there was little of the administrative supervision from the capital that prevails today.

Thus, a general pattern of intergovernmental relations, already tested and fairly well known, was ready to be used to ease the transition from colonial to independent status. The relations between the colonies and the imperial government in England could be converted into a relationship between a new central government of the United States and the governments of the thirteen states. The relations between the several colonies, between them and local units, and, to the extent there were any, relations between local units, could be carried over pretty much intact to relations between the states and between them and their subdivisions of government.

It should be noted finally that American federalism is the product of a specific situation in American history. The Articles of Confederation, which went into effect in 1781, were an instrument of revolutionary freedom rather than of union. Conceived in the spirit of liberty, they did not provide for the exertion of power necessary to hold the colonies-turned-states together. In many respects the Articles set up a system like that created in the modern world by the Charter of the United Nations, with state sovereignty given the same primacy that national sovereignty has in the Charter. The Articles provided for little more than a debating society, in which the debate became increasingly unrelated to the pressing needs of American society. By 1785–86, the new nation was approaching a crisis. The power vacuum created by the Articles had been filled by the state governments, each acting independently and with little regard either for the nation as a whole or for a strict adherence to the principle of limited government. Delinquency in meeting Congressional requisitions under the Articles for money and troops during the Revolutionary War was only their first contribution to the crisis. Several states issued depreciated paper currency, which had disastrous consequences for creditors. With no effective safeguards to protect them in state law, the propertied classes began to search for ways to protect their interests. Together with those who were concerned over the lack of power in Congress, as Alexander Hamilton was, they combined to demand an occasion to review the national situation and to devise ways of meeting its exigencies. The result of their joint concern was the calling of the Annapolis Convention of 1786 and of the Philadelphia Convention of 1787.

The Philadelphia Convention constitutes one of the best-known chapters of American history and so does not need any lengthy discussion here.[2] The delegates to the Convention were by and large from among the most eminent men in America. If not quite the demigods Jefferson later proclaimed them to be, they were as well qualified as any group could have been to undertake their difficult task. For over three months the delegates wrestled with the two major proposals put before them—the Randolph (Virginia) Plan submitted in behalf of the large states, and the Paterson (New Jersey) Plan offered in rebuttal by the small states. What they produced is a remarkably practical document. They agreed through the Connecticut Compromise on a two-chamber Congress. Representatives in one house would be chosen on the basis of population and in the other on the basis of equality of the states. They agreed on a single executive with largely undefined power and on the creation of a system of federal courts to interpret and enforce laws and treaties of the United States, if not to exercise the function of judicial review of state and federal legislation which some called for in the Convention. They set up a system of checks and balances among the three branches of government and were careful to make provision for

2. See Max Farrand, *The Framing of the Constitution of the United States* (New Haven: Yale Univ. Press, 1913); Carl Van Doren, *The Great Rehearsal: The Story of the Making and Ratifying of the Constitution of the United States* (New York: Viking Press, 1948).

future amendment of the Constitution they were devising. Finally, they made the Constitution of the strengthened Union both law and supreme, "Anything in the constitutions or laws of any State to the contrary notwithstanding." All of these agreements were set into brief and concise statements, and together they form the explicit backbone of the Constitution.

With federalism, it was quite a different story. None of the framers went to Philadelphia determined to create a federal system. Some went to try to secure a stronger center of power in the United States to serve pressing public needs; others went determined to protect the states against that very centralization. They were agreed on a few basic principles: that government power is a potential threat to individual freedom and therefore must be restrained and limited in its exercise; that power divided is power inhibited; and that power inhibited is tyranny prevented. And most of them were pluralists by long habit, they and their English ancestors having been accustomed to a number of small units of political, religious, economic, and social organization. But they were far from certain where acceptance of these principles would lead them in the quest for a stronger union. As Grant McConnell has observed, "The founders of the American federal system were . . . not entirely clear in their intentions. What they created was partly an inheritance from their recent past, partly a pragmatic compromise of contemporary issues, in which different men among them saw different virtues." [3]

Of necessity, whatever they devised had to take into account two opposed forces. There were forces which drove Americans apart from one another—state patriotism; long and distinct state histories; the vested interests of state political leaders; the variety of economic interests pursued by the states; the religious and cultural differences among them; and the real difficulties of transportation and communication up and down the land. But there were also forces which tended to pull Americans together—the fact that state leaders had worked together to achieve independence; the slowly developing idea of "Americanism"; the desire for better trade relations among the states and with foreign powers; the

3. Grant McConnell, *Private Power and American Democracy* (New York: Knopf, 1967), p. 92.

common language, social background, and values of most of the people; a common legal structure; and the feeling that in a stronger bond among them lay their safety from foreign aggression.[4]

What sort of system would take into account all of these factors and still result in a workable whole? The framers had few places to look for help in their dilemma. They knew of course of the examples of antiquity and of Holland [5] and Switzerland, but none of these offered much that was applicable to the American situation. In the final analysis, they had only their own experience and background and their strong theoretical orientation toward limited government to guide them in their deliberations. As it turned out, these were enough. To what degree each of these contributed to the form and substance of federalism as it emerged from the Convention it is impossible to say. All of them contributed. To attempt, therefore, to make federalism appear to be the product of one or another theoretical concept—or the result of some particular historical force or of accident—is to ignore the facts of the case.

Unfortunately the facts cannot be proved by recourse to the Convention debates, for the Convention did not actually debate federalism at all. The Virginia Plan, which served as the basis for discussion in Philadelphia, assumed the continued existence of the states at the same time that it proposed an extensive enlargement of the powers of the central government. A careful reading suggests (1) that that plan proposed to solve the dilemma created by having two levels of government by giving Congress the power to define the extent of both its own authority and that of the states, and (2) that the authors of the Virginia Plan had not thought much about its implications for a multilevel system of government. The closest to a theoretical discussion the Convention came was in a Committee of the Whole session just after the Virginia Plan had been presented. Gouverneur Morris suggested and Edmund Randolph offered a resolution that no "Union of the

4. For a fuller exposition of these points, see Loren P. Beth, "The Supreme Court and American Federalism," *Saint Louis University Law Journal* 10: 376 (Spring 1966).

5. See William H. Riker, "Dutch and American Federalism," *The Journal of the History of Ideas* 18: 495–518 (October 1957).

States merely federal" would be sufficient. Rather, "a national government ought to be established consisting of a supreme Legislative, Executive and Judiciary." The resolution was adopted, with only Connecticut voting in the negative. Before what was meant by the resolution could be developed in debate, however, the representatives of the small states offered a counter-proposition based on quite different precepts. They had listened to the discussion of the Virginia Plan with mounting dismay at the centralization of power it visualized and now were ready to present an alternate plan which amounted to little more than a strengthening of the Articles of Confederation. The New Jersey Plan called for an expansion of the powers of Congress and would have made all treaties and acts of Congress the supreme law of the land in the several states, enforceable in state courts; but it would have retained the principle of equality of states in Congress and made the proposed national executive directly subject to the control of the states.

Though it thus appears that the stage was set for a lengthy and revealing debate on federalism, in fact such a debate did not materialize. Instead, the energies of the Convention were devoted to solving the problem of reconstituting Congress, which was, after all, the central item at issue between the proponents of the nationalistic Virginia Plan and those who favored the state-oriented New Jersey Plan. That problem was eventually resolved by the fashioning and adoption of the Connecticut Compromise. From then on (it was already early July, the Convention had been in session since May 25, and it was becoming clear to everyone that an end to deliberations would soon have to be called), the Convention turned to a series of practical matters—the form and powers of the executive branch, the proper construction of the judicial system, the devising of a workable amendment process—and it never came back again to the question of the nature of federalism. In the end, the Constitution emerged with no real clues as to what was in the framers' minds as they voted on the several resolutions before them or how they expected the federal system they had brought into being to work in practice.

The reasons the framers avoided what now seems to be such a vital question are not hard to imagine. The very necessity for compromise in getting the Constitution drawn up and promulgated virtually ruled out an exhaustive excursion into theory. The framers were agreed on the need for a limited government; they saw the possibilities of federalism in this connection. But they also saw the dangers of going beyond that point of general agreement into the thicket of theoretical niceties which lay just on the other side. So they avoided theoretical considerations and advanced in their place the more utilitarian matter of preserving the union. They set about to produce an instrument of action.

For the Constitution is above all a practical document. Its main purpose was to provide a government adequate to the exigencies the new nation faced in the late 1780's. To do this the founding fathers settled upon a system likely to accomplish the one philosophical objective to which they were unanimously committed—that of limited government—and within this framework they resolved most issues by resort to practical rather than theoretical considerations.

Thus while there is no doubt that the framers visualized two levels of government, each exercising power over the nation's affairs at the same time, they failed to make clear what should be the precise relationship between them or how either level might relate to local and private sources of power. Neither in Article IV, where a few necessary points of federal-state and interstate but no other intergovernmental relations were dealt with, nor in Article VI, section 2, the so-called "supremacy" clause, which was carried over almost word for word from the defeated New Jersey Plan, did they deal with specifics, and nowhere else in the document did they address themselves to questions of federalism at all.

Nor was the deficiency remedied later. Even the several excursions into the subject of federalism by James Madison and Alexander Hamilton in *The Federalist* and the addition of the Tenth Amendment in 1791 served more to confuse than to enlighten. Madison and Hamilton disagreed as to what federalism implied,[6] and the Tenth Amendment, by introducing "the peo-

6. See especially *Federalists* Nos. 9 and 16, written by Hamilton, and Nos. 39 and 40, written by Madison; see also Alpheus T. Mason and Richard H. Leach, *In Quest of Freedom. American Political Thought and Practice* (Englewood Cliffs, New Jersey: Prentice Hall, 1959), pp. 152–155.

ple" as another element to be considered in the relationship, turned what otherwise might have been a heavy weight on the side of the states into an empty phrase.

It has been suggested that as a compromise rather than an ideal solution, federalism was offered not as a permanent and binding choice but rather as a temporary expedient, intended, as Professor Beth hypothesizes, "to endure until cohesion gr[ew] to the point at which a centralized regime be[came] possible, or until cohesion [broke] down to the point at which no union [was] possible." [7] There is no direct evidence that this is what the framers intended. In any case, in practice, vested interests, the force of tradition, mere inertia—and the startling fact that the "system" worked—combined to make federalism permanent and indeed to turn it into a given in American politics and government and endow it for later generations with the aura of wisdom and desirability.

It is very possible that today, were the choice still open, the United States would not opt for federalism. America today is virtually a national state in terms of economics, culture, education, athletics, labor unionization, employer organization, and most of the other indices that could be used to measure nationalization. That it would seem desirable now to begin a nation with a pledge to small constituencies and a division of power in their behalf is doubtful. Be that as it may, the United States is a federal state today and very likely will remain one into the indefinite future.

But precisely what "federalism" means is not now and never has been clear. We can only be sure that the framers of the Constitution regarded it as one of several ways to limit the power of government in the United States. Thus any attempt to argue for a particular relation between the national government and the states—in particular for a precise division of powers between them—must fall flat for lack of constitutional corroboration. Nor are clear directions given with regard to other aspects of federalism. Instead of a rigid set of principles, what the framers gave us was a flexible instrument concerned with function and the practice of government. Federalism is thus something which is able to respond to changing needs and circumstances and is not bound

7. Beth, *op. cit.*, p. 378.

by the tenets of a particular political theory.

But that there is in effect no basic theory of American federalism has not prevented both plain and eminent men from arguing vehemently that such a theory exists. So many and so vociferous have proponents of various conceptions of federalism been over the years that the literature is voluminous. The leading theoretical contentions are summarized under two main categories in the paragraphs that follow.

COMPETITIVE THEORIES

1. Nation-centered Federalism

The concept of nation-centered federalism was the first to be advanced. Alexander Hamilton laid the basis for nation-centered federalism in his numbers of *The Federalist*, in his state papers, and by his actions as Secretary of the Treasury under George Washington. Later, John Marshall, as Chief Justice of the United States, constantly emphasized national power and indeed visualized judicial review "as a means of keeping the states within bounds." [8] The nation-centered theory of federalism posits the idea that the Constitution is a document emanating from and ratified by the American people as a whole. It follows that the government which the whole people created is the focal point of political power in the United States and that it has the principal responsibility for meeting the needs of the American people. Between them, Hamilton and Marshall expounded the idea that, in Marshall's words in *McCulloch* v. *Maryland*,[9] the national government "is the government of all; its powers are delegated by all; it represents all, and acts for all . . . The nation, on those subjects on which it can act, must necessarily bind its component parts. But this question is not left to mere reason; the people have, in express terms, decided it by saying, 'this constitution, and the laws of the United States, which shall be made in pursuance thereof, . . . shall be the supreme law of the land' . . ." Nor is it merely its popular base which gives the nation primacy. As Abra-

8. The phrase of Benjamin F. Wright, *The Growth of American Constitutional Law* (Boston: Houghton Mifflin, 1942), p. 38.
9. See Ch. II, pp. 27, 30 for a brief description of the case.

ham Lincoln pointed out in his first Inaugural Address, "The Union is much older than the Constitution. It was formed, in fact, by the Articles of Association in 1774. It was matured and continued by the Declaration of Independence in 1776. It was further matured, and the faith of all the then thirteen States expressly plighted and engaged that it be perpetual, by the Articles of Confederation. . . . And finally, in 1787, one of the declared objects for ordaining and establishing the Constitution was 'to form a more perfect Union.' " What else needs to be pointed out to demonstrate the centrality of the Union at the outset? And the intervening years did nothing to alter the original emphasis on the national government.

Nor is there anything incompatible in emphasizing the national government and at the same time defending the existence and utility of states and state governments. As Chief Justice Roger Taney put it in 1869 in *Texas* v. *White*[10] (the case which tested whether the government of Texas was responsible for the bonds issued by the state's Confederate government during the Civil War),

. . . the perpetuity and indissolubility of the Union, by no means implies the loss of distinct and individual existence, or of the right of self-government by the States. Under the Articles of Confederation each State retained its sovereignty, freedom, and independence, and every power, jurisdiction, and right not expressly delegated to the United States. Under the Constitution, though the powers of the States were much restricted, still, all powers not delegated to the United States, nor prohibited to the States, are reserved to the States respectively, or to the people. And we have already had occasion to remark at this term, that "the people of each State compose a State, having its own government, and endowed with all the functions essential to separate and independent existence," and that "without the States in union, there could be no such political body as the United States." Not only, therefore, can there be no loss of separate and independent autonomy to the States, through their union under the Constitution, but it may be not unreasonably said that the preservation of the States, and the maintenance of their governments, are as much within the design and care of the Constitution as the preservation of the Union and the maintenance of the National government. The Constitution, in all its provisions, looks to an indestructible Union, composed of indestructible States.

10. 7 Wallace 700 (1869).

Thus the national government has a dual responsibility to the people under the Constitution, a responsibility for the preservation and defense of both the Union as a whole and each and every individual state, which adds but a further reason for its primacy.

2. State-centered Federalism

State-centered federalism developed in resistance to the nationalism of Hamilton and Marshall and was first articulated in the Virginia and Kentucky Resolutions of 1798. Later on, the full-blown theory of state-centered federalism was polished and perfected, particularly by southerners, as its usefulness in rationalizing the differences between that section of the country and the rest of the nation became more apparent. Thomas Jefferson and John C. Calhoun were the chief (but far from the only) developers of this variation on the theme.[11] The theory of state-centered federalism holds that the Constitution resulted from state action. It was, after all, the states which sent delegates to Philadelphia, and state ratifying conventions which confirmed the completed document. Moreover, to protect the states, the framers set absolute limits to the power of the national government in Article I, section 8, and specifically guaranteed state power in the Tenth Amendment. James Madison spoke to the point in *Federalist 45:*

. . . is it not preposterous, to urge as an objection to a government, without which the objects of the Union cannot be attained, that such a government may derogate from the importance of the governments of the individual states? . . . The powers delegated by the proposed Constitution to the federal government are few and defined. Those which are to remain in the State governments are numerous and indefinite. The former will be exercised principally on external objects. . . . The powers reserved to the several States will extend to all the objects which, in the ordinary course of affairs, concern the lives, liberties, and properties of the people, and the internal order, improvement, and prosperity of the States.

The chief focus of citizen and governmental attention, believers in this theory are convinced, should be to guard against any en-

11. See Alpheus T. Mason, *The States' Rights Debate*. A Spectrum Paperback (New York, 1964).

largement of national power. For basic to the theory of state-centered federalism is the conviction that there is only a limited amount of power available to government in the United States and that the constitutional delegation of power, as narrowly construed as possible, is all that safely can be exercised by the national government. Any expansion beyond those narrow limits amounts to usurpation of power which rightfully belongs to the states.

3. Dual Federalism

In one sense, the Civil War was fought between the proponents of nation-centered and state-centered federalism. With the victory of the North, it might be assumed that the nationalist concept became the dominant and unchallenged interpretation of federalism in the United States. In fact, this was not the case. Even before the war, the Taney Court had begun to develop the concept of dual federalism, which the Supreme Court after the war embellished and utilized well into the twentieth century; and it gained adherents outside the bar and the judiciary as the corporation, which sought freedom from the restraints of both national and state government, came fully into its own. Proponents of dual federalism profess to believe that the Constitution created a governmental system with "collateral political spheres," to use John Taylor of Caroline's phrase. The national and state governments form two separate centers of power, from each of which the other is barred and between which is something like a jurisdictional no-man's land, into which both are barred from entering. Each government in its own sphere is sovereign, and there is an essential equality between them. As Taylor put it in his *Construction Construed and Constitutions Vindicated*, published in 1820, "the federal constitution, so far from intending to make its political spheres morally unequal in powers, or to invest the greatest with any species of sovereignty over the least, intended the very reverse"—the distribution of equal power between the states and the national government. "The reason," Taylor continued, "why great spheres derive no authority from magnitude to transgress upon small spheres, is, that both are donations from the same source [i.e., the people]; and that the donor did not intend, that one donation should pilfer another, because it was smaller." The donation is inviolable, and it is the clear duty of the several branches of the national government, as well as of state governments, to maintain it so, not so much to protect the governments involved, but to assure the freedom of the people. For "the strength of the government lies in the people," Taylor concluded.

They are the protectors and supervisors of the collateral political spheres, which they have created. If one of these spheres should acquire sufficient power to controul the others, it would, like an officer of a monarch, who can controul all the other officers of the government, obtain a supremacy over the monarch himself. . . .

COOPERATIVE THEORIES

4. Cooperative Federalism

Despite the triumph of dual federalism in the years following the Civil War, neither the nation-centered nor the state-centered varieties were abandoned, in part probably because the heat of the Civil War was so long in dying down, both sides continuing to fight the battle long after the war was over. Perhaps because the arena of argument seemed to be full, the concept of cooperative federalism was slow in jelling and was not given explicit expression much before Morton Grodzins described it in the 1950's. The flavor of the cooperative theory is best caught in the title of a book by Grodzin's student, Daniel Elazar, *The American Partnership*.[12] Elazar illustrates how from the very beginning all levels of government in the United States have collaborated in performing governmental functions. Far from comprising separate and independent layers of government as suggested by proponents of the competitive theories, the American form of government is cooperative, a blending of governments, resembling a "rainbow or marble cake, characterized by an inseparable mingling of differently colored ingredients, the colors appearing in vertical and diagonal strands and unexpected swirls. As colors are mixed in a marble cake, so functions are mixed in the American federal system." [13] In this view, the Constitution visualized a sin-

12. Daniel Elazar, *The American Partnership* (Chicago: Univ. of Chicago Press, 1962).
13. Grodzins, "The Federal System," Ch. 12 in *Goals for Americans, op. cit.*, p. 265.

gle mechanism of government in the United States, with many centers of power, which among them were to perform all the functions required of government by the American people. Even before the Constitution, intergovernmental cooperation was utilized to establish primary and secondary education; and the framers of the Constitution were so conscious of "the essential unity of state and federal financial systems"[14] that they provided for the federal government's assumption of the states' Revolutionary War debts. It is a fundamental principle of American federalism that the national government will use its resources in harmony with state and local programs and policies. During the nineteenth century that principle was manifest in steadily increasing intergovernmental cooperation in all the important functional areas of American government, and the twentieth century confirmed the practice. Shared functions, without regard to neat allocations of responsibility, is thus the core of American governmental operation and of the theory of federalism as well. Intergovernmental collaboration rather than the priority of particular governmental levels is the working principle of the federal system.

5. Creative Federalism

Creative federalism is that theory of federalism first used and described by Governor Nelson Rockefeller in his Godkin Lectures at Harvard in 1962.[15] The idea was picked up and made central to his program by President Lyndon B. Johnson after his election in 1964. Creative federalism is an extension of cooperative federalism in that it emphasizes cooperation. It differs in its recognition of local and private centers of power as well as national and state centers, and in its concern for the development of cooperation not only between the national and state governments but between them and local governments and private organizations as well. All are regarded as a working team, dedicated to positive action in solving the problems facing the nation, with perhaps a different combination of forces at work in each different problem area, and with the national government not always the senior partner. In both its stress on the responsibility of the

14. *Ibid.*, p. 268.
15. Nelson A. Rockefeller, *The Future of Federalism* (Cambridge: Harvard Univ. Press, 1962).

private sector of American life in the problem-solving process and its concern that action and innovation take place before problems become critical, it is unique among the theories of federalism so far espoused in America.

6. New Federalism

President Richard Nixon described his concept of "new federalism" in a nationwide television speech on August 8, 1969, and again before the National Governors Conference on September 1. It was later given more explicit form in testimony before Congress by the assistant director of the Bureau of the Budget.[16] Its major theme is to rechannel "power, funds and authority . . . increasingly to those governments closest to the people . . . to help regain control of our national destiny by returning a greater share of control to state and local authorities." [17] It stresses *responsible decentralization*: "Washington will no longer try to go it alone," President Nixon said. Washington will "refrain from telling states and localities how to conduct their affairs and [will] seek to transfer ever-greater responsibilities to the state level." [18] To make the transfer possible, a system of revenue sharing must be established. It also emphasizes *a strong concern with basic systems*. Instead of piecemeal action on parts of problems, intergovernmental strategies for attacking broad problem areas must be worked out. Welfare and manpower programs were the first two such areas to be singled out for attack. Finally, the "new federalism" places *greater emphasis on the effective implementation of government policies*, particularly at the state and local level, where acceptance of the concept "would impose . . . new obligations and new challenges" on government in terms of improved quality of performance. The thrust of the "new federalism" is to deemphasize the national government's role in the partnership of governments and to strengthen that of state and local governments. "Washington will no longer dictate," President Nixon

16. See the statement of Richard P. Nathan, September 25, 1969, reprinted in *Congressional Record* 115: S11429 (September 26, 1969). The italicized phrases are from his testimony.
17. President Nixon before the National Governors Conference, reprinted in *Congressional Record* 115: H7533 (September 4, 1969).
18. Quoted in *The New York Times*, September 3, 1969, p. 1.

promised. "We can only toss the ball; the states and localities will have to carry it." [19] The new federalism has not yet developed the specifics as to how to make this possible, particularly in financial terms, and until it does, *The New York Times* remarked editorially, it will likely be little "more than a rhetorical phrase." [20]

A recital in chronological order of the several theories of federalism which have been developed in the United States should not be misinterpreted; the subsequent development of one theory by no means served to crowd its predecessors off the stage. Not only did the first two claimants of attention continue to make themselves heard, but as each new concept was developed, proponents of the earlier theories hardened their positions. Thus the stage became more crowded, more confused, and certainly more noisy.

To a large extent the "debate" over the theories of federalism has not been a debate at all. For the most part, it has been conducted at presidential press conferences and in political addresses, in legislative committee chambers and court rooms, in the pages of the daily press and in scholarly journals and reports, but not in the streets and by the people as a whole. Indeed, it would be difficult to demonstrate that there is now or ever has been a widespread public understanding of federalism. If some southerners seem to have consistently supported one theory as opposed to any of the others, their advocacy is based not so much on participation in the debate and understanding derived therefrom as on habit and stereotype. It has always been difficult to find out what the popular conception of federalism is, and this is because the people are very likely confused as to what federalism means, as much by the several interpretations of the "truth" offered them through the years as by the vacuum left by the framers.

An example of that confusion is found in a survey of federalism as viewed by governmental officials concerned with the administration of federal grant-in-aid programs, recently conducted by the Senate Subcommittee on Intergovernmental Relations.[21]

19. *Ibid.*
20. *Ibid.,* p. 46.
21. *The Federal System as Seen by Federal Aid Officials.* Committee Print. December 15, 1965. 89th Congress, 1st Session.

The survey showed that, while none of those interviewed had consciously articulated a theory of federalism or even given much thought to the need to do so, "the respondents [did] have a general idea of what intergovernmental relations are and how they should operate. In short, the survey made it clear . . . [that] they [had] a theory of federalism . . . ,"[22] and that state and local officials involved in federal grant-in-aid programs hold views of federalism quite different from those of federal officials. Moreover, the study revealed that neither the state and local officials nor the federal officials were in agreement among themselves as to the several elements of the theories they espoused. As the report itself put it, "These contrasting [theories] . . . are based on contrasting emphases and principles." The federal officials were chiefly concerned with doing a professional job of administering aid programs and generally held an anti-state and anti-local official bias, which understandably made their views "completely unacceptable" to the state and local officials, who generally insisted on a more formal statement of principles and were concerned with such concepts as "balance" and "parity."[23] The views of neither group of officials, however, conformed in every respect to one of the theories described earlier in this chapter. Indeed, the subcommittee concluded, governmental officials probably held atypical views of the federal system.

One is left at the end of even so careful an analysis of concepts of federalism more confused than ever as to just what the theoretical bases of American federalism are—or one's confusion is finally dispelled as he is led to understand once and for all that considerations of theory are irrelevant to an understanding of federalism. For the most important conclusion to be drawn from the Senate study is that most respondents agreed their commitment was to a *process*, to *a way of doing things*, rather than to a set of abstract principles. The most frequently occurring words in the views of both sets of officials are *function, program, activity, administration,* in considering all of which *collaboration* and intergovernmental *relations* are fundamental. Federalism from both points of view—more from the federal than from the state

22. *Ibid.,* p. 95.
23. *Ibid.,* pp. 96, 97, 99.

and local, to be sure—is seen as a complex working arrangement to permit the accomplishment of commonly held objectives. It is an arrangement whose virtue lies in what it permits to be accomplished rather than in the degree to which it adheres to a set of binding tenets. And accomplishment can only be secured by a large amount of interrelation. Above all, the conclusion is inevitable that intergovernmental cooperation is the key to modern federalism. Meeting the problems of modern America with the right programs and policies involves *all* levels of government, working together in a variety of ways. The older competitive theories of federalism took into account only the actions of and relations between the government of the United States and those of the states, and even the more recently developed theories of cooperative and creative federalism are focused chiefly on them. Yet federalism is much more than that. It involves as a matter of inheritance and practical necessity at least three levels of action—national, state, and local—and five sets of relations—national-state, interstate, state-local, interlocal, and national-local. To the extent that theories of federalism overlook this elemental truth, they are inapplicable and invalid from the outset. Only the theory of creative federalism seems to take interaction between all levels of government into account.

Just as it cannot be shown that any of the theories of federalism developed over the years fully fit the facts of the case, so it cannot be demonstrated that a certain pattern of action and intergovernmental relations must always be followed. Variation and adaptation to changing needs have characterized American governmental actions and intergovernmental relations. The particular nature of each action and relationship has been determined largely by the area of activity in which governments are involved. In the area of environmental pollution, for example, no clear pattern of action or of intergovernmental relations has developed at all. In other fields, such as education and health, well-defined programs and sets of relations have come into use. Seldom is the same pattern followed in two action areas; new varieties of actions and relations are constantly being introduced and adopted. What Luther Gulick said about the burgeoning activities of the national government in the area of business regulation and control applies with equal pertinence to the development of American federalism. Regulatory activity, Gulick wrote,

did not come about as a matter of social theory. It came about because . . . problems arose. . . . The people most affected took what steps they could to establish the controls and the services they found to be needed . . . Each move was a pragmatic Yankee solution designed to meet a condition, not a theory.[24]

As a comparable response, working federalism is marked by diversity, trial and error, and experimentation on the one hand, and it is problem-oriented on the other. The possibilities for new actions and relationships to handle the diverse problems coming within the scope of governmental action today are far from exhausted.

But if there is no universally agreed-upon theory of American federalism on which to build a positive understanding of American government, it should be noted that a diversity of theories may have a negative effect. As the Subcommittee on Intergovernmental Relations noted, disagreements over theory create tensions in intergovernmental relations by the mere fact that those who hold different points of view often occupy critically important positions, and they permit their divergence to impede program operation. Inevitably, concluded the subcommittee, the particular theories held by government administrators condition "their official behavior." [25] Nor are the tensions created among administrators the most serious ones. The gaps in understanding and appreciation created by rigid adherence to one of the several theories of federalism in legislative halls and judicial chambers—and in political parties and among the people as well—may make it difficult, if not impossible, for administrators to function at all in certain areas of need. The very slowness with which American governments have reached out to attack major problems—those arising from urbanization are a good case in point—is in large part due to irreconcilable differences over theories of federalism felt by policy makers at different levels. Their obduracy may at times serve to paralyze the decision-making process.

24. Luther H. Gulick, *The Metropolitan Problem and American Ideas* (New York: Knopf, 1962), pp. 15–16.
25. *The Federal System as Seen by Federal Aid Officials, op. cit.,* p. 100.

Thus it is important to recognize the role of theory and the hold of certain theoretical positions on men's minds, because theoretical beliefs qualify practical applications. But to understand the American federal system at work, one must focus his attention chiefly upon the operations and operators of that system. As Senator Edmund S. Muskie remarked, "When we speak of . . . federalism, we are concerned, as were the founders, [with] the *means* by which we organize our common efforts [to] adapt to the new and larger challenges which we face." [26] Only by concentrating on those means—on the processes of federalism—will it be possible to obtain the insights that permit understanding.

The practical basis of federalism has not prevented political scientists from developing a theoretical explanation for federalism.[27] In "modern" political science there is an unfortunate tendency to demand "tools of analysis," "conceptual frameworks" of one kind or another, as the only way of studying and understanding political phenomena. The goal of these efforts is a "useful model" for study. The number of political scientists who have attempted to devise such a model for federalism is large, and it is growing as the number of federal states in the world increases.

The British political scientist David Mitrany postulates a theory of functionalism to explain federalism.[28] Another British student of federalism, K. C. Wheare, constructed an institutional model of federalism.[29] The American W. S. Livingston defines federalism in sociological terms and sees it as resulting from the presence of a particular set of social relationships in a society.[30] Another American, Charles D. Tarlton, offers the view that the principal "element in federal relationships, both essential to understanding federalism and too often not carefully distinguished

---

26. *Congressional Record* 113: S2159 (February 17, 1967). Italics supplied.

27. The variety of approaches is discussed in A. H. Birch, "Approaches to the Study of Federalism," *Political Studies* 14:15–33 (February 1966).

28. Remarks of David Mitrany to the International Course on European Integration, University of Amsterdam, February 12, 1968.

29. See K. C. Wheare, *Federal Government* (London: Oxford U. Press, 1946).

30. See W. S. Livingstone, "A Note on the Nature of Federalism," *Political Science Quarterly* LXVII: 81–95 (March 1952).

and recognized, is the symmetry of the federal system. What I mean by symmetry is the level of conformity and commonality in the relations of each separate political unit of the system to both the system as a whole and to the other component units." [31] Karl W. Deutsch and his collaborators see federalism as an aspect of the phenomena of communications between groups,[32] and William H. Riker sees it as a bargain struck between competing interests and political groupings.[33] On the basis of such academic postulates, students have come up with a number of "conditions" which they feel must be met if federalism is to be established and successfully maintained as a system of government, particularly in emerging states.

But one looks through the literature on federalism pretty much in vain for a theoretical discussion by a practicing political decisionmaker, one who holds elective office or an appointed administrative post, a legislator or a judge. They may be—indeed, they probably are—adherents of one of the variations of theory growing out of the Constitution's vagueness which are described earlier in this chapter. But they ordinarily are too busy to concern themselves with theoretical niceties. Those involved in making modern intergovernmentalism work are among the most pragmatic of people, working for the most part without a binding conceptual framework, model, theory, or system in mind, faced with a particular set of facts and guided by a reservoir of experience and common sense. They know the instrument they are working with has immense possibilities for adaptation and development, and they do not feel themselves limited by the requirement of meeting ideal conditions before they act. Political scientists can set conditions which must be met; men on the front of intergovernmental action cannot do so. They must take things as they find them and attempt to work out solutions with less than optimum conditions prevailing.

31. See Charles D. Tarlton, "Symmetry and Asymmetry As Elements of Federalism: A Theoretical Speculation," *The Journal of Politics* 27: 861–74 (November 1965).

32. The chief proponents of this view are Carl J. Friedrich and Karl Deutsch.

33. See William H. Riker, *Federalism: Origin, Operation, Significance* (Boston: Little, Brown, 1964).

There is nothing wrong with theorizing. It may be fun as well as instructive as an exercise in reasoning. All the hypothesizing in the world, however, will not reveal what the framers of our Constitution had in mind when they set the American intergovernmental system we call federalism into motion, if indeed they were clear in their own minds about it. Moreover, the federal system in the United States—and presumably in any nation—is always in flux. Thus hypotheses based on observation must always be somewhat out of date, and hypotheses based on prediction and projection may be entirely off base.[34] The very size of the federal system in the United States makes observation—and therefore theorizing—difficult. It is possible to look closely at one city or county, as Dahl did in *Who Governs?* and as Paul Ylvisaker did in *Blue Earth County*,[35] but beyond that, even with computers, close scrutiny becomes difficult. How can all the action and intergovernmental aspects of any state, to say nothing of those involved in even one branch of the national government or of the national government as a whole, be observed and understood? And to study simultaneously all the units of American government as they act and interact is manifestly impossible. Thus there can be theories with some validity about certain aspects of the federal spectrum, but hardly a viable theory about federalism as a whole.

Implicit in all the theorizing about federalism is the belief that men plan an act rationally in devising their governmental systems. There is no clear evidence that they do. Even the revered framers of the American Constitution were men affected by many forces, only some of them within the control of their reason, as they worked to create the federal system. It is all well and good to speak, as Paul Ylvisaker does in *Area and Power*,[36] of "the proper areal division of powers." Proper according to what logic? what criteria? what reasoning? Persons working in practi-

34. See W. J. M. Mackenzie, *Politics and Social Science* (Baltimore: Penguin Books, 1967), pp. 290 ff.
35. Robert Dahl, *Who Governs?* (New Haven: Yale Univ. Press, 1961); Paul N. Ylvisaker, *Intergovernmental Relations at the Grass Roots. A Study of Blue Earth County* (Minneapolis: Univ. of Minnesota Press, 1956).
36. Arthur Maass, ed., *Area and Power. A Theory of Local Government* (Glencoe, Illinois: Free Press, 1959).

cal intergovernmentalism are more likely fettered than aided by such notions of "propriety."

American federalism is based on the theory of limited government. Beyond that, it answers not to theoretical dictates. Nor is it likely that it will be adjusted to meet theoretical demands in the future. Theory, in other words, has not been causative in American federalism. The framers of the Constitution bequeathed us an open-ended system. We can only be the losers if we try to close it off by adopting any set of theoretical principles, any model, any construct. As in so many other areas, the framers in building federalism built better than they knew—and we are the beneficiaries.

FEDERALISM AND GOVERNMENTAL POWER

THERE ARE THREE MYTHS about power in a federal system that must be disposed of at the outset. One is that power is wholly a governmental prerogative. Because government's role in society has increased so markedly in recent decades and power exertions by government have been so central to American political debate, government and power appear synonymous. They are not, of course. Man is subject to many nongovernmental, i.e., private, power factors as well: his family, his religion, the groups to which he belongs, social customs and mores, and especially economic forces. It is not necessary to list them all to demonstrate that government is but one of the governing forces in society—or, to put it another way, one of the wielders of power. Thus, no consideration of powers is complete without reference to the important part played by private power. In a free society such as ours, indeed, the private power forces taken together probably impinge with greater impact on the individual than the governmental power forces.

Another myth is that the functions of government are so neatly divisible among the levels of government—national, state, and local—that power to carry on particular functions can be clearly allocated to each level, until all functions and the power to conduct them have been assigned, and none are left over. Except for foreign affairs, national defense, and a monetary system, which are pretty clearly functions assignable to the national government, there is no clearcut allotment of governmental power in the United States. Rather, the governmental functions needed by the American people can be performed only by exertions of power at two or even three levels of government simultaneously. There are functions to be performed and powers to be exercised separately or cooperatively, with no precise formula governing who gets what.

The third myth is that the total amount of governmental power available for use in the American system is constant and to enlarge power at one level is necessarily to decrease it at another. The truth is that about as much power is available as the people want to exercise. Total power has constantly expanded to meet the demands of the twentieth century, and it is still expanding. Thus it is possible for the power exertions of the national government to increase at the same time that state and local power, and that of the private sector as well, are growing, without any diminution taking place. For power is a flexible and evolving force in society, not a static and frozen one. The amount used depends not on the calculus of a mathematical equation but on the needs of a people and how they determine to satisfy them.

The heart of the question of power in a federal system is how powers are distributed among its units. The Constitution of 1787 set about to create a system which would work, in the words of its preamble, so as to "establish Justice, ensure domestic Tranquility, provide for the common defense, promote the general Welfare, and secure the Blessings of Liberty" to all generations of the American people. It did not go on, however, to describe in any detail how the new national government was to exercise its power toward those ends in conjunction with the pre-existing state and local governments. To be sure, some powers which had heretofore belonged to the states (in theory if not in practice) were *delegated* to the national government. Certain other powers which it was important that all levels of government possess the states and their local subdivisions were allowed to keep even while the same powers were delegated to the national government; thus some powers were made *concurrent*. And a number of powers, in accordance with the framers' concept of limited government, were *denied* to all units of government.

In addition, *implied* powers were made available by the words of Article I, section 8, clause 18 of the Constitution, which gives Congress power "To make all laws which shall be necessary and proper for carrying into Execution the foregoing Powers, and all other Powers vested by this Constitution in the Government of the United States, or in any Department or Officer thereof." It was not until John Marshall applied his reasoning to this constitutional provision in *McCulloch* v. *Maryland* in 1819 [1] that the full potentiality of the clause became evident. In that case, which tested Congress's power to charter a national bank in the absence of any specific Constitutional authorization, Marshall declared that a constitution by its very nature requires that only the "great outlines" of power "be marked, its important objects designated," not that every means to attain the ends so described be specified as well.

> . . . we must never forget that it is a constitution we are expounding . . . can we adopt that construction . . . which would impute to the framers of that instrument, when granting . . . powers for the public good, the intention of impeding their exercise by withholding a choice of means? . . . Let the end be legitimate, let it be within the scope of the Constitution, and all means which are appropriate, which are plainly adapted to that end, which are not prohibited, but consist with the letter and spirit of the Constitution, are constitutional. . . .

The national government in other words needs only to demonstrate the existence of "legitimate ends," and the power it seeks is its to exercise.

Finally, certain *inherent* powers reside in the national government as a consequence of its existence as a sovereign entity on the state of world politics. What is left in the armory of power is *reserved* to the states, in part by indirection and in part directly but ambiguously, by the terms of the Tenth Amendment, which leaves those powers to the states or to the people thereof.

But if the Constitution dealt thus broadly with power, it did not describe how these various kinds of power were to fit together, how they were to be utilized jointly to accomplish the

1. 4 Wheaton 316 (1819).

objectives set forth in its own preamble. This the framers left, probably by necessity, to be worked out in practice as the national, state, and local governments began to exercise their respective powers. There was bound to be controversy, and controversy there was, more over the nature of national power than over the power of the other levels of governments. That controversy continues to the present day.

What is "national power" in the division of power among governments in the United States? On the face of it, it would appear fairly easy to define. But even a short discussion of the variability of the several elements that together constitute the national government's share of power will demonstrate that students of American federalism must be content with only a blurred image. Controversy has revolved chiefly around the two kinds of power the national government has under the Constitution—delegated and implied. It is obvious that the framers were not niggardly in delegating power. The occasion for the Constitutional Convention in the first place was chiefly the deficiency of power in the central government under the Articles of Confederation. It would have been surprising if the framers had not generously made up that deficiency. Article I, section 8, constitutes a very broad grant of power indeed, in terms of both the number and the breadth of the different powers granted to Congress. They range from the essential taxing and borrowing powers to the regulation of interstate and foreign commerce, the establishment of inferior federal courts, and the declaration of war. Several other powers are granted to Congress elsewhere in the Constitution. Article II, for example, gives Congress power to set the time for presidential electors to cast their votes; Article III, power to set the appellate jurisdiction of the Supreme Court and to punish treason; and Article IV, power to admit new states and govern territories. Still other powers have been granted in amendments to the Constitution. The framers conceived of none of these powers narrowly. Not only did they not try to define such terms as "commerce" and "war" and so left their exact meaning to be determined by Congress (and ultimately by the Supreme Court), they went on, as we have seen, in the last clause of Article I, section 8, to grant authority to Congress to choose its own means of converting the powers granted to it into effective national policy.

The delegation of certain powers to Congress, however, does not mean their automatic or full exercise. Indeed, Article I, section 8, merely provides the springboard from which Congress can convert authorization into action. On some grants of power—the power to regulate commerce, for example—Congress acted slowly and for many years only in part; on others, such as the power to constitute tribunals inferior to the Supreme Court, it acted with dispatch and in detail. To this day, Congress continues to exercise discretion in implementing the powers available to it. Moreover, the difficulties imposed on the actual exercise of power by the fact that Congress is bicameral must not be forgotten. Differences in point of view between the two houses arise not because the Senate represents the states (if in fact it ever did, and since the addition of the Seventeenth Amendment it clearly has not) and the House represents the people. They arise rather as a result of the fiercely individualistic organization and operation of each house; the dissolution of both houses for working purposes into semi-autonomous, and often autocratic, committees; the curious party split in each house, which in reality ignores party labels and makes discipline virtually impossible; and the relationship between the two houses, which is often marked by asperity, if not hostility.[2] Differences also stem from the relationship of leaders of the two houses with members of their own parties in their respective chambers and with each other. Disagreements inevitably arise between the houses. When they do, they serve to slow down or paralyze altogether the use of power by Congress. The use of power by Congress is further affected by the ever-changing relationships between each group of Congressional leaders and the President, between Congress and the other parts of the executive branch, and between Congress and the Supreme Court. If Congress has from the first accepted suggestions from the President, executive officers and agencies, and the Supreme Court as to which powers to act upon and what kind of action to take, it has also balked at such suggestions and provided inaction instead of

2. For a more detailed discussion of the friction between the two houses, see Richard H. Leach, *Governing the American Nation* (Boston: Allyn & Bacon, 1967), pp. 241–243.

action in reply.[3] Nor does Congress have the final word on the exercise of its power. Presidents have not been loath to use the veto, and the Supreme Court has not been reluctant to keep a particular exertion of power from becoming effective.

Thus the mere lodgment of power in Congress has not been equivalent to the full exercise thereof. If Congress makes fuller use of its powers now than it did in earlier days, it is still guided in that use by public opinion through reliance on pressure groups and party leaders and by a healthy sense of respect for the role of the state and local governments. And in some broad areas, Congress has in effect delegated its powers to independent regulatory agencies in the executive branch. Even with regard to the specific powers granted to Congress in the Constitution, then, it is clear that there is no one pattern of application which must be followed. Rather, Congressional power remains, as it has always been, a variable within the federal system.

If this is the case with the delegated powers, it is of course even more so with the implied powers. Acting in response to Alexander Hamilton's urging as Secretary of the Treasury in Washington's first administration, the first Congresses demonstrated the possibilities of action implicit in several of the delegations in Article I, section 8, and once the example was advanced, other Congresses followed suit. Since *McCulloch* v. *Maryland*, it has been clear that if in the first instance Congress may determine the appropriateness of means—and if not contested, the Congressional choice stands until changed by Congress itself—in the last analysis the federal courts, and in particular the Supreme Court, become parties to that determination. Since different forces operate to bring about a court test of an exercise of implied power, and different reasoning may prevail in a judicial determination of appropriateness than was the case when the decision was first reached in Congress, those who oppose the particular exertion of power still have a recourse left to them to try to stop it. In this way, separation of powers works hand in hand with federalism to do just what the framers of the Constitution intended: to make it

3. See in this connection Walter E. Travis, *Congress and the President: Readings in Executive-Legislative Relations* (New York: Teachers College Press, 1967).

difficult, if not impossible, for Congress to exert its power at all. On occasion, as when an income tax was levied on income rather than on persons, it has been necessary to change the Constitution to permit the exercise of power.

Whereas the framers were quite clear in their grant of power to Congress, they were far from precise in dealing with the broad grant of power to the national government as a whole. Congress was given considerable power to enact laws on specific subjects; but elsewhere, the President was granted "the executive power" of the United States, and "judicial power" was vested in a Supreme Court and such inferior courts as Congress might from time to time establish. These two kinds of power were not spelled out in any detail, and only a negative relationship was established between them as parts of a check-and-balance, separation-of-powers system of government. If the framers of the Constitution considered the power of the national government to be a composite of the powers delegated to its three branches, they did not say so. Perhaps because they were more familiar with legislative power than with the kinds of power the newly devised President and Supreme Court would exercise under the Constitution, they dealt with Congress in greater detail. But by saying so little about the other two kinds of power, they made the national government a virtual unknown in the American power equation.

In any case, the broadest grant of power contained anywhere in the Constitution is the statement in Article II, section 1, that "The executive power shall be vested in a President of the United States of America." No attempt was made to define the nature of that power any further, with the result that each President was left free to define the term for himself, subject only to such emendations as Congress and the courts might make in the operation of their power of checking and balancing. Thus executive power too is a variable in American government and so contributes its share to the fluid nature of federalism. Presidential power depends on a number of factors—on the President's majority in the election, on his powers of public persuasion, on the men and women he is able to recruit to work with him and on their performance in the job, on the attitude of the federal bureaucracy toward him, on his own personality, on his control of his party,

on the relationship he is able to establish with the leaders of the
other party, on the nature and demands of the times, on the precedents set by his predecessors in office, and on the composition
and leadership of Congress. For executive power depends also on
what Congress gives the President and the agencies of the executive branch to do. In recognition of the impossibility of developing detailed legislation for the many new areas of government activity undertaken since 1933, Congress has delegated an increasing
amount of its power to the President and to executive agencies to
provide the detailed implementation of general legislative di-
rectives. And like Congressional power, executive power finally
depends on what the Supreme Court will let its agents do. To be
sure, the Court has been much more permissive with regard to
executive power than it has with Congressional power, but it has
not foresworn its power of restraint altogether.

Given the right combination of these several factors, the arse-
nal of power available to an American president is truly formidable. The President is not unlimited in the exercise of his powers,
however. He is limited first of all by his ability to get the many
power elements in the American system of government—and this
includes in a prominent position the governments of the fifty
states and their many subdivisions—to do what he considers to be
in the best interests of the country. For he lacks the power to
command and must rely instead chiefly on the power of persuasion. The President is also limited by the power of a free and active press and by the constant watchfulness of the opposition
party. He is limited by the power of the people to defeat him
after one term in office. And he is limited by law. He cannot
move very far or for very long without Congressional support
(he can count on greater leeway in foreign affairs and defense
measures than in domestic affairs). To the extent that Congress is
amenable to his leadership and responds to it with action he
wants, the President's power is augmented; but every time Congress refuses to act in accordance with presidential wishes or acts
more slowly or with more opposition than he would like, or im-
poses on him a set of demands of its own, presidential power is
restricted. The President of the United States, in sum, has power,
but he has not achieved absolute power, even within the execu-

tive branch. Indeed, the division of that branch into a multitude of departments and agencies—far too many for a President ever to control effectively—is perhaps the greatest restraint of all on presidential power.

And last but not least, the power of the national government as it affects the federal system includes the power of the Supreme Court and of the lower federal courts as well. Though the framers of the Constitution were careful to list the general kinds of cases in which federal judicial power might be exercised, they did not define the phrase "judicial power" itself. Nor has Congress attempted to do so. Thus the courts—and particularly the Supreme Court—have been able to define it themselves. The traditionalists have held that the judicial function is merely to maintain and enforce the law and to administer justice under it, while the activists hold that judges should use their power to achieve reform and bring about improvement, i.e., to legislate.[4] In more recent years, the latter view has come to be predominant. Generally speaking, the federal courts have not often deliberately sought to encroach on either executive or legislative power. But since the courts sit continually in judgment on legislative and executive acts as they relate to the Constitution, even the restrained exercise of judicial power may well serve to qualify legislative and executive power. Thus judicial power remains a variable too, though perhaps not quite as great a one as either legislative or executive power, thanks to the courts' reliance on the doctrine of *stare decisis*[5] in rendering their decisions. Yet times and circumstances change, as do the justices themselves, and there have been enough reversals of court rulings to justify the assertion that there is no guarantee at all of a particular judicial point of view

4. See Fred V. Cahill, Jr., *Judicial Legislation. A Study in American Legal Theory* (New York: Ronald Press, 1952), especially Ch. 1.

5. ". . . whatever philosophy of law one may choose to adopt or follow," writes Francis H. Heller in *Introduction to American Constitutional Law* (New York: Harper, 1952), p. 11, "the central element of law is that it provides rules of conduct for the members of a given community. The idea of a *rule* connotes certainty and constancy. But the decision of a given controversy does not become a rule unless it is followed in subsequent like situations, unless it is accorded the strength of a *precedent*. . . . Lawyers speak of the principle of *stare decisis* (meaning 'to stand by what has been decided') which demands that prior decisions should be followed in like cases."

prevailing over the long pull with regard to the exercise of national power. Some of the best examples of change in the Court's attitude include reversals on the appropriateness of separate-but-equal, i.e., segregated, facilities for Negroes—compare *Plessey* v. *Ferguson*, 163 US 537 (1896) and *Brown* v. *Board of Education of Topeka*, 349 US 294 (1954)—and decisions with regard to federal action in providing representativeness in legislative districts—compare *Colegrove* v. *Green*, 328 US 549 (1946) and *Baker* v. *Carr*, 369 US 186 (1962).

Thus the concept of *the* national government as a unified participant in the federal system is largely mythical. To be sure, there are occasions on which the many elements in the national government hold nearly identical positions on a matter or are at least in fair alignment with one another—emergencies and war especially provide such occasions. But for the most part, the separate branches of the national government, and even the various units within each, speak with different emphases, opinions, and conceptions, and make different demands about what ought to be done. Or one part or several may speak while the others are silent. The number of possible permutations and combinations is large. Thus charges that "Washington Seeks to Dominate American Education" or that "The national government has once again encroached upon the states" in some area or another may be dismissed as entirely inaccurate, because they fail to take into account the division of and competition for power within the national government itself. To think of the national government as monolithic in the exercise of its power in the federal system is to misunderstand its nature altogether.

On the other hand, Luther Gulick points out correctly that the delegation to the national government of "responsibility for interstate commerce, for all foreign affairs, and for taxing . . . 'to promote the general Welfare' inevitably placed the federal establishment in control of our economy and of our social evolution."

Once the Constitution was adopted and made effective, the several states had no individual economic "skin." Only the nation was endowed with an economic geographic boundary. The states were thus individually all but powerless to influence the free flow of capital, of people, and of economic activity. This not only placed the states individually in a position where they could not act vigorously, but set each major economic or social problem in a framework where little could be done about it except on a national scale.[6]

Thus the potential for a powerful national role in American governmental affairs is great; when the several different power elements in the national government all work together, as they have occasionally, the results of national action can be very impressive. Perhaps because it can effect so much, the frequent failure of the national government to act or to act fully enough seems to many all the more depressing. Indeed, the national government seldom functions as a team, with the result that vast powers for good are likely to lie fallow. For, unreasoning claims to the contrary, state and local governments seldom walk in where the national government fears to tread.

If it is difficult to pin down the national side of the American power equation, it is even harder to determine the state side. What powers did in fact remain with the states after power had been allocated in various ways by the Constitution? It is no more possible to define the exact range and depth of state powers than to describe accurately the totality of national power. To make such a definition, it would be necessary first of all to know what the total available governmental power was prior to the framers' allocation, then to know just how much was deducted in the course of delegation, implication, and prohibition. The residue might fairly be called "state power." But neither political speculation nor political science has been able to supply even approximate figures for either part of the equation, so that to attempt any such determination is an exercise in futility. The reservoir of state power cannot be described in detail.

Something concrete of course can be said about state power, even so. Something should be said about "states' rights," if only because the term has come into common usage and may seem to connote something which in fact it does not. Clearly the states have a right to a share of the power exerted in the federal system, but not to any particular share, either quantitative or qualitative. The framers must have intended to leave state power open-ended

6. Gulick, *The Metropolitan Problem and American Ideas, op. cit.*, p. 34.

and certainly not to make it a rigid barrier against the exercise of national power. Dumas Malone tells how it became that barrier. Thomas Jefferson first enunciated the doctrine of states' rights in the Kentucky and Virginia Resolutions. His decision to do so "was determined by the actualities of the situation." The three branches of the national government, all of which were under Federalist control, were united in their support of the Alien and Sedition Acts of 1798.[7] Hence Jefferson and the Republicans turned to the states and to state power because there was nothing else with which to oppose the national government. In a "dangerous political situation," Malone tells us, "he and his party resorted to the Constitution for defense. Naturally, they followed the line of strict construction and, against what they regard as an unwarranted assumption of power by the federal government, they talked of the reserved rights of the states." Jefferson "had said very little about the rights of the states before he became fearful of Hamiltonian consolidation. Now, under pressure of circumstances he found intolerable, he took the most extreme position . . . with regard to state rights." He "never attempted to put into practice the extreme theory. . . . [It] was a theoretical matter altogether. . . . [It was a] weapon which he never regarded as anything but a threat and which in fact he afterward discarded."[8] Most historians agree with Malone's basic thesis.

If Jefferson afterward discarded the idea, however, it was too attractive a gimmick for others to ignore. Soon it was utilized again, much in the way Jefferson used it, as a stick with which to beat whatever power exertions of the national government were

7. There were four acts: the Naturalization Act, repealed in 1802, raised from five to fourteen years the period an alien had to wait to acquire citizenship; the Alien Act empowered the President to order out of the United States all aliens he judged dangerous to the peace and safety of the nation and to cause their imprisonment or forcible removal if necessary; the Alien Enemies Act empowered the President in case of war to remove or detain as enemy aliens all male subjects of a hostile power; and the Sedition Act provided punishment by fine or imprisonment of any persons conspiring against any measures of the United States government, impeding the operation of any United States law, or uttering malicious statements against United States officials. The latter law expired in 1801.

8. Dumas Malone, "Jefferson, Hamilton, and the Constitution," in William H. Nelson, ed., *Theory and Practice in American Politics* (Chicago: Univ. of Chicago Press, 1964), pp. 21–22.

unpopular with some particular group. Thus John Taylor of Caroline attacked the national bank, and John Calhoun launched an attack on the tariff, on states' rights grounds. Indeed, Calhoun argued that the states, far from having lost their sovereignty upon coming into the Union, had merely created a central government whose function it was to act as agent of the states. Should the government go beyond the narrow limits within which it was authorized by the Constitution to operate, a state might, through a constituent assembly, nullify whatever law it deemed objectionable and attempt to aid other states to act similarly. Thus the doctrine of nullification was created. Relying on Calhoun's reasoning, a South Carolina convention actually did adopt an "ordinance of nullification" on November 19, 1832, and the state legislature passed the legislation necessary to put the ordinance into effect. For a while actual hostilities threatened. No other states followed South Carolina's lead, however, and the counteraction of President Jackson's proclamation of December 11, which declared nullification unconstitutional, the passage of a compromise tariff bill, and the threat of the passage of the Force Bill in March, 1833, led South Carolina to repeal the ordinance. Later, both sides were to claim victory, and southern leaders continued to have recourse to the doctrine of states' rights, if not to nullification, as a defense of the institutions and customs peculiar to their region.

Though the doctrine has never received any other official sanction, it has continued to be used with great effect, and not only by southerners. Frank E. Smith, in his excellent study, *The Politics of Conservation*, relates how interests in the west were long able (and still are in some natural resource fields) to hold back national conservation programs by claiming that conservation, not being delegated to the national government in the Constitution, was thus a power reserved to the states. All the while, of course, those same interests controlled the state legislatures and made sure that the states did next to nothing in the conservation area. After Gifford Pinchot finally was able to put regulations upon grazing in the national forests in 1905, "Throughout the West, cries went up for state control of forests, along with strident attacks on federal bureaucracy and regimentation." Smith quotes President Theodore Roosevelt in his speech to the Second

National Conservation Congress in 1910, " 'It is not a question of
hair-splitting legal technicalities . . . [or] of state against nation.
. . . It is really a question of special corporate interests against
the popular interests of the people. . . . It's a comical fact that
the most zealous upholders of states' rights are big businessmen' "
who stand to profit from lax state regulation and control. " 'The
most effective weapon is federal laws and the federal executive.
That is why I so strongly oppose the demand to turn these matters [conservation] over to the States.' " [9]

Adherence to the principle of states' rights has never been allowed to interfere with economic benefit, however. The ardent
states' righters in the Mississippi delta country saw no contradic-
tion in encouraging federal flood control activities in their region,
for example. "There was no doctrine of state's rights in solving
flood control problems in Mississippi, Arkansas or Louisiana,"
Smith observes. "Lawyers in New York or Washington might
express doubts about the constitutionality of federal flood control
but none did in the Mississippi delta." [10] Thus the proponents of
states' rights sought to have it both ways. When their interests
were being served by national action, no voice asserting states'
rights was to be heard. Only when a national program seemed to
them harmful to their interests was the challenge made. Today
the argument is relied on by southern opponents of national action in the fields of education and civil rights, and it will very
likely continue to be utilized whenever a sizable opposition to a
particular national program or policy develops. It remains a hol-
low argument and is to be regarded with skepticism. As a political weapon it does affect the power equation, however, and so has
to be taken into account in any treatment of federalism.

Questions of the validity of the states' rights doctrine aside,
the states simply are not well organized for the exercise of power.
Characterized by restrictive constitutions, weak governors, often
ineffective legislatures, unsystematized courts, and public disinterest and neglect, they do not make ideal participants in the power
arena.[11]

9. Frank E. Smith, *The Politics of Conservation* (New York: Pantheon,
1966), pp. 99, 122.
10. *Ibid.*, p. 128.
11. See Chapter V below for a general discussion of the weaknesses of
state government.

For all these reasons, it is easier to discuss what the states cannot do than what they can. Beyond question, the states do not have certain powers which the framers felt the national government should exercise and which they therefore delegated to it. Nor were the states given powers which the framers felt would detract from the strength of the national government they were then creating. Section 10 of Article I thus prohibits states from entering into treaties or alliances with foreign nations; from coining money; from levying imposts or duties on exports; from keeping troops in time of peace; and from entering into compacts or agreements with other states and from engaging in war, without the consent of Congress. In addition, out of the framers' concern for the rights of private property, the states were denied the power to pass bills of attainder and *ex post facto* laws and were kept from passing legislation impairing the obligation of contracts. These flat prohibitions are easy to understand, and by and large the states have accepted them *in toto* and have not tried to find ways to get around them.

The states clearly have suffered a further loss of power by the adoption of the Fourteenth Amendment [12] and by the Supreme Court's extension through it to the states of most of the limitations on the power of Congress given in the first eight amendments. Thus the area of action left open to the states today is smaller than the area the framers originally foreclosed to them in Article I, section 10. Precisely how much smaller it is not possible to say, for the Supreme Court is still at work—and presumably always will be—defining and redefining the extent to which the Bill of Rights applies to state governments.

Even so, it is possible to say something about what the states can do. In general, they can exercise all those powers which have not been removed from their jurisdiction by prohibition or by federal preemption, constitutional or otherwise. Their most important power has always been the police power, which in effect endows them with responsibility for protecting the health, morals, safety, and general welfare of the citizens of the United

12. "No state shall make or enforce any law which shall abridge the privileges or immunities of citizens of the United States; nor shall any state deprive any person of life, liberty, or property, without due process of law; nor deny to any person within its jurisdiction the equal protection of the laws."

States. Under its broad coverage, all kinds of intimate regulations of individual life and conduct are enacted by state governments, or, by delegation from the states, by local governments. This does not altogether rule out federal regulation of some of the same subjects; Congress can and does enact police regulations in the exercise of some of its delegated and implied powers. But by and large, it is the states which provide legislation in this broad and basic area.

In addition, the states are competent to handle their own internal organization, structure, and procedures. Although the Congress was able to prescribe limitations and/or restrictions on territories before they were admitted to statehood, once they came within the union, states were free to draw up their own constitutions and frame their governments as they wished and to alter them as it suited them later on. This is a very significant power, inasmuch as even when the financing and many of the standards for programs of a wide variety are provided by the national government, their administration continues to be handled by state and local governments. The states also clearly have jurisdiction over the local governments within them. Local governments are regarded legally as creatures of the states and may, like state government itself, be cast in whatever molds the state legislatures may decide and be assigned whatever functions the states wish them to perform. Much of the states' power over education, for example, is given to local school boards.

Finally, the states handle most of the administration of justice in the United States. Federal courts are primarily intended to enforce federal laws and the federal Constitution; for the adjudication of most disputes between individuals and most crimes against society, state and local courts are utilized.

Other state powers can be described. The need here, however, is less to provide an exhaustive list of individual state powers than to indicate the broad range and scope of state power. Indeed, the full extent of state power has not yet been probed in any state. Despite the fact that, as Grant McConnell points out, "the states are perceived as presenting opportunities for experimentation and as sources of innovation in government," and are viewed as such precisely because the capacity of their reservoir of power is still unknown, "the total list of . . . innovations is not long. . . ." [13] In other words, the states can probably do a good deal more than they have in the implementation and development of their powers in the federal system.

For the fact is that the states have not made as much of their power position within the union as they might have. This is probably the result of a combination of factors. One important factor is without doubt the limitations the states have placed on themselves. To a much greater degree than the national Constitution, the state constitutions were written with the object of limiting governmental power. They are more restrictive than they are permissive and have as a result had to be amended almost yearly to permit governmental movement at all. Secondly there is the matter of leadership. State legislatures (the dominant part of most state governments) were for a long time not fully representative of the people [14] and are only now being forced to represent the urban majority more adequately. The long-powerful rural interests in the states were conservative in their concerns, more interested in preserving the *status quo* than in developing new departures in government and administration to meet changes they did not fully comprehend or approve. Under such dominance, neither strong governors nor strong political parties were allowed to emerge. As a consequence of all these factors, the states came to have a low visibility in the eyes of their citizens, who became habituated to look either to local governments or, latterly, to the national government for action in response to their needs. In any case, at least in recent years, action by Congress to solve a host of problems which might have been tackled by the states has been sought successfully, as even a cursory glance at legislation enacted since the inauguration of the New Deal attests. The growth of a leviathan in Washington, it can safely be asserted, is due in large part to the default of the states in exercising power in areas where they had a legitimate claim and every reason to act.

13. McConnell, *Private Power and American Democracy, op. cit.*, p. 167.
    14. Thus the chapter on state legislatures in a book on state government is subtitled "Over, Under, and About Equally Representative." John C. Buechner, *State Government in the Twentieth Century* (Boston: Houghton Mifflin, 1967), Ch. 4.

Thus it is false to argue a case for national "encroachment" into the power area of the states. The national government responded to the expressed demands of the people while the states did not. It is that simple. It cannot be successfully argued that any recent president, or Congress, or majority of the Supreme Court has set out to put into effect a revised theory of the division of powers between the national government and the other governments in the federal system. What can be demonstrated is that the national government filled a power vacuum when, in the words of the Chief Justice of New Jersey, the "inexorable sweep of scientific and economic events . . . dictated the readjustment of responsibility and power" in the United States.[15] To a large extent, the states turned a deaf or closed ear to that sweep of events, and the only recourse the people had was to turn to Washington for help in adjusting to it.

Just as it is impossible to argue that the national government is a single power force in the federal system, so it cannot be asserted that the states collectively are participants in that system, or that each is an equal partner therein. Although a number of regional groupings of states have emerged from time to time on a variety of issues, and though some of them have even exercised a a limited amount of power—the New England states in relation to industrial development, the Appalachian states in an attack on poverty, and the Southern and Western states with regard to higher education, for example—for the most part the states play their power roles in the federal game alone. There are thus fifty power points on the state side, and the differences among them are large and vary with the passage of time. The states differ in history and background, in social and racial composition, in economics and resources, in topography and climate, and in a variety of other ways. Thus they differ greatly in their potential for the exercise of power. And as a result of so many differences, the states inevitably assume different stances with respect to the federal system. There is a vast difference between Virginia, which for a while maintained a Commission on Constitutional Government as a state agency designed to "develop and promulgate in-

15. Chief Justice Joseph Weintraub, quoted in *Congressional Record* 105: A687 (February 2, 1959).

formation concerning the dual system of government, federal and state, established under the Constitution of the United States and those of the several states" to support the theory of state-oriented federalism,[16] and New York and many other states, which have established state liaison offices in Washington, the better to work with units of the federal government. The likelihood of any two states picked at random for that matter viewing the federal system and their own and the national government's role within it in the same light is not great. Thus the states inevitably lose some of their power in their very individualism and separateness.

The states lose another portion of power to their local governments which constitute the third important focal point of power in the federal system. The Constitution contains no reference at all to local governments. They have been assumed to be creatures of the states, by whom they may be subject to the most intimate and vital regulation and control. "Home rule" has done little to alter this basic relationship. But if local governments seem in theory not to have an independent existence, in fact they do have a life of their own, increasingly since a number of federal aid programs have begun to be based on direct contacts between the federal government and local units without the intercession of the states. They have a life of their own in any case, because no state is constituted so as to render its local units neuters. And the facts of life—local needs to be met, vested interests to be served, political pressures to be taken into account, party politics to be heeded—all contribute to their independence. Thus local governments must be considered on the same plane as the national government and the states as participants in the power process, even if there is no constitutional imperative for it.

Their power remains circumscribed, however. They have no inherent powers, no reserved powers, no powers by right at all. They have only those powers which the states wish and permit them to have. For the tasks facing them in the mid-twentieth century, these powers are usually not enough. The states have been notoriously slow in recognizing local problems and giving local units enough power to solve them. Mayor Samuel W. Yorty

16. An act to create a commission on constitutional government, Chapter 223, General Assembly of Virginia, approved March 7, 1958.

of Los Angeles once observed that "cities can't do anything" in California.[17] In problem area after problem area, he alleged—and he ticked off smog, crime, schools, and rapid transit in quick succession—the state denied local governments the necessary powers to act or granted them in too small a quantity or too late to be effective. The problem is not a simple one. It is aggravated by the prodigious number of local units, by the states' deeply entrenched habit of neglecting them, and by the local units themselves expecting very little state response to their pleas. Whether cities can convert their voting power now that legislative reapportionment is becoming a reality vis-à-vis the states is still not a sure thing. In 1966 the Deputy Mayor of New York, Robert Price, demanded that urban areas use their political power to force a revaluation of "the whole scope of Federal, state and municipal priorities." "The metropolitan areas," Price declared, "must become the primary political and governmental power in the United States, or else we are never going to have the tools or the money to do the work which must be done." In particular, Price thought, a plan must be devised to give cities an independent and primary taxing power that would free them from the penury imposed on them by their present position at the bottom of the fiscal totem pole. He called for a national conference, to be held at the initiative of the cities themselves, to consider their power plight and work out some way to overcome it.[18]

The diversity among local units has an even greater effect on their power than has the diversity within the national government and among the states. For there is often little to hold local units together, even within a single state, what with city-county, rural-urban, central city-suburban, and special-versus general-purpose unit conflicts. Nor is there an over-all local position or attitude. There are real differences which may be explained historically and in terms of function. Time and tradition have operated to exaggerate these differences and the necessity for independence until most local units are touchy and suspicious of other units on the same level. Of late there has been an increasing number of instances of interlocal cooperation, especially in the larger

17. Quoted in *The Christian Science Monitor*, May 4, 1966, p. 15.
18. Quoted in *The New York Times*, June 5, 1966, p. 40.

metropolitan areas. But it will probably be a long time before all local antagonisms are removed, and in any event, the sheer number of units undermines the status of local government as a single power entity within the federal system.

It is evident that, regardless of their exact power circumstances, all three levels of government act upon domestic problems.[19] Power in the United States is not compartmentalized but is shared. "This is one country with 50 states," the late President Kennedy once remarked. "We are all engaged, both on the State and Federal levels, and on the local level, in a common effort. . . . The important point is . . . that we are allies under the Constitution, that we must work closely together . . . for the benefit of our country which all of us seek to serve." [20] Governmental power in the United States is, in sum, a matter for the joint exertion of the several units of government who among them share the responsibility for serving the people of the nation. There is no formula for the exact distribution of that responsibility; it is something that has to be determined in each case by the need to be met, the pressures involved in bringing it to the attention of government, and the availability of resources to provide for it. Every time an exertion of power is called for, how it shall be made becomes a subject of debate and controversy, often protracted and sometimes bitter. Power is always in contest. That is the key to understanding the federal system.

But if there is continuing debate over the use of power in the American federal system, there is agreement with regard to certain fundamentals. There is agreement, first of all, that government in America, at whatever level, exists to serve the people of

19. As Professor Kenneth Boulding makes clear (Kenneth E. Boulding, *The Impact of the Social Sciences* (New Brunswick, New Jersey: Rutgers Univ. Press, 1966), p. 55, "The distinction between domestic and foreign affairs . . . is not a clear one and has become increasingly clouded in recent years. Many aspects of the organization and behavior of a national state which are thought of as concerned primarily with domestic matters in fact have a profound influence on the international system. A good example of this is American agricultural policy. . . ."

20. President John F. Kennedy, Remarks at the Opening Session of the Fifth Annual Legislative Conference of State Legislative Leaders, Boston, Massachusetts, September 21, 1963.

the United States as they wish to be served, and that power
wherever it is used is to be directed only to that end. There is
agreement also, at least since the Civil War, that *both* the national
government and the states are entitled to power and that neither
should be allowed to eclipse the other in exercising it. The federal government has come, particularly in the middle of the present century, to occupy a larger role in managing the internal affairs of the nation than it once had, but in the process the states
have not been frozen out. Rather, what Morton Grodzins reported in 1960, that "state and local governments are touching a
larger proportion of the people in more ways than ever before;
and they are spending a higher fraction of the total national
product" as they do so, has become steadily more the case each
passing year.[21] The enlargement of the federal sphere has resulted from the terrible demands of depression and war, from the
demands of aggrieved minorities, and from the fact, as already
suggested, that the states and local units failed or were unable to
take action where action had become necessary. It was made possible by the willingness of the Supreme Court to broaden the
construction of the commerce clause (or to restore it to the Marshall conception thereof) and to nationalize civil rights by use of
the Fourteenth Amendment. The Supreme Court has also broadened its view of the General welfare clause so as to permit national support of a much broader range of programs. But even as
national power came to be exerted more frequently, it was exerted in such a way as to involve the states. The national government has come to be chiefly financier and standard setter, the
states, executors and administrators. What has developed is a partnership in power between the national government and the states
and their local units for the most effective handling of the country's domestic governmental business. The end product of that
development is a single interlinked instrument of government to
perform the varied tasks and services the American people require. Thus it probably is no longer correct to speak of the governments of the United States, as if they were contestants in a
ring, each vying with the others for a share of attention and

21. Grodzins, in *Goals for Americans, op. cit.,* p. 261.

power. The American governmental process should rather be regarded as a single process, carried on at different levels by units of government with different personalities, as it were, but who are joined in a common enterprise and who share the same overall objective—the enhancement of the welfare of the American people.

Such a process obviously does not always work smoothly or with lightning speed. Sometimes, if debate is not concluded and a consensus reached, it is hard to get movement at all. The framers of the Constitution, however, were not concerned with how debate comes out, with what mix of power is finally brought to bear in each particular case. They were concerned that debate be held and hopeful that, however time-consuming, it might prevent the excesses and the harmful exercise of power.

Nor is the shared governmental process an easy one. Not the least among the difficulties it presents is the great number of governmental units among which the power debate must be waged. The total number of independent governmental units at the beginning of 1967 was 81,299, with an average per state of 1,626 units and a range from 20 in Hawaii to 6,454 in Illinois. The table below shows the breakdown of units over a twenty-five–year span.

TABLE 2.1 *Units of Government in
the United States at Intervals 1942 to 1967*

Type of unit	1942	1957	1962	1967
National	1	1	1	1
State	48	50	50	50
County	3,050	3,050	3,043	3,049
Municipality	16,220	17,215	18,000	18,048
Township	18,919	17,198	17,142	17,105
School district	108,579	50,454	34,678	21,782
Special district	8,299	14,424	18,323	21,264
Total	*155,116*	*102,392*	*91,237*	*81,299*

The national government was created by design, and thirteen states had of necessity to be included in the system, as did the relatively large number of local units of government in existence in 1787. But the rest of the units—other states, cities, townships, special districts—were all created later, willy-nilly, in response to ir-resistible political and economic demands in Congress and in the state legislatures. There were a good many struggles over power as new units were brought into existence—the seaboard resisted the mountains, the free states resisted slave states, residents of agricultural areas resisted stockmen—but there was no stopping their creation. And the process, below the state level at least, has not yet come to a halt. The same pressures that have always been present are still at work to bring new local units of government into existence. As the table demonstrates, the 1967 census of governments showed a further increase in the number of both municipalities and special districts, though through consolidation of school districts the total number is smaller than it was in 1962.

With no foreordained plan from which to build, and no clear guidelines to help the old and the new units adjust to one another (how would such a plan and such guidelines have been drawn up?), so many contenders for power produce a great deal of overlapping, duplication, and conflict, as well as waste of effort and resources.

Moreover, the development of the over-all system, left as it was to time and circumstances rather than to the requirements of a generally accepted plan, was spotty. Power was exerted generally in response to crisis situations, to problems after they had developed, rather than prospectively, in an attempt to prevent their emergence. Great strides have been made in solving a number of problems facing the American nation in this way, problems of education, highway and airport construction, housing and urban renewal, and public health and welfare, to name only a few. But other problems have been neglected, and some of them are critical ones. In this context, asked Senator Edmund S. Muskie of Maine not long ago, "How do we make sure that the powers of government [will] continue to be diffused while at the same time the chores of government are effectively performed? This is the great dilemma which faces us with increasing urgency." [22]

For a long time there was no answer to this dilemma. Neither

22. Edmund S. Muskie, Speech to the American Municipal Congress, 1961, in *Proceedings of the American Municipal Congress* (Washington, 1961), p. 18.

the federal government nor the states have indulged to any great extent in planning for the future use of governmental power. Indeed, *planning* has been a suspect word in the United States, and the process it suggests has been regarded as an alien one. Government at all levels has been pretty much a pragmatic affair with policy framed on an *ad hoc*, after-the-event, basis, and individually at each level of government, and compartmentalized even within states and municipal boundaries. It has not been part of the process of federalism to draw up a coherent program of action based on a joint analysis of emerging problems and future trends in order to develop devices to meet them cooperatively. There have been a few exceptions, to be sure. Some of the interstate compact agencies [23] have set prospective programs of action for themselves, and such federal-state programs as those for highway, hospital, and airport construction and such federal-local programs as urban renewal have been based on joint analysis and planning, as well as on subsequent cooperative action. But no general across-the-board effort to anticipate problems and devise ways to attack them cooperatively has been made by the parties to the federal system. President Eisenhower did appoint a Commission on National Goals, whose report went a long way in that direction.[24] But it came too late in Eisenhower's second term for him to initiate action on the basis of its contents, even if he had been so inclined. While Presidents Kennedy and Johnson professed interest both in implementing the report's suggestions and in continuing the process followed in developing national goals, very little concrete was done in either direction. Thus the policy-planning function of American governments is still exercised by and large as it has been all along, much of it in Washington, some of it in state capitals, some in county courthouses and city halls, but with no provision for the integration of all the action and little advance arrangement for cooperative administration. That the intergovernmental system works as well as it does is a tribute to the hard work of the thousands of federal, state, and

23. See Richard H. Leach and Redding S. Sugg, Jr., *The Administration of Interstate Compacts* (Baton Rouge, Louisiana: Louisiana State University Press, 1959).

24. The report was published under the title *Goals for Americans, op. cit.*

local administrators who somehow pick up the loose threads and weave them into a semblance of order.

There has been some improvement in the situation, however. As the crisis years of depression and war moved on, during which swift and effective governmental action was imperative, the number of intergovernmental programs grew in virtually geometric proportions, until by the mid-fifties a nearly chaotic situation was the result. So dominant did the national government's part appear to be, no one was sure just where the states and their local subdivisions stood any longer. In an attempt to find out, the second Hoover Commission, the Commission on Intergovernmental Relations (the Kestnbaum Commission), the two Congressional Committees on Government Operations, and the Joint Federal-State Action Committee, as well as the President's Commission on National Goals, all devoted at least part of their efforts to an examination of the workings of the federal system. All of them reached the common conclusion that the greatest problem was the lack of a systematic method to bring into the open the problems and difficulties which arise between the many governments involved in the system. The great need, all of them agreed, was to provide a regular forum for the discussion and resolution of such problems. Acting on a specific recommendation of the Kestnbaum Commission, Congress established in 1959 a continuing agency for study, information, and guidance in the field of intergovernmental relations as an arm of the national government.[25] The permanent Advisory Commission on Intergovernmental Relations, as it is called, is a bipartisan body of twenty-six members, who represent governors, mayors, county officials, state legislatures, Congress, the executive branch of the national government, and the public at large—all the parties involved in modern functional federalism. The commission derives practically all its financial support from the national government, but it responds "to the needs of all three major levels of government." It "encourage[s] discussion and study at an early date of emerging public problems that are likely to require intergovernmental cooperation" for their solution.[26] It thus provides for the

25. Public Law 380, 86th Congress. 1st Session.
26. Advisory Commission on Intergovernmental Relations, *Third Annual Report* (Washington, 1962), p. 2.

first time an impartial agency to study trouble spots in intergovernmental relations which might interfere with the effective exercise of power at any level of government and to make recommendations for their alleviation or removal. Once recommendations are made, the commission works to implement them by stimulating and encouraging their adoption by national, state, and local governments. The commission regularly prepares draft legislative proposals to be considered by the states.

It is too soon to expect the commission to have rationalized the use of power in the federal system, if indeed that is a logical expectation at all. But in the years since its creation, the commission has tackled some of the thorniest problems of intergovernmental relations. In 1968, for example, it issued a two-volume report on fiscal balance in the American federal system; released a study of recent urbanization trends in the United States with recommendations for national and state policies to deal with them; completed a study of intergovernmental problems in medicaid; made progress on an analysis of state aid to local governments; and began to study state-local responsibilities for labor-management relations in public employment. A large number of its recommendations have been adopted every year, and if it is strengthened internally [27] and supported adequately by appropriations, it can be expected to be a force of considerable importance in the future of American federalism. Its creation at least gives the United States a steady force at work concerned with establishing better working relations between levels of government, so that each level will make more effective use of the power vested in it. The commission's continued existence promises that power in the federal system may come to be used to better advantage than it ever has been before.

One other aspect of the nation's ability to use power effectively must be mentioned. The United States has traditionally been opposed to planning, to looking ahead and making long-term calculations as to what goals to achieve and how to achieve them. What Terry Sanford said about the states applies with equal pertinency to all levels of government:

27. See the recommendation concerning the Commission by W. Brooke Graves in his monumental *American Intergovernmental Relations* (New York: Scribners, 1964), p. 916.

From my observations of a number of states and my own experience in the governor's office, I have concluded that one major weakness of the states is that too often state government is "flying blind." Governors and state legislators, with the best of intentions for improving the effectiveness of state government, frequently have difficulty knowing where they should lead the state. When they want to lead, and have the capacity to lead, they are not quite sure how to chart the course.

For one thing . . . turnover of state officials, both elective and administrative . . . is so high that continuity of programming is most difficult. With each change of administration, there is a shift of emphasis—new goals are set, often with little or no relation to the old. Change is initiated for the sake of change. I am not saying that this is always bad, but it isn't necessarily good. Add to this the fact that most states simply don't have the experience for long-range thinking that will allow them to plan ahead with any degree of certainty that where they are going is where they ought to go. Lack of knowing where we ought to go hampers our getting there.[28]

Sanford called for the initiation of long-range programming by the states as an answer to the problem. The same remedy might be utilized by all governments in the American federal system.

But even with the Advisory Commission at work, and programs of long-range planning in effect, the problems arising out of the use of power in the American federal system would not all be solved. For not only is federalism always in motion, as power units are added to and subtracted from the system and power adjustments are made by and between units, thus constantly introducing new problems, but some of the power problems are probably beyond analysis and treatment altogether. Moreover, while power is in part institutional, involving in its exercise government councils, bureaus, agencies, boards, legislatures, and courts, much of the power in any governmental system is personal. Power is wielded by individuals, senators and representatives, committee chairmen and agency heads, governors and mayors, county commissioners and city managers. Personal power cannot be eliminated in a democratic system; it can only be restricted and supervised. Finally, as suggested earlier, much of the power held and

28. Terry Sanford, "A New Strategy for State Initiative," An Address delivered at the 72nd Annual Conference of the National Municipal League, November 15, 1966. Mimeo copy. Pp. 3-4.

exercised in the United States is private, not governmental at all, exercised by the press and other communications media, industrial and commercial firms, labor organizations, and a variety of religious, social, scientific, and educational groups. How are the power relationships of all these groups to be regularized and harmonized with exertions of public power? How indeed! James MacGregor Burns was conscious of the importance of these power factors in his study, *Presidential Government*. Noted Burns, "Stripped to its essentials, the Presidency requires two cardinal political skills: the ability to appeal directly to mass publics, at home and abroad, and the ability to negotiate with rival leaders holding independent bases of power." [29] The President must use his power over the public, in other words, to reach the wielders of political and economic power in the nation, and he must negotiate with them to accomplish his objectives. What is true of the President is true only to a lesser degree of governors and mayors —and not only of executive officers but of legislative leaders as well. But how these negotiations will be carried on and with what success cannot be predicted or described. Much negotiation goes on behind the scenes in any case. And all such power relationships depend on the persons involved—their intelligence, their tractability, their integrity, their willingness to bargain. Even the best institutional arrangements cannot mitigate the difficulties personality clashes and rivalry for power pose for the governmental process.

The rivalry between political, i.e., governmental, power and private economic power has been a central issue in the United States ever since the formation of the Union. From the beginning the relation between the two forces has chiefly been one of conflict, as political power (numbers) has sought to enlist the support of and then to control economic power (interests). The power of giant industrial units, corporations, trusts, banks—and latterly of unions—in the United States is incalculable. For a while, after the Civil War, the conversion of the nation into a plutocracy did not seem impossible. Even in the heyday of the Jacksonian period, there had been foreshadowings of a new tyr-

29. James MacGregor Burns, *Presidential Government* (Boston: Houghton Mifflin, 1966), p. 299.

anny. DeTocqueville noted the development of a manufacturing aristocracy in the United States and warned against its harshness.[30] By Charles F. Adams's time, the Gilded Age had come fully into its own. The industrial potentates who dominated that age, Adams wrote,

> declared war, negotiated peace, reduced courts, legislatures, and sovereign States to an unqualified obedience to their will, disturbed trade, agitated the currency, imposed taxes and boldly setting both law and public opinion at defiance, have freely exercised many other attributes of sovereignty.[31]

An equally somber assessment of the situation was made a few years later by Grover Cleveland in his 1888 annual message to Congress:

> . . . we discover the existence of trusts, combinations, and monopolies, while the citizen is struggling far in the rear or is trampled to death beneath an iron heel. Corporations, which should be carefully restrained creatures of the law and servants of the people, are fast becoming the people's masters.[32]

Gradually, resistance developed to such usurpation of power, as between them the Greenback, Granger, and Populist movements, aided by an array of brilliant thinkers—Henry George, Edward Bellamy, Henry Demarest Lloyd, Lester F. Ward, Louis D. Brandeis, and Woodrow Wilson prominent among them—and by the muckrakers, mounted an offensive in behalf of political power. Their efforts culminated first in the Progressive Era and later in the New Freedom and the New Deal. If the worst abuses of private power were corrected in the process, the power conflict itself was not finally resolved. It not only continues to the present day but will likely always be a part of the American political milieu.

Nor, finally, has any attention been paid here to military power. Despite adherence to the principle of civilian control of the military, the United States is affected by a military psy-

30. Alexis DeTocqueville, *Democracy in America*, Tr. by Henry Reeve (London: Oxford Univ. Press, 1953). 4 vols. See Vol. 4, Chapters 5–7.

31. Charles F. Adams, Jr., "An Erie Raid," *North American Review* 112: 242 (April 1871).

32. James D. Richardson, *Messages and Papers of the Presidents* (Washington: Government Printing Office, 1909), Vol. 8, p. 724.

chosis,[33] so much so that in his farewell address to the American people, President Eisenhower warned against the power of the industrial-military complex. "In the councils of government," he declared, "we must guard against the acquisition of unwarranted influence, whether sought or unsought, by the military-industrial complex. The potential for the disastrous rise of misplaced power exists and will continue to exist." The possibility of the abuse of power, President Eisenhower felt, arose chiefly out of the tremendous stake American industry has in defense supply, an interest which it might use with the acquiescence of the American people to force a build-up of military power or to perpetuate or accelerate a war when the need to do so did not in fact exist. By such techniques, the nation might be converted into a garrison state. President Kennedy repeated the warning in an early message to Congress, and since then it has been issued a number of times.[34]

There is no indication that the dire forebodings of Presidents Eisenhower and Kennedy have come about. In fact, the distinguished political scientist, Hans Morgenthau, has concluded that such fears are groundless. "The military are indeed a center of power," Morgenthau writes,

competing with other centers of power, old and new, for the determination of policies relevant to its tasks. But, far from being a single-minded colossus, it reflects within itself the same variety of philosophies and policy commitments that characterize American opinion in general. Contrary to popular assumptions, the power of the military vis-à-vis the civilian centers of power has steadily declined in recent times.[35]

If Morgenthau is right, the problem is not as severe as feared. The danger of concentration of power in the military, however, is always present, and its influence in American society needs constantly to be guarded against. As with the conflict with economic power, the rivalry of military power with political power

33. See Tristram Coffin, *The Armed Society: Militarism in Modern America* (New York: Macmillan, 1964).
34. See C. Wright Mills, *The Power Elite* (New York: Oxford Univ. Press, 1965) and Fred J. Cook, *The Welfare State* (New York: Macmillan, 1962), among others
35. Hans Morgenthau, "Who's Running the Country?" *Saturday Review*, April 25, 1964, p. 31.

cannot be overlooked in any analysis of power in the federal system.

Karl W. Deutsch may be correct in asserting that the question of power is not the most important one after all in considering government. "Power," Deutsch believes, "is . . . neither the center nor the essence of politics. It is one of the currencies of politics, one of the important mechanisms of acceleration or damage control where influence, habit, or voluntary coordination may have failed, or where these may have failed to serve adequately the function of goal attainment. . . . [It is] important . . . [but it is] secondary to what now appears . . . as the essence of politics: the dependable coordination of human efforts and expectations for the attainment of the goals of the society." [36] In any case, as the studies of Deutsch, Maass, Ylvisaker, and others show, political scientists are not agreed on either the role or the importance of power in government, nor have they settled on a satisfactory definition of it. Such a discussion as this, therefore, can at best be only partially reflective of the issues involved. There can be no doubt, however, that the power aspects of federalism are vital to its functioning and understanding.

36. Karl W. Deutsch, *The Nerves of Government* (London: Free Press of Glencoe, 1963), p. 124.

III

THE DYNAMICS OF
FEDERALISM

THE FRAMERS OF the American constitution devised a number of ways—separation of powers, checks and balances, judicial review, and federalism—to prevent the abuse of power in the system they were creating and at the same time to preserve the largest possible area of independent action for the individual. But the same devices were also able to prevent the governments of the new nation from doing things easily and quickly. Federalism, in other words, was designed as one of a parcel of negative devices which inhibit the use of power in the United States. It was not designed to facilitate that use. It thus serves as a *static* element in American society, not as a *dynamic* one at all. In a sense therefore, it is wrong to seek the dynamics of federalism.

On the other hand, the federal system in operation has become noted for the numerous and diverse opportunities it presents for the positive exercise of governmental power, a development which has been an incidental result of the vast number of power points in the system. Centralization of power in a unitary system would very likely have imposed a large degree of uniformity and a generally accepted pattern of what constituted "proper" governmental action in this country, even as it has in others. Decentralization has virtually guaranteed a large degree of difference among the courses of action which may be taken by the many centers of governmental power in the United States (not too large a degree, of course, since most Americans in the formative stages of the union shared the same racial, legal, cultural, and even social background). At the beginning of the republic, the popular orientation against any use of governmental power and the relatively few problems requiring its exertion kept the potentials for difference largely hidden. But as the number of units in the system proliferated when the American people began to move across the continent, and as needs were discovered which could only be met by governmental action, differences in approach and method began to appear in quantity. Before long, the fact that units of government in the federal system *could* differ was converted into the principle that they *should* differ. Each unit of government in the system came to be recognized as an independent focal point of power, directed to the purposes and ends of its particular constituents.

Thus federalism has built within it two opposing concepts. One views power with distrust, seeing the division of governmental power as a method by which its exercise is slowed down in deference to individual self-reliance. The other views power expectantly, seeing the division of power as providing additional opportunities for its use in ways that accord with local, not with national, determinants. Our concern in this chapter is with the use of power, not with the forces that restrain it. It is necessary only to remember in the pages that follow that federalism was not designed primarily as a device for facilitating the use of power and that as a consequence the power dynamics of the system were not developed at all by our founding fathers. They were left instead to evolve in the course of time, to be ground out of experience; even now, they are neither clearly articulated nor fully understood.

There is no data bank for power factors; lacking hard data, it is impossible to develop a completely accurate picture of power in the American federal system. Therefore only a series of propositions will be advanced. Until the "social laboratories" Professor Lasswell called for recently [1] are developed and in operation, such propositions will have to suffice.

PROPOSITION I. It is a misconception to view American federalism as a power system. Despite common usage, power is not ex-

1. Harold D. Lasswell, "Do We Need Social Observatories?" *Saturday Review*, August 5, 1967, pp. 49–52.

ercised systematically in the United States. Indeed, it is probably wrong even to use the suffix "ism" for federalism, for the danger is always present that it will be read to mean adherence to a system rather than to a process, which is all its use should imply. "System" suggests a regularly interacting group of power units, a power network, which performs its functions in a steady flow. That simply is not descriptive of federalism. Units there are aplenty, and interaction in great quantity, but there is nothing regularized about it, nor is there a steady flow of output. Power in the federal system moves irregularly, in spurts, even as water overcomes obstacles and flows on again until it meets another. It is characterized by disorder and seldom moves twice precisely in the same way to accomplish its objectives.

PROPOSITION 2. Federalism is procedural in nature and so devoid of specific goals in operation. It fulfills its purpose in its functioning, not in meeting a set of predetermined objectives. Thus despite the inclusion of a "more perfect Union" among the phrases describing the goals of American government in the wording of the preamble to the Constitution, federalism is merely a means to be employed in achieving those goals. Nothing in the debates at Philadelphia or in *The Federalist* suggests that the framers intended otherwise. And what they did not provide for has not been added subsequently either by direction or indirection. Federalism remains process. To read anything else into it is to misread it altogether.

PROPOSITION 3. Action in the American federal state is not confined to governments alone. Although it is common to refer to federalism as an inter*governmental* process, it is necessary to remember that we have recognized from the outset "that the nation's public purposes are considerably more extensive in scope than its governmental purposes, and . . . a wide variety of private institutions [have been] chartered to accomplish certain *public*, though *non-governmental*, purposes. . . ." [2] Table I below attempts to suggest the traditional primary and secondary points of responsibility for action in major program areas in the United States. It is obvious from the table that governments have only part of the burden to bear.

2. Carnegie Corporation of New York, *Annual Report 1968*. "The Report of the President" (New York, 1968), p. 6.

TABLE 3.1   *Traditional Responsibilities for Action in the United States in Selected Program Areas*

	Transportation & communication	National defense	Education	Social security	Highways	Property protection	Metropolitan development	Health	Natural resource development
Federal government	x	X	x	X	X	x	x	x	x
State governments	x	x	x	x	X	x	x	x	x
Local governments	x	—	X	—	x	X	X	X	—
Private sector	X	—	X	X	—	—	X	X	X

— minimal or no responsibility
x secondary responsibility
X primary responsibility

PROPOSITION 4. Action in the American federal state is not automatic. It must be triggered by one or more forces within the state. Like the Constitution itself, federalism is only a contrivance which must have life breathed into it. The nature of the legislative process is such that it is not often activated until overwhelming pressures bring about motion on the part of legislators and legislative committees. And administrative procedures are apt to become rooted in the habits of administrators and so to become rigid with the passage of time. The essential conservatism of both legislators and administrators works to slow innovation at all levels of government. If innovation is to be secured—if power, in other words, is to be exercised—there must be sufficient counterpressure to overcome this inertia. Sometimes that pressure emanates from the judiciary, sometimes from state and local governments, but more often it comes from outside the formal structure of government altogether.

PROPOSITION 5. The inputs into the federal process, *i.e.*, the power agents which may trigger action, are numerous. Those which, singly or in combination, account for action in a particular instance cannot always be identified. A diagram of some of them might be useful to illustrate the point (see p. 62). Some issues will attract one combination of inputs, others will enlist the interests of quite a different set. Federal court decisions, for example, along with presidential prodding and popular demand, are generally regarded as the chief inputs in the power move which brought about change in the area of civil rights, whereas urban needs and pressures and the leadership of the national Department of Housing and Urban Affairs were the prime movers in bringing about the development of the model cities program. The possible permutations and combinations in the federal process are unlimited.

PROPOSITION 6. Federalism lacks any single point of responsibility for triggering the process into action. Although both the national government and the states have ample power under the Constitution on which to base action, there is no clear statement or implication therein to guide either as to when or how to exert it, either singly or in combination. The only reference to intergovernmental action in the Constitution occurs in Article 1, section 10, which requires the states to seek the approval of Congress when they conclude an interstate compact or agreement among themselves, and even there neither its absolute necessity nor the mode of action is specified. Nor is there any guidance to the private sector as to when or how it should act. Since there are no directions as to who should instigate a power move in the United States, it is done by chance, it often is done too late to be fully effective, and it frequently produces conflict among the several forces involved.

PROPOSITION 7. Action in American federalism is for the most part confined to parts of a problem rather than to a problem as a whole. Action is brought about more often in response to a narrow pressure than to a broad one. Thus action can be secured on individual urban ailments (mass transportation, slum clearance, rat control), but not on the over-all urban problem; or on highway safety or airport construction or railroad regulation, but not on the faltering American transportation network.

PROPOSITION 8. Action by one of the input forces listed above in a single program area is often taken independently of action taken or being contemplated by other input forces. No mechanism for correlating power exertions in diverse program areas has

*Diagram Suggesting Power Inputs
in the American Federal System*

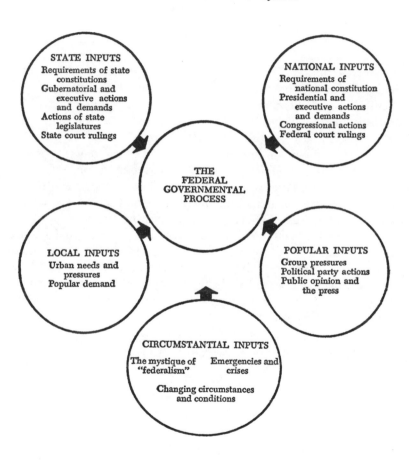

ever been developed in American federalism. Thus there is no sure way of preventing overlap, duplication, and conflict of efforts.

PROPOSITION 9. Exertions of power in the federal system do not always produce a positive result. Although with Locke the framers of the Constitution believed in man's essential reasonableness, and so were confident that a multi-partite governmental system like federalism could be made to work, they were realists enough to be aware as well of man's toleration of inaction (witness Jefferson's "long train of abuses" in the Declaration of Independence) and of his proclivity for conflict and dissension in devising alternatives for positive action (witness their experience under the Continental Congress and the Articles of Confederation). If the power exertions of American governments have made a major contribution to the conversion of a wilderness to the world's most industrialized nation, there have been many occasions when a negative result ensued. The Civil War stands out as the major, though far from the only, example of conflict, not cooperation, as the result of the intergovernmental power process at work in the United States. Just as often, no action at all results as relatively equal power forces resist each other to a draw.

PROPOSITION 10. The outputs of the federal governmental process, *i.e.*, the results of the exercise of power in the federal system, can be listed under headings, as follows:

Unilateral action	Cooperative action
National action	*Interlocal action*
State action	*State-local action*
Local action	*Interstate action*
Private action	*National-state action*
	Multigovernmental action
	Governmental-private action
Conflict	Inaction
Interlocal conflict	
State-local conflict	
Interstate conflict	
National-state conflict	
Multigovernmental conflict	
Governmental-private conflict	

PROPOSITION 11. Power in the federal process, as it is in politics generally, is circular. No output is final. Each output is fed back into the system and must be considered as constituting another input in the process. No "solution," thus, is ever final. Federalism involves constant change and movement. Conflict, for example, at any of the levels, is apt to result in a suit in court, the decision of which, as in interstate boundary disputes, may trigger still another reaction by the parties involved. Similarly, the success of a cooperative output, such as that achieved by the Port of New York Authority in the years after its creation in 1921, may come to constitute a force (or input) of its own toward further interstate accommodation along the same lines. The possibilities are endless.

The federalism the workings of which are suggested by the foregoing propositions is thus an unstructured process, a process without required form or practice, a process constantly in flux and under evolution. So many forces make an impact on the dynamics of the federal process that far more research needs to be done before more can be said definitively about them or about the process itself. One contribution the behavioral sciences can make to an understanding of federalism is to subject as many of those forces as possible to careful scrutiny. But constitutional law, administrative science, and legislative process all have contributions to make as well. One hopes that before too long their joint efforts will result in a better understanding of the dynamics of federalism than has been achieved so far.

Some of the difficulty lies in the part American political parties play in the dynamics of federalism. Political parties have aptly been described as the engines of American government; they stand between the private sector of American life (more properly, the voters) and the agencies of government at every level and provide much of the drive which causes the power of those agencies to be restrained or exerted. Moreover, political parties provide a way to select candidates to fill the elective positions of government at the national, state, and local levels; they support candidates in their subsequent races for election; they stimulate voters to think and act politically at election time and occasionally between elections; they provide a major forum for the discussion of issues at all levels of government; they help shape public policy and control the machinery by which it is carried out; and they stand as one device of surety for the satisfactory performance of governmental officials in office.

They do not, however, perform these functions monolithically and that is the first point to be made about their power. *The* Republican Party or *the* Democratic Party is a myth. Indeed, the outstanding feature of the American party system is its decentralized, even fractionated, nature. Rather than there being simply two parties at the national level, there may be at least four, if Professor Burns's reasoning is accepted: two Congressional parties and two presidential parties [3] and an occasional "third" party [4] as well. And at the state level it is virtually impossible to count the many widely differing state and local party units, each of which functions pretty independently of the others. This decentralization is the result of forces which began to operate early and which by and large have not changed. It resulted naturally from the tremendous size of the United States and the early lack of adequate transportation and communication facilities to link diverse regions. It resulted too from the deep American attachment to the ideology of localism and from a strong belief in the democratic value of small autonomous units of power. The small, geographically defined, single-member constituency and the long ballot, which came into vogue in Jackson's time, still survive throughout the United States and serve to keep parties decentralized. From the outset, districts small enough to keep a fairly low ratio between representatives and the people were favored in the United States; and after the Jackson era, when, in order to bring government closer to the people, the Jacksonians brought about extension of the suffrage, rotation in office, and minimum qualifications for holding government offices, that type of district was made virtually inviolate. Most of the offices to be filled on the lengthening ballots were local ones, and as a result party activities became locally oriented. Centralization of party affairs made little sense to leaders whose support

3. See Burns, *Presidential Government, op. cit.*, pp. 159–76.
4. See Howard P. Nash, *Third Parties in American Politics* (Washington: Public Affairs Press, 1959).

came from small segments of the total population, and it makes no better sense to them today. As Edward Banfield and James Wilson have said, even "Congressmen and Senators are essentially local politicians and those of them who forget it soon cease to be politicians at all." [5]

If parties have taken their shape from the federal mold into which the nation was cast by the framers, they have also contributed a great deal to the preservation and hardening of that mold to the present day. In a landmark study of American political parties, Morton Grodzins described the effect of our undisciplined, locally oriented political parties as preserving "both the existence and form of the considerable measure of governmental decentralization" which is characteristic of the United States. "The constitutional fathers," Grodzins noted, "rigged a government to dissuade the formation of political parties and to prevent concentration of power under the aegis of parties in the national government. They did this by establishing a system of separation, within the federal government and between the federal government and the states." By now, the formal separations of power have become relatively unimportant, but the separation of parties has continued and become rigid. As it has worked out, instead of preventing the formation of parties, the framers' scheme only prevented the formation of strong, nationwide parties. Parties developed all right, but they developed as small, separate units, and to this day they have by and large maintained their aloofness from one another, so much so that Grodzins is tempted to call them "antiparties" instead of parties, if one defines *party* in the usual sense of one group dedicated to bringing segments of power together and welding them into one in order to tackle common problems and attempt to achieve common goals.[6]

Parties thus represent the main support of the traditional decentralized structure of government units in the United States today. Lacking a central focal point, it is in the interest of each party unit first to maintain and strengthen its own position vis-à-vis the local electorate and only after having done so to work

5. Edward C. Banfield and James Q. Wilson, *City Politics* (Cambridge: Harvard Univ. Press, 1963), p. 2.

6. Morton Grodzins, "American Political Parties and the American System," *The Western Political Quarterly* 13:974 (December 1960).

with other units in pursuit of broader common objectives. Unlike British parties, which are organized from the top down and respond to elected national leaders and to a single national program of action, American party units are most effectively organized at the local level—county, city, and precinct—and respond primarily to local interests, problems, and political cultures. As Frank J. Sorauf has demonstrated, American political leaders are more apt to try to live up to local constituency expectations than they are to any more general, not to say national, party norms.[7] Their influence follows the pattern of their structure and is fractionated. Indeed, Grodzins concludes, "the peculiar and unique nature of the American political parties provides the dynamics of the system: that the chaos of party explains the chaos of governments and the characteristics of government that flow from this chaos."[8]

This being the case, parties as such do not exert their power in American government in any coherent or steadily maintained pattern.[9] Members and units of the same party often work in opposition to each other and/or in cooperation with members and units of the other party to achieve differing objectives. Even the national and state platforms arrived at by conventions of delegates from below are regarded not as binding but as entirely dispensable in the face of contrary local or even personal pressures and interests. With parties constituted as they are, it has been impossible to develop a system of party discipline which would control individual party members in legislative bodies, and the legislators' voting has thus been free to respond to dictates other than party "lines." As a result, party membership itself has never come to have much meaning in the United States.

All these factors must be kept in mind when considering parties as power agents in the federal system. Clearly, party units do

7. Frank J. Sorauf, *Party and Representation* (New York: Atherton Press, 1963), a study of local parties in Pennsylvania.
8. Grodzins, "American Political Parties and the American System," *op. cit.*
9. Karl M. Schmidt insists that a "quiet revolution" in federalism has been brought about by "the work of pragmatic leaders of both political parties who have found in our system the flexibility to adapt to modern needs." Karl M. Schmidt, ed., *American State and Local Government in Action* (Belmont, California: Dickenson, 1966), p. 3. If he is right, they have done so as individuals and not as leaders of parties as such.

tackle and propose solutions to current problems. Their proposals, however, are cast for the most part so as to utilize existing
governmental units and skirt the fundamental question of the division of power among the national government, the states, and
local units of government. Neither party goes far beyond repeti-
tion of slogans in an attempt to analyze the limited role they in
fact play in activating change and innovation in the federal system or to suggest ways of increasing their contribution toward
that end. In 1968 the Republican Coordinating Committee did
issue a 22-page report entitled "The Restoration of Federalism in
America" in *The Republican,* the official publication of the Republican National Committee, but the report merely examined alleged "excessive centralization of power in Washington" and
made recommendations to alleviate it.[10] Generally the parties shy
away from a direct confrontation with the concept of federalism.
Nowhere is this more obvious than in the party platforms. Parties
speak with one voice only quadrennially, when each draws up its
platform as part of the presidential nominating process. Platforms
thus provide the only succinct statement of party beliefs and
principles. One might suppose that platforms would cover all the
points which the parties feel to be of primary importance in defining and clarifying their positions, and therefore include a discussion of federalism. But while they deal with a great many individual program areas in which problems of intergovernmental
relations and the division of power between units and levels of
government are present, and make a large number of unrelated
pronouncements about appropriate federal, state, and local action
therein, neither party sees its platform as a vehicle for the systematic and analytic treatment of a subject such as federalism. In its
1968 platform, the Democratic Party reaffirmed the hallowed idea
that "citizen participation in government is most meaningful at
the levels of government closest to the people." For that reason,
it went on,

we recognize the necessity of developing a true partnership between
state, local, and Federal governments, with each carrying its share of
the financial and administrative load. We acknowledge the tremen-

10. "The Restoration of Federalism in America," *The Republican,*
Vol. 4, No. 2 (February 5, 1968), pp. 5, 9.

dous strides made by President Johnson in strengthening federal-state relations through open communications with the governors and local officials, and we pledge to continue and expand on this significant effort.

The complexities of federal-state-local relationships must be simplified, so that state and local communities receiving federal aid will have maximum freedom to initiate and carry out programs suited to their own particular needs. To give states and communities greater flexibility in their programs we will combine individual grant programs into broader categories.

As the economy grows, it is the federal revenue system that responds most quickly, yet it may the states and local governments [*sic*] whose responsibilities mount most rapidly. To help states and cities meet their fiscal challenges, we must seek new methods for states and local governments to share in federal revenues while retaining responsibility for establishing their own priorities and for operating their own programs. To this end, we will seek out new and innovative approaches to government to assure that our Federal system does, in fact, deliver to the people the services for which they are paying."

The 1968 Republican Party platform addressed itself to federalism in a section on "The Individual and Government." "Decentralization of power," it observed, "is urgently needed to preserve personal liberty, improve efficiency, and provide a swifter response to human problems."

Many states and localities are eager to revitalize their own administrative machinery, procedures, and personnel practices. Moreover, there is growing inter-state cooperation in such fields as education, elimination of air and water pollution, utilization of airports, highways and mass transportation. We pledge full federal cooperation with these efforts, including revision of the system of providing federal funds and reestablishment of the authority of state governments in coordinating and administering the federal programs. Additionally, we propose the sharing of federal revenues with state governments.

Obviously, neither of these sections speaks directly to the dynamics of federalism. What constitutes a "true partnership" of governments? When exactly is "maximum freedom" obtained? What is the relation between the national government and efforts of state and local governments to "revitalize" themselves? How is revenue to be divided among competing units of government so as to achieve the most appropriate fiscal balance? To such questions, neither platform supplies any answers.

Nor are the party platforms any more relevant to the actual dynamics of federalism in their many references to intergovernmental relations in program areas. The 1968 Democratic Party platform asserts in relation to the solution of urban problems that "Democrats have invigorated local effort through federal leadership and assistance." And elsewhere it declares:

Under our constitutional system of federalism, the primary responsibility for law enforcement rests with selected local officials and with governors, but the federal government can and should play a constructive role in support of state and local authorities.

We will help the states to establish consumer fraud and information bureaus, and to update consumer credit laws.

We urge local governments to shape their own zoning laws and building codes to favor consumers and hold down costs.

Our aim is to maintain state-local control over the nation's educational system, with federal financial assistance and help in stimulating changes. . . .

The Republican platform is not significantly different. Like the Democratic platform, it relies throughout on verbs such as "support," "encourage," "assist," "finance," and "share" to describe its concept of the proper working relationship between the national government and the other levels of government in the United States. Thus the Republican platform pledges the party to "Presidential leadership which will buttress state and local government," "vigorous federal support to innovative state programs," and "an all-out, federal-state-local crusade against crime." The platform also notes that

Air and water pollution, already acute in many areas, require vigorous state and federal action, regional planning, and maximum cooperation among neighboring cities, counties and states. We will encourage this planning and cooperation.

Local communities will be encouraged to adopt uniform, modern building codes . . . and innovative state and local programs will be supported.

We believe that states which have not yet acted should reevaluate their positions with respect to 18-year old voting, and that each such state should decide this matter for itself. We urge the states to act *now.* We will encourage state, local or private programs of teacher training . . . To help assure excellence and equality of educational opportunity, we will urge the states to present plans for federal assistance which would include state distribution of such aid to non-public school children.

Additionally, we will work with states and local communities to help assure improved services to the mentally ill. . . .

To judge from such statements, the role the parties see for themselves in effectuating national policy is largely an exhortative one. Without saying so, both parties seem to recognize the fact of their inability to do anything more forceful vis-à-vis state and local governments and acknowledge the limited effect of their operations on them. As Morton Grodzins expressed it,

> The political parties of the United States are unique. They seldom perform the function that parties traditionally perform in other countries, the function of gathering together diverse strands of power and welding them into one. . . . the American parties rarely coalesce power at all. Characteristically, they do the reverse, serving as a canopy under which special and local interests are represented. . . . [11]

Their dominance of governmental systems at all levels in the United States (even where nonpartisanship is formally called for in certain state and local elections, candidates are identified with parties and parties are active in elections) assures that legislation —i.e., the basis for governmental programs—always provides important roles for state and local governments without clearly prescribing the power relationship between levels of government. "This is as true of Democratic as of Republican administrations and true even of functions for which arguments of efficiency would produce exclusive federal responsibility," [12] Grodzins states, adding that the lack of cohesion and discipline in parties further affects the character of the federal system not only "as a result of senatorial and congressional interference in federal administrative programs on behalf of local interests," but also because of the necessity of administrators themselves taking a politi-

11. Grodzins, in *Goals for Americans, op. cit.,* p. 272.
12. *Ibid.,* p. 273.

cal role. "The administrator must play politics for the same
reason that the politician is able to play in administration: the
parties are without program and without discipline. In response
to the unprotected position in which the party situation places
him, the administrator is forced to seek support where he can
find it." [13] Finally, "the way the party system operates gives
American politics their over-all distinctive tone. The lack of
party discipline produces an openness in the system that allows
individuals, groups, and institutions (including state and local
governments) to attempt to influence national policy at every
step of the legislative-administrative process." [14]

Political parties, in sum, aid and abet the devolution of power
in the United States. They serve to break up power and keep it
in the hands of the many divergent power groups in the United
States, and they provide a means by which those groups can either achieve their several objectives or alter governmental programs and policies in their behalf. They thus often serve to inhibit governmental action or to render it ineffective. But parties
so constituted and so operating accurately reflect the American
civic culture, and their influence can be expected to continue as
long as that culture remains unchanged.

There is little indication that a change is in the works. Basically, the prevailing civic culture in a nation is the product of the
history and traditions of its people. In the United States, the people as a whole lack understanding of the political system in general and of federalism in particular. They tend to see federalism,
like political parties, as consisting of sharply individual levels, the
layer cake Morton Grodzins describes, rather than seeing it in its
intergovernmental reality, Grodzins's marble cake. Thus the people tend to be rigid in assigning new functions and responsibilities
to levels of government and to regard mingling of functions in
government negatively as "encroachment" or "interference"
rather than positively as helpful and indeed necessary to the successful functioning of the system as a whole. In other words, the
people's concept of federalism is more likely to reinforce its static
qualities than to help it adapt to changing circumstances. But at

13. *Ibid.*, p. 274.
14. *Ibid.*

times—during the Depression, for example—the people seem to forget this conception of federalism entirely and to demand action and service from a level of government without regard to its supposed position in the governmental firmament.

The problem is further complicated by the fact that when the people speak—that is, try to exert their power—they do so through a variety of channels. Not only the local governments, but also the states, the President, and Congress—as well as parties, pressure groups, and agencies of public opinion such as polls and the press—all presume to reflect the popular will. The chances are great that each reflects it differently. How, then, is the people's power, even assuming they have a firm grasp of all the issues and a correct understanding of federalism, to be exerted with telling effect? The answer is that it often is not so exerted. Instead, it may be lost in a maze of different and conflicting expressions until it loses its potency altogether.

The people of course do not function as a single entity, nor indeed do many of the people ever take positions on public issues. Those who take positions with any effect do so primarily by joining or forming groups. In Earl Latham's view, indeed, pressure groups grew out of the very nature of the American governmental system: "Pressure groups exist because political power in the United States is divided between the federal government and the states, and, within each of these jurisdictions, it is further divided among . . . three branches of government. There is no institutional arrangement for the concentration of these separated and decentralized powers." Congress, because of the local orientation of political parties and their consequent lack of discipline, does not provide such an arrangement. In its failure is to be found the "scope of pressure group activity, and [it] may even make it necessary. It provides scope because a Congressman normally depends for re-election upon his own efforts and not those of [his political] party. He looks, therefore, beyond his own party for aid at the polls and for guidance in policy in some matters after he is elected. The pressure group may even be a necessity because it fills the need for the representation of functional interests as well as those of territorial localities." "The growth of pressure groups," Latham concludes, "has actually created two systems of representation in the United States which mesh with and supplement each other—the geographical and the functional. The first is formal and the second is informal. An understanding of the principle of political representation in the United States must take these elements into account." [15]

There are a number of difficulties with Latham's thesis. For one thing, there are so many groups that many of them stand for policies and programs in direct opposition to those of other groups and so tend to cancel each other out, leaving Congress, or the President, or state or local government, with no clear guide to action. For another, while there are a great many groups—perhaps as many as two thousand actively at work in Washington—they differ widely from one another in their resources and abilities. Several groups each year list expenditures of over $100,000 with the Congress under the terms of the Regulation of Lobbying Act, and their actual spending is undoubtedly larger. Others spend very little. There can be little question whose voice and recommendations are heard most clearly, whose power, in other words, is most readily acknowledged. Nor is there any assurance that every point of view is covered by pressure groups. To overcome the lack of a consumers' lobby, for example, President Johnson appointed the first Special Presidential Assistant for Consumers Affairs in 1964, and Mayor John Lindsay of New York followed suit with regard to city affairs in 1969.

Not many pressure groups include a position on federalism among their concerns. The National League of Cities and the United States Conference of Mayors attempt to represent cities directly, while the National Association of Counties, the Council of State Governments, and the National Governors Conference speak for their membership. A number of the program-oriented pressure groups occasionally take a stand that bears on federalism. Thus the electric-power lobby has for years criticized the idea of action by the national government in the power field and advocated, at the most, local control (but preferring private control) over the distribution of electric power. Similarly, groups repre-

15. Earl Latham, "Interest Groups in the American Political System," in Stephen K. Bailey, ed., *American Politics and Government: Essays in Essentials* (New York: Basic Books, 1965), p. 153.

senting national resource interests have tended to push for state and local control rather than national control, fearing that the latter would be harsher in its effects.[16]

Thus pressure groups make major inputs into the federal process. If parties are not concerned with the issues of current federalism, if they emphasize the continuation of traditional patterns of governmental conduct and operation within the federal system, pressure groups work the other way. The strongest of them are national in scope and may emphasize national power. In any case, they have made it their business to seek to effect changes in the power structure of federalism and do so consistently and ably.

Much more needs to be known about how each part of the national government serves as an input in the federal process. On issues involving federalism, as on most others, the national government is not monolithic. Rather, it is much divided and split within itself. The president has potentially the most force as a power input, although no two presidents have exactly the same views about power or about relationships in the federal system and so do not act in the same way. President Eisenhower, for example, felt that in a number of areas the national government had improperly invaded the rights and responsibilities of the states. He was for each level of government performing "its proper functions—no more, no less." He was against "excessive centralization of power in government" and concerned that the major tasks of government be performed by the "government nearest the people and not by the far-off reputedly 'rich uncle' in Washington, D.C." [17] President Kennedy was more concerned that needed functions be performed than he was with niceties about who performed them. In his message to Congress transmitting Reorganization Plan No. 1 of 1962 (creating a Department of Urban Affairs and Housing), he noted that the "federal government must act to carry out its proper role of encouragement and assistance to States and local governments, to voluntary efforts

16. McConnell, *Private Power and American Democracy, op. cit.,* *passim.*
17. Eisenhower's major address on federalism was his speech to the 1957 Governors Conference at Williamsburg, Virginia, given in *Public Papers of the Presidents. Dwight D. Eisenhower* (Washington, 1958), pp. 486–497, from which these quotations are taken.

and to private enterprise, in the solution of [common] problems." But he noted that the national government had the additional role of seeing to it that unmet needs were filled. Often there is a need, he observed, "and no one responds to it, and the national government, therefore, must meet its responsibility to the people." [18] President Johnson, early in his administration, gave considerably more attention to questions of federalism than either of his two immediate predecessors. He made the concept of "creative federalism" central to the thesis of his 1964 commencement address at the University of Michigan and shortly thereafter elaborated on it in his book, *My Hope for America:* [19]

There has been much loose talk about the Federal Government versus the states' governments—as if they were enemies of one another . . . The Founding Fathers in their wisdom set up both state and national governments. Their purpose was for each to do what it could do best. The Federal Government was not, as some would have it, an alien invention. Both the Federal and state governments have always exercised leadership in solving the problems of the nation. They are not, they must not be, rivals for the citizens' loyalty. They are separate agencies, each with special resources, each with special capabilities, but both joined in a united attack on the common problems of our country. At times one or another has not pulled its full weight. Early in the twentieth century [it was] the Federal Government. . . . Today we are moving into another era . . . an era of revitalization of our states . . . The best government is the one closest to the people but also one which can accomplish its proper tasks . . . That is why I am intensely interested in efforts to determine who can best do the job. . . . The White House has not the slightest interest in directing such efforts. We live by the belief that our Federal Government exists not to grow larger itself, but to encourage the people to grow larger. . . . The Federal Government does not exist to subordinate the sovereign states. We exist to support them.

If Johnson was not entirely correct in his assertion that the Founding Fathers "set up" state governments and was oversolicitous in his reference to the "sovereign states," he nevertheless made it clear then and often later that he saw federalism not so much as a limiting division of power but as an enabling combina-

18. *Public Papers of the Presidents. John F. Kennedy* (Washington, 1963), pp. 78, 93.
19. Lyndon B. Johnson, *My Hope for America* (New York: Random House, 1964). The quotation is from pp. 119–121.

tion of forces to accomplish what the people want done. Unlike Eisenhower, for whom maintaining a balance between the levels of government was the important thing, Johnson, even more than Kennedy, saw jobs to do and governments to do them and was not so concerned about just what combination was utilized as long as action was taken.

Not only can each president be expected to react differently when issues of federalism arise, he is limited in a great many ways in the exercise of his power. He must be painfully aware that his control over the decision-making processes in states and even more in local governments is remote, if it exists at all. Nor can he prevent a determined Congress or the Supreme Court from taking action contrary to what he is persuaded should be done. He must make his decisions to exert power within the framework of both public and party opinion and has always to remember the binding power of the mystique of federalism on both the people at large and on state and local politicians.

The president cannot even speak for the entire executive branch. The study of the Senate subcommittee on intergovernmental relations revealed that the "continuing debate on . . . our federal system . . . apparently has exerted little impact on many Federal program administrators." Few federal officials, it found, were fully aware of the changes taking place in state and local government, and only "a few analyzed the future of their individual programs in the light of these developments." Most federal officials confined their interests to the administration of their own programs. "Only a few . . . dealt with the . . . broader intergovernmental context" of what they were doing. "Indifference, stand-pattism, and a narrowly defined functionalism . . . were the themes that dominated the majority of responses." [20]

Such a lack of concern in the rank and file of the bureaucracy (though fortunately not in all of it) poses problems and creates tensions within the executive branch itself. A president can never count on moving the bureaucracy along with him, even on an issue where he has voiced particular concern. Differences in program goals, professional interests, and clientele pressures combine to blind federal executives to the broader problems of coordina-

20. *The Federal System as Seen by Federal Aid Officials, op. cit.,* p. 22.

tion and lead them to give "comparatively little thought . . . [to] such intergovernmental niceties as cooperative planning, appraisal, and administration," [21] presidential pressure notwithstanding.

Undoubtedly, program administrators have little awareness of questions of an intergovernmental nature largely because little in their legislative mandate requires it. In other words, Congress makes an impact on the federal process independent of that of the executive branch. Generally speaking, Congress does not view questions broadly. Instead it acts in response to specific problems: it is action oriented, accustomed to taking short-range thrusts in the direction of resolving urgent issues rather than evolving an over-all policy on which to base all actions. Thus no policy of intergovernmental relations has been agreed upon, no common attitude toward federalism adopted, despite the fact that the programs Congress has enacted over the last thirty years have altered the federal system a great deal, and altered it inevitably in the direction of national power. Congressional committees are in the main designed to facilitate the passage of legislation in a single area. Each committee and its chairman are thus most concerned with how power is exercised in one particular subject-matter area. When issues of federalism do arise, they are apt to be dealt with compartmentally without being coordinated with other actions in Congress that may involve the very same questions. Individual members of Congress sometimes have definite views on federalism, which they declaim in debate or advance in committee considerations. Thus former Representative Jim Gardner of North Carolina told a local group on one of his first home visits that "the Federal Government is exceeding more power [*sic*] than was originally granted in the Constitution. . . . As long as I represent the Fourth District," he promised, "I will vehemently oppose federal control of the states." [22] Exactly what he meant, Representative Gardner did not make clear. Like most of his colleagues, past and present, he probably spoke from stereotype rather than from any careful analysis of his own and because that is what he felt his constituents wanted to hear. What a junior

21. *Ibid.*
22. Quoted in *The Evening Telegram* (Rocky Mount, N.C.), February 23, 1967, p. 1.

Congressman thinks may not be important, but as he rises in power and influence, his opinions may become of central importance to the quality and/or passage of legislation. Generally members of Congress have not been responsible for much innovation in the area of federalism, but have reflected the public's conception of federalism and tended to confirm its stereotypes. A few members of both houses—Senator Edmund S. Muskie preeminent among them—have begun to develop a broad philosophy of federalism and act from it rather consistently, but they are exceptions to the rule. From his unique vantage point as chairman of the Senate subcommittee on intergovernmental relations, Senator Muskie has been able to see the dynamics of the federal process perhaps more clearly than any other member of Congress. He understands the interwoven nature of American governmental action and sees the necessity of finding ways to bridge rather than to preserve or widen the jurisdictional gaps between units and levels of government in the United States. But with only isolated exceptions (the passage of the Intergovernmental Personnel Act of 1968, for example), he has not been able to persuade his fellow Senators to accept his thinking, and there is no evidence that such a concept has caught the imagination of even a small portion of the electorate.

The federal courts, especially the Supreme Court, often act on matters of federalism and thereby constitute a major power input. No one can pay even the most cursory attention to the Marshall Court without seeing its impact on the nation's conception of federalism,[23] and although the precedents it set were not followed in every instance by later courts,[24] they have become the foundation on which twentieth-century federalism is based. Today the Supreme Court is expected to provide leadership in federalism, perhaps because of all the branches of government it is the least shackled by stereotype and vested interests. In any

---

23. See Edward S. Corwin, *John Marshall and the Constitution* (New Haven: Yale Univ. Press, 1919). The key Marshall cases concerning federalism were *McCulloch* v. *Maryland* 4 Wheaton 316 (1819) and *Cohens* v. *Virginia* 6 Wheaton 264 (1826).

24. See the classic statement of the principle of dual federalism in *Hammer* v. *Dagenhart* 247 US 251 (1918). See also *In re Neagle* 135 US 1 (1890) and *Missouri* v. *Holland* 252 US 416 (1920).

case, in such areas as integration of educational facilities (*Brown* v. *Board of Education* [25]), legislative reapportionment (*Baker* v. *Carr* and *Wesberry* v. *Sanders* [26]), and punishment for sedition (*Pennsylvania* v. *Nelson* [27]), it has wrought major changes in modern American society. Nor are such landmark cases isolated examples. Indeed, in the everyday course of its work, the Court tackles questions of federalism as frequently as any others. Thus during 1968, for example, it announced that "it would decide whether or not states can order residency requirements for welfare recipients . . . the lower courts [having] held that the requirements [were] unconstitutional because they violate[d] the right to travel"; [28] held that a Texas loyalty oath for state employees was unconstitutional and agreed to decide if Congress had exceeded its constitutional power to regulate interstate commerce when it extended the federal minimum wage and hour standards to about 1.7 million state employees; and agreed finally to decide whether states may ban the teaching of the theory of evolution in the public schools. All of these issues were full of import for the federal system.

The Supreme Court may have the most important role to play of any of the input forces involved in the federal system. However, its input is largely in one direction, that of national power. Only because of the crucial role it plays in "mitigating an almost unworkable system of government by ameliorating some of its worst defects," says Loren P. Beth, can the system itself be tolerated. "In the long run," Beth argues, "the component parts of a federal system must be brought under a larger measure of central control; the price of not doing so is first, ineffective government and substantial losses of individual liberty, and later, perhaps, the . . . breakup of the federal system itself." [29] As America has developed, it has become more and more unified and national in its orientation until the only preventative of a unitary state may be the fact that the nation is held constitutionally together in a federal

25. 347 US 483 (1954); 349 US 295 (1955).
26. 369 US 186 (1962); 376 US 1 (1964).
27. 350 US 497 (1956).
28. *International Herald Tribune*, January 16, 1968, p. 3.
29. Beth, "The Supreme Court and American Federalism," *op. cit.*, p. 376.

form. As the country becomes more national in its orientation, federalism is inefficient, slow, and cumbersome, and to overcome these difficulties, the combined efforts of public opinion, economic and social pressure, and political and legislative action find ways to bypass its limitations. The Supreme Court, by legitimizing these short cuts, in a sense enables the nation to have its cake and eat it too, in that it provides the mechanism by which the major national needs and aspirations can be satisfied with at least some dispatch and efficiency and without forcing the issue and arousing the ancient forces of disunion once again. The Supreme Court thus serves as the major nationalizing agency in the American system of government, either by nationalizing itself, as it did in the area of civil rights, or by suggesting nationalization to Congress, as it did in the classic case of *U.S. v. Southeastern Underwriters Association* [30] in 1944, in which it found that insurance was in interstate commerce and so "eligible" for regulation by the federal government under the commerce power instead of by the several states.

It is not possible to pursue each of the other power forces labeled "inputs" in this chapter. Indeed, to embark on a discussion of state and local power inputs alone would require writing another book, and a description of some of the other inputs would involve nearly as much. In any case, it is clear already that power in the federal system is scattered and divided. There is no single decision-making process in the United States; there are many, and this is what the framers of the Constitution expected us to have. Their original mix was complicated enough—a new national government imposed on thirteen pre-existing states and their many subdivisions. But in the years since 1787, the problem has been infinitely complicated by the steady addition of new states and their subdivisions, so that by now, even with the reduction in numbers in more recent years, the parties to federalism—the agencies of power—are prodigious in number. Provided with no method of interlooping them, and working within an over-all atmosphere that denied a large place to governmental exertions of power at all, the framers could not have been expected to do

30. 322 US 533 (1944).

other than they did. They left the units of government in the
new nation to function largely as islands unto themselves, which,
once ingrained as a habit, was very hard for those units to shake.
Inertia, vested interests, the very size of the nation with the early
difficulties of transportation and communication it posed, the
rules of the political game which emphasized a local or at best a
statewide point of view for most players—all of these contributed
to the continuation of a fractionated power process. And all this
diffusion of power among governments was exacerbated by considerable separation of power within governments.

Indeed, though in certain program areas there are exceptions,
it must be concluded that federalism in the last analysis works not
by design but by accident, by the lucky fact that there is, as
Lyndon Johnson used to remark so often, a broad consensus
among Americans that permits them to work together to accomplish important national goals. For somehow the federal system
does work. Popular needs and desires are expressed, ideas for
meeting them are advanced, and policies and programs are finally
adopted. It has not been an easy or efficient system, nor has it met
each need as well or as quickly as it might have been met. But
the net result of this operation since 1789 has been remarkable.
No one can argue successfully that the American people have not
been well served by the federal system in operation.

IV

EDUCATION:
A CASE STUDY IN
FEDERALISM

LIKE OTHER ASPECTS OF a political system, federalism takes on meaning only in actual situations, when solutions are sought to substantive problems. For the purpose of a political system is action toward the solution of society's problems and needs; structural devices like federalism are intimately related to governmental function. Thus what federalism involves and how it works can best be seen in a program area, and no program area provides a better illustration of federalism in operation than that of public elementary and secondary education.

Probably no society has been as education-conscious through its whole history as American society. From the first days of settlement, the colonists made education a basic commitment. Both to participate properly in a Bible-based religion and to govern themselves as free men, they recognized the promotion of education as a major goal. Ever since, and with increasing zeal, the virtue of education has been advanced in the United States. "Enlighten the people generally," Thomas Jefferson once said, "and tyranny and the oppressions of mind and body will vanish, like evil spirits at the dawn of day." So dedicated, Americans have always taken education seriously. It is by now "simply an article of faith in this country that children need more and better schooling to enter and to succeed in the changing world of work."[1] Education has come to receive about 7 per cent of the annual gross national product, and that percentage seems likely to increase. Education and education-related activities have become the nation's second biggest business, next only to national defense. Even so, education has traditionally been regarded as a matter of local or private responsibility. Although state legislatures early authorized taxes for local support of schools and chartered academies and colleges, they went no further in exercising initiative or control in educational affairs. And in 1787 the new national Constitution was drafted without a single reference to the subject, even while the expiring Congress under the Articles of Confederation was drawing up the famous Northwest Ordinance of 1787, which, like the earlier Ordinance of 1785, provided that national public land revenues be directed to school support.

As population began to increase and along with it a speed-up of the democratization process which culminated in the Jacksonian era, free public schools became the common expectation of the people. The states, recognizing the change, began to pass compulsory education laws, requiring local communities to maintain schools and to compel children within specified ages to attend them. The states moved also into training for teachers by establishing normal colleges and state universities and later by certifying their ability to teach. Eventually the states began actively to supervise the schools, prescribing curricula and approving textbooks. Localism was not abandoned, however, nor was the private role, especially in the field of higher education, where the small denominational college proliferated all through the nineteenth century.

As for the national government, it continued to make public lands available to the new states for public school purposes,[2] and

1. Samuel Halperin, "Some Implications of the New Role of the Federal Government in Education," an address at Wayne State University, February 23, 1966, reprinted in *Congressional Record* 112:8398–8400 (April 25, 1966). The quotation is from p. 8399. Dr. Halperin was then the Deputy Assistant Secretary for Legislation, Department of Health, Education and Welfare.

2. For the first few states, "Congress appropriated one section of land in each township (one square mile in each thirty-six). . . . By 1830 the grant was increased to two sections in each township; later states received

in 1862, in the Morrill Act, it offered support to agricultural and mechanical colleges. Later, it began to provide grants-in-aid for specific educational programs.

Thus the pattern was set which has continued to this day, a pattern of both public and private involvement, in which all levels of government take part. As Morton Grodzins wrote, "All planes of government in the United States participate in the function of education. . . . Education is not simply a function of local school districts. Rather, [it] is provided through the joint efforts of many governments." [3] He might have added, of private groups as well.

Despite the large involvement of governmental units, education has long been felt by the American people to be *a*political. Very little attention has been paid to the politics of education. Early in 1969, Douglass Cater, a former special assistant to President Johnson, undertook under grants from the Carnegie Corporation and the Ford Foundation to conduct a study of the "political structure which underlies education in America on the Federal, state, community and campus level." [4] Hopefully, his findings will go far both to reveal the political facts of the educational apparatus in the United States and to provide the people with a clearer understanding of its political nature.

The educational function is not uniformly assigned to equivalent units of government in the American federal system. In three states, Alaska, Hawaii, and Maine, elementary and secondary education, like higher education, are a function of the state. In several of the Southeastern states, they have been delegated to the county. A good many municipalities (309 in the 1967 Census of Governments) include education among other municipal functions. And the township is charged with that responsibility in much of New England and in New Jersey. Pennsylvania has a

four sections. Between the admission of Ohio in 1802 and Arizona and New Mexico in 1912, the national government granted over 29 million acres to new states. . . . These school lands were sold or leased by the states and the proceeds" invested to help pay for local school operations. John F. Cramer and George S. Browne, *Contemporary Education. A Comparative Study of National Systems* (New York: Harcourt, Brace, 1956), p. 41.

3. Morton Grodzins, *The American System. A New View of Government in the United States* (Chicago: Rand McNally, 1966), p. 5.

4. *The New York Times*, January 6, 1969, p. 12.

unique system of joint boards. But by far the most important governmental unit in education is the local independent school district, and it is to that unit that attention will chiefly be devoted here.

When free public schools were first established, they were run as parts of the existing units of state and local government, as they are in parts of the United States today. But those levels of government fell into serious disrepute in the nineteenth century. Riddled with graft and corruption, they became the prime targets of muckrakers and reformers. In the process of amelioration, and reflecting a concern to prevent schools from ever being so sullied again, the education function was commonly broken off from the other functions of state and local government and entrusted to separately elected, nonpartisan school boards, each responsible for a particular geographical school district. As long as transportation facilities remained limited, individual school districts were quite small and so were very numerous. Even as late as 1940, well over 115,000 school districts existed. By the Census of Governments of 1967, the number had been cut drastically by consolidation to 21,782, and the next census will undoubtedly show a further decline in numbers.

Although districts were originally utilized to keep the schools out of politics (or politics out of the schools), a rationale has been built up for them which emphasizes other virtues as well. Local school districts, it is argued, are in keeping with the American spirit of localism; geographical decentralization of school responsibility provides the best opportunity for local differences and desires to be accommodated in the most important of all governmental areas, the instruction of the young. By preserving a substantial degree of local automony, the basic pluralism which is America's chief hallmark is preserved and strengthened. Moreover, decentralization gives those closest to the children concerned the responsibility for meeting their actual needs, rather than entrusting that responsibility to a more remote and therefore less knowledgeable group. This argument was advanced most recently by a blue-ribbon panel of experts in a report on New York City schools which recommended that primary responsibility for the city's schools be taken out of the hands even of the existing city-wide board of education and vested instead in some thirty "local" boards serving neighborhood districts within New York.[5] Finally, it is argued that all schools in a free society should be subject to popular control, and that only by the agency of a board of citizens elected by the people in relatively small geographical divisions can education be kept truly democratic.

Such arguments suggest that local school boards are effectively free agents in their handling of elementary and secondary education (only a few school boards have responsibility for higher education). They *are* free to a large extent in administrative matters—deciding tax rates within a permissive range, hiring certified teachers, building and operating school plants, and determining many of the details of school operation. But they are not completely independent of the authority of other government agencies. Their powers are prescribed and limited by the action of state legislatures. Indeed, the state is free to impose requirements as much on school districts as on any other unit of local government. Thus the so-called Taylor Law in New York, which attempts to discourage strikes by public employees, applies to those employed by school districts. It requires employers—in this case school boards—to bargain collectively with employees and provides a system of flexible penalties for those who go out on strike. Moreover, in all states local districts are dependent, in varying but usually large degree, on state financial aid. In 1963–64, for example, local sources accounted for 56.3 per cent of school revenues, state governments for 39.3 per cent, and the national government for 4.4 per cent. By 1967–68, the local share had fallen to 52 per cent and the national share had risen to nearly 8 per cent, but the state share remained right at 40 per cent. Local schools are subject too to "state teacher certification, state prescription of textbooks, and state inspection of performance in areas as diverse as building maintenance and the caliber of Latin instruction." [6] The actions of schools and school districts are also subject to judicial review and to the normal procedures

---

5. See *Saturday Review*, December 16, 1967, pp. 70–71; see also Fred M. Hechinger, "Board Hearings to Focus on Decentralization Plan," *The New York Times*, January 2, 1969, p. 22.
6. Grodzins, *The American System, op. cit.*, p. 4.

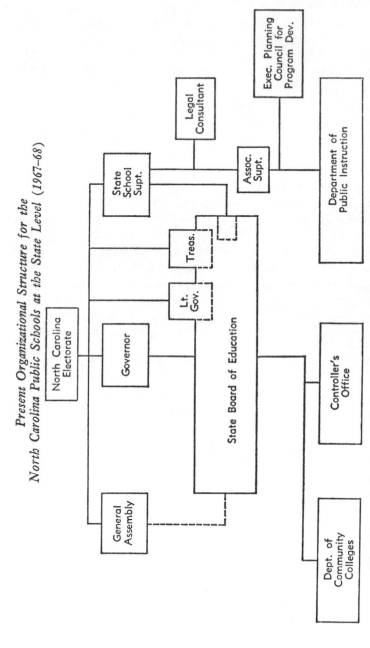

*Present Organizational Structure for the
North Carolina Public Schools at the State Level (1967–68)*

North Carolina Electorate

General Assembly

Governor

Lt. Gov.

Treas.

State School Supt.

Legal Consultant

Assoc. Supt.

Exec. Planning Council for Program Dev.

State Board of Education

Controller's Office

Dept. of Community Colleges

Department of Public Instruction

SOURCE: *The Report of the Governor's Study Commission of the Public School System of North Carolina* (Raleigh, 1968), p. 145.

for auditing the expenditure of state funds.

State boards of education, state school superintendents, and state departments of education exist in every state; the organization of North Carolina's state educational apparatus is typical. State boards of education are chosen in a variety of ways: election, appointment by the governor, selection by the state legislature. Generally, they establish state-wide standards and control state educational funds, and often they determine curricula. The superintendent is the administrative head of the state's efforts in school affairs, and the department of public instruction backs up the work of the superintendent. Together, these state bodies serve local districts "by accreditation, evaluation . . . and surveys," and by regulation of school-building construction. State departments "write out a program and translate [it] into a building which will house [it]." In addition, departmental specialists organize statewide programs and spend time in the field advising and guiding teachers in the classroom. Even so,

About all a state department can do as far as control is concerned is minimums. At the local level, [it] . . . encourage[s] them to go beyond the minimum, to provide incentives where they can improve the situation. . . . About all a state department can do is require a foundation upon which . . . a greatly enriched program [can be built].[7]

Local school boards also entertain relations with other governmental units. They have many "Intricate and diverse relationships with county and city governments: the latter, for example, often act as tax-levying and tax-collecting agencies for the districts; they are responsible for certifying that standards of health and safety are maintained on school property; they . . . provide . . . police protection to students".[8] And county governments are intimately related through the provision of transportation to students, a particularly important function in the increasing number of large consolidated rural school districts. In addition, "There are many areas, such as recreation, parks and play grounds, health services, community planning, and others, where the local school district and the local [government] author-

7. Quoted in Clayton Braddock, "Do the States Have a Place in Education?" *Southern Education Report*, April 1967, pp. 29–31.
8. Grodzins, *The American System, op. cit.*, p. 4.

ity must work very closely together. The problems of control and of budgetary relations have not been solved. . . . The trend seems to favor a greater degree of voluntary and legal co-operation between school administration and city [and county] management." [9]

Long before the national government came to play the role it now does in education, it too had an important, if random, impact on local districts. An extensive vocational education program in agriculture, home economics, and industrial arts was begun by the Smith–Hughes Act of 1917 and expanded by the George–Dean Act of 1936; the United States Office of Education (founded in 1867) and the Library of Congress both developed an extensive program of technical assistance to schools; a school lunch program was established; federal surplus property was made available to meet the needs of local school districts for school equipment; and teachers were given a variety of opportunities for special training through programs of the National Science Foundation and other national agencies. And in the so-called "federally impacted areas," where a heavy influx of population due to federal activity there created special school problems, special grants for construction and school support have been made since the days of World War II. For a long time, however, even as the national government turned its attention to the over-all betterment of the national health and welfare, there was virtually no effort or interest in developing a comprehensive federal program "for the upgrading of education . . . When interest in Federal aid to education finally did become a major national sentiment, the struggle to enact [it] was intensely bitter and, usually, totally frustrated . . . Victory for . . . aid [legislation] was close a number of times. The issues which complicated and on several occasions doomed it—such as reluctance to spend money, fear of Federal control, the church-State issue,[10] racial segregation—each

9. Cramer and Browne, *Contemporary Education. A Comparative Study of National Systems. Op. cit.*, p. 55.

10. The church-state issue cannot be regarded as settled. The Supreme Court of the United States heard arguments in March, 1968, in a case brought against the Elementary and Secondary Education Act of 1965 by seven New York taxpayers on the grounds that the act of giving away funds for library materials, text books, and remedial instruction to a religious

had to be overcome in turn." [11] Finally in 1965, with the passage of the landmark education legislation of the 89th Congress, the national government achieved full status as a major participant in the American educational process.

Of special importance to local school boards is the Elementary and Secondary Education Act of 1965, immediately coded ESEA in educational circles.[12] It was the first general aid-to-education law ever enacted by Congress. It authorizes aid on the basis of the number of pupils from low-income families in each public school district. Money appropriated under its terms must be spent on poor children, but it can be spent pretty much the way each individual school district decides. The act authorizes grants for textbooks and library materials, for the creation of educational centers to provide programs which individual school districts cannot afford, and for the improvement of educational research and administration. Under its terms somewhere near one billion dollars has been handed over every year to school districts, chiefly those in urban centers. Perhaps no other act has had the impact on intergovernmental relationships that ESEA already has. And since it represents a continuing commitment to the improvement of educational quality in the United States on the part of the national government, its effects will continue to be felt in intergovernmental relations for many years to come.

Almost simultaneously with the impact it made on public school education with ESEA, under the terms of the Civil Rights Act of 1964 the national government also was empowered to become a sort of guardian of the national conscience in educational matters. That act made it illegal for any recipient of federal aid to use it in a racially segregated activity or facility. Specifically, it authorized the cut-off of federal funds to any state or local governmental unit, including school districts, which practiced dis-

school contravenes the separation of church and state guaranteed by the First Amendment.

11. Halperin, "Some Implications of the New Role of the Federal Government in Education," *op. cit.*

12. See Stephen K. Bailey and Edith K. Mosher, *ESEA: The Office of Education Administers a Law* (Syracuse: Syracuse Univ. Press, 1968), for a study of the historical setting of the law, its enactment, its implementation during the first year of its operation, and a number of conclusions and reactions to it.

crimination in carrying out federally aided programs. All such agencies are required to submit assurances of compliance with the requirements of the act.

In connection with grants in the education area, the Office of Education first laid down desegregation guidelines only for school systems that had once been segregated by law, nearly all of which were in the South. But in March 1968, those guidelines were extended to every school system in the nation. According to the Office of Education at that time, all school systems have an "affirmative duty" to eliminate racial segregation and discrimination. Schools are not required to change racial imbalances resulting from private housing patterns, but they are prohibited from disproportionately crowding mainly Negro schools, assigning less-qualified teachers to them, or making lower expenditures on them. If a school system refuses to correct violations found by the Office to exist in these areas, it risks losing all federal aid. Obviously the difficulties involved in implementing such requirements are many and profound. The school district retains the right to refuse to comply with the guidelines and so give up the federal funds which otherwise would be coming to it, as the school board in Jeff Davis County, Georgia, for example, chose to do. But with many school systems already running an operating deficit, this is often not a viable alternative.

Very recently, the national government has moved dramatically closer to the center of the educational stage as both the legislative and executive branches have come to see education as the key to the solution of a good many of the nation's most critical problems as well as the main way to help individual citizens find rewarding and useful personal lives. In the words of former Secretary of Health, Education and Welfare John W. Gardner,

Nothing has been more striking than the emergence of education as a well-nigh universal ingredient of all our attempts at social betterment—education in and out of school, at all ages, Headstart, the three Rs, vocational skills, special training for dropouts, adult literacy programs, courses for parents, graduate and professional training and so on.

One reason for this is that in modern society the requirement for trained manpower is basic. But quite aside from the requirements of modern society, education is the prime means we use for the liberation and strengthening of the individual which is our ultimate aim.[13]

Some measure of that process is provided by statistics on federal support for education in recent years. At the elementary and secondary levels alone, federal support increased from $670 million in Fiscal 1964 to $3.3 billion in Fiscal 1968.

To date, the programs of the national government in aid of education have generally featured financial aid and program support rather than program operation and control. The basic pattern of federal action has been the appropriation of funds to national, state, local, or private agencies for specific purposes, programs which had been initiated by those organizations (though often in response to the availability of funds from the national government) and administered entirely by them. Federal funds have generally supported activities in four categories: construction (10 major programs in Fiscal 1969), programs of instructional development and administration (62 programs in Fiscal 1969), teacher and other professional training and student assistance (31 programs in Fiscal 1969), and research (15 programs in 1969). No national program to date has been devised to help pay teachers' salaries or to provide general support for elementary and secondary schools.

When one turns from elementary and secondary education to higher education, the same over-all intergovernmental pattern of operation is found. A sizable proportion of the collegiate student body in the United States today still attends private institutions of one sort or another, and in absolute numbers such institutions predominate. The majority of college students, however, attend public institutions, and the leading public universities are among the best in the nation. For the most part public colleges and universities are state institutions, though there are a number of municipal and county universities, some of them part of a local school system and so under the jurisdiction of a local school district (or of a separate higher education district), others independently administered. Generally, each university is run by its own

13. Remarks by John W. Gardner delivered at a luncheon of The Women's National Press Club, Washington, D.C., March 22, 1967. Mimeo copy, p. 8.

board of trustees or as one of several institutions in a system by a state university board of regents. A number of states have created statewide higher education coordinating boards for the state-supported institutions. Although state legislatures are vitally related to the universities through the appropriations process and sometimes through a specific program in one or more universities in the state, most policy matters are determined by the institutional board of regents, in some cases subject to approval by the state coordinating authority. Higher education has become such big business that governors very often intrude upon internal university matters (as Governor Ronald Reagan of California has felt compelled to do several times in connection with units in the California university system), and occasionally university issues are decided at the ballot box. There is thus a definite political aspect to public higher education at the state level even as there is with regard to elementary and secondary education at the local level.

The national government has come to have a heavy impact on higher education as well, through the continued implementation of the principle of the Morrill Act, the series of "G.I. Bills" providing higher educational benefits for veterans and their widows since World War II, and the passage of such recent acts as the National Defense Education Act of 1958 (designed to encourage education chiefly in the sciences, mathematics, engineering, foreign languages, and teacher education through loans and funds for graduate fellowships),[14] the Higher Education Facilities Act of 1963 (which authorizes grants and loans for construction of public and private academic facilities), and the Higher Education Act of 1965 (a multiple-program act authorizing funds for scholarships, work-study programs, guaranteed low-interest loans, aid to developing colleges, funds for college and university community service programs and the development of library resources, the establishment of a National Teachers Corps, and fellowships for present and future teachers). Federal grants to

14. NDEA also has had an impact on public schools in that it provides funds for public schools for the purchase of equipment and for testing and guidance services. See re NDEA, Wilbur J. Cohen, "National Defense Education Act: An Idea That Grew," *American Education* 4:2-4 (September, 1968); Joyce Rothschild, "The NDEA Decade," *ibid.*, pp. 4-11; and "NDEA Financial Aid Roundup," *ibid.*, pp. 12-13.

higher education rose from $1.5 billion in Fiscal 1964 to $3.8 billion in Fiscal 1968; and for adult, vocational-technical, and continuing education, the increase was from $200 million to $1.1 billion. Nor is this likely to be the end of such increases. The Carnegie Commission on Higher Education recommended in its report at the end of 1968 a wide-ranging package of twenty-two related proposals for increasing national expenditures for higher education alone to some $7 billion in 1970–71 and to almost $13 billion in 1976–77.

Unlike many other countries, the United States has never had a national university, although the service academies and the institutions of higher education in the District of Columbia are federal instrumentalities, and the newly created Eisenhower College in Seneca Falls, New York, occupies a special position with the national government pledged to match up to $5 million in private donations as a token in honor of President Eisenhower.

Perhaps the most impressive involvement of the national government in education is that of the Defense Department. As former Secretary Robert S. McNamara said,

The Defense Department today is the largest single educational complex in history. The services provide enlisted men with professional training in some 1,500 different skills in more than 2,000 separate courses. In addition, 65,000 officers a year continue their professional education. The Department operates 327 dependents' schools around the world, employing 6,800 classroom teachers for 166,000 students, making it the ninth largest U.S. school system, with a budget of $90 million. More than 30 correspondence-school centers are sponsored by the military departments, offering over 2,000 courses and enrolling nearly a million students scattered about the globe. The United States Armed Forces Institute currently has enrolled more than 250,000 students in hundreds of courses ranging from the elementary school level through college. During the five years through 1967, an annual average of 95,000 individuals earned a high school diploma or its equivalent through this hugely beneficial program.

This immense educational complex exists specifically for the needs of the Defense Department, but it nevertheless has a gigantic spin-off into American society as a whole. The services return over half a million personnel annually to the country's skilled manpower pool. A very substantial number of civilians currently employed in such skilled occupational fields as electronics, engineering, transportation management, machine-tool operation, automotive and aircraft maintenance, and the building trades . . . have been trained in the armed forces.

Thus the imperatives of national security in our technological age make the Defense Department the world's largest educator of highly skilled men. Those same imperatives require that it also be the world's most efficient educator. As a result, the Defense Department has pioneered some of the most advanced teaching techniques. Indeed, it has been in the vanguard of a series of innovations in education technology. Its findings and its philosophy are making a significant contribution to the modernization that is sweeping throughout the American school system.[15]

But merely to list the ways in which the several levels of government in the United States are involved in education does not fully suggest the many diverse ways in which education at all levels in the United States is an *inter*governmental operation. It does not suggest, for example, the professional relationships among teachers, administrators, professors, and other educational specialists, "ties that criss-cross governmental boundaries and from which a good fraction of new ideas and new programs emerge." [16] When such ties are taken into consideration, the multipartite nature of the basic educational picture of the United States is made even clearer.

As a result of the way education has been handled in the United States, the nation has never had either a national education policy or a national system of education. Instead, it has innumerable centers of educational policy-making and administration, which receive most of their support from state and local sources, as well as a good many independent and parochial schools and colleges, which are outside of most state or local control but are nevertheless involved to some degree with those in the public sector. In all the states, higher education is coordinated only loosely with education in the lower grades, and there is very little coordination of systems across state lines, although a beginning has been made in that direction by the several regional commissions on higher education established by interstate compact since World War II.[17] Thus the quality of education any given person

15. Robert S. McNamara, *The Essence of Security. Reflections in Office* (New York: Harper & Row, 1968), pp. 132–133.
16. Grodzins, *The American System, op. cit.,* p. 5.
17. See for example Redding S. Sugg and George Hilton Jones, *The Southern Regional Education Board: Ten Years of Regional Cooperation in Higher Education* (Baton Rouge, Louisiana: Louisiana State Univ. Press, 1960).

receives in the United States is largely dependent on where he happens to live. Educational resources and opportunity vary widely among the states and among different parts of the same state, especially among city and suburban school systems. Some school districts spend several times as much as others on each elementary pupil and high school student. The percentage of gross personal income spent on elementary and secondary education in 1964 ranged from 6.8 per cent in Utah to 2.8 per cent in the District of Columbia, with 4.7 per cent constituting the national average. Ten per cent of the school districts in the country spent less than $237 per elementary pupil in 1964, while another 10 per cent spent more than $534. The worst educational disparities were to be found in the central city portions of the nation's largest metropolitan areas and in the rural districts in the south and south central states, although under financing is not confined to any one region of the country. Such disparities are not easily resolvable. A "one child, one dollar" rule might be as unfair as the traditional system, since the needs of some children are greater than those of others. Moreover, as taxpayers, parents probably have the right to spend at differing rates for meeting the educational needs of their children. Recently, suits have been instituted in four large cities —Detroit, Chicago, Los Angeles, and San Antonio—to force state legislatures to provide a more equitable distribution of school funds among school districts. The cases, which seek to prove that through educational disparities the states are denying city children the equal protection of the law required by the Fourteenth Amendment, involve a test of the whole system under which American schools are financed.

It is exactly this kind of evidence which led President Johnson to give education top priority among domestic programs in his administration. Although his predecessors had become increasingly conscious of the mounting importance of educational improvement if the nation's objectives were to be reached (President Eisenhower sponsored a White House Conference on Education in 1956 and President Kennedy's interest in education was deep and far-ranging), it was President Johnson who in rapid succession recommended and secured Congressional enactment of legislation which expanded and improved vocational education programs, provided special programs for the benefit of deprived children, established a teachers' corps, vastly increased the student loan program, and expanded the program for the education of the handicapped. By the end of his administration he had signed sixty education bills.

As for President Nixon, his role in relation to education was laid out for him in a report prepared by the task force on education he appointed under the leadership of Alan Pifer, president of the Carnegie Corporation of New York.[18] "Any Administration today, and every one from now on," the report began, "must be an education-minded Administration. Education has become clearly established as a top concern of the national government. . . . It would seem to us, therefore, that establishing his image as an education-minded President must be one of Mr. Nixon's highest priorities . . . in office. His concern for education must become vivid and real—not only to the one American in four who is now either a student or teacher in the educational system but to the American populace at large." No other president has had national expectation with regard to his own and the federal government's role vis-à-vis education made so explicit.

As a result of the stepped-up tempo of federal interest in education, it is not surprising that some concluded that the national government was well on its way toward taking over education, lock, stock, and barrel.[19] That has not been the case, however. To be sure, as former Commissioner of Education Harold Howe II declared, "The relationship of the federal government to state and local education authorities is a tender one," not only because some national funds go for specific activities designated by Congress rather than for purposes determined by state and local authorities and must be spent within the spirit of the Civil Rights Act, but also because recently appropriations have been made to "finance a new educational system which local and state educational authorities do not control. Headstart, the Job

18. The full text of that report was reprinted in *Congressional Record* 115: H1658–1666 (March 12, 1969).

19. Thus Representative Robert L. F. Sikes of Florida introduced House Joint Resolution 292 on February 13, 1967, proposing an amendment to the Constitution which would declare that "The right of each State to determine the curriculum of, the facilities provided for, and the qualifications of the personnel in, the public schools of that State shall not be abridged either directly or indirectly by the United States."

Corps . . . [and] the Neighborhood Youth Corps . . . have been somewhat outside the umbrella of duly constituted local and state educational authorities [and so have added] to the complexity of federal-state-local relationships concerning education." [20] But if public school authorities would look to the higher education field, Commissioner Howe suggested, they would feel less menaced by what they believed to be incursions by the national government into their bailiwicks.

Higher education, which absorbs a little more than one-third of the funds spent annually by the Office of Education, presents a special problem in relationships. Through the National Science Foundation, the National Institutes of Health, the Defense Department, and other federal sources, higher education long ago learned to live with the federal funds without getting nervous indigestion over problems of federal control. It will receive $1.5 billion from the Office this year [1966] without any complaints except for the general one of wanting more money.

Indeed, funds from the national government notwithstanding, curriculum, personnel, and administration in local schools and colleges and universities alike remain outside of federal control, both in theory and in fact.

Control by the national government does not raise problems as much as the way in which federal aid-to-education programs are administered. Thus the American Council on Education recently observed that "the most obvious weakness in the government-university relationship is that to date there has been no way that institutions [can] be sure that apparent commitments made in one year [will] be honored by the government in a succeeding year." [21] As with other legislation, there is no necessary connection between authorizing legislation, which in the case of education has been passed by large majorities in both houses of Congress, and the appropriations process. "We do not suggest that every program, once begun, must be continued regardless of merit," the Council said. "We suggest that the launching of a

20. The quotations in the next few pages from Commissioner Howe are from *Saturday Review*, December 17, 1966, pp. 68–70 *seq.* They will not be footnoted individually.

21. American Council on Education, *Higher Education and National Affairs*, Vol. 18, No. 6, February 28, 1969. Subsequent quotations from the Council are from this source.

program at a given level of support should signify the government's intent to continue at that level of support unless the program fails in its purpose or the need for it has been fulfilled." To illustrate the problem, the Council pointed out that the National Aeronautics and Space Administration announced in 1962 a traineeship program expected eventually to produce 1,000 Ph.D.'s a year. The program reached an input of 1,300 in 1966, but, by 1968, "the new input had been reduced to 75, leaving institutions with heavy commitments, greatly expanded capacity to produce, and limited, if any, resources to support those who sought this kind of education." The Council cited a similar example: in 1958 Congress identified as one of the nation's critical needs a vastly expanded number of college teachers at the Ph.D. level and passed legislation which envisioned a gradual growth of the program as newly involved and newly expanded institutions increased their capacity to meet this need. In 1966, the input of new fellows in the NDEA Title IV program reached 6,000. In 1968, it had dropped to fewer than 3,000. The council's comment was that

If the government had suggested that these were temporary programs, to be phased out as a short-term need was met, institutions could have planned accordingly. But the need was not short-term; it has not been met; institutions did not make only temporary commitments. On the contrary, they believed it was in the interest of the nation, the government, and themselves to build this greater capacity and to establish a carefully planned and tightly budgeted program. The sharp reductions have brought in their wake both severe financial hardship and uncertainty about responding to new national demands.

President Nixon's Task Force on Education concluded that what is needed, besides rectification of this fundamental weakness, is (1) a clearer definition of the federal role; despite its magnitude, "there is at present considerable ambiguity in it"; (2) more adequate machinery for policy formulation; and (3) better arrangements for inter-Governmental coordination."

The Federal effort has . . . in recent years been characterized by a multiplicity of uncoordinated, and sometimes conflicting, initiatives from many different departments and agencies of the Executive Branch and from the Congress. Although much of great importance has been accomplished, there has, nonetheless, been a serious lack of coherent planning and coordination within the Government and an absence of any mechanism for centralized appraisal of the net effect of the myriad Federal initiatives on state and local education authorities and on educational institutions.[22]

Moreover, "a new way of federal involvement in the financing of education," perhaps grants for general institutional purposes, at least in higher education,[23] and "a consolidation and rationalization of the many existing programs," are required. The many new programs which have been developed in education in the last few years have not been "enacted . . . on a carefully planned basis, but in the ways that were politically possible." Now the need is to "look over the spectrum of programs to see how they might be welded together and made more useful . . . by making . . . dealings with the federal government less complex." [24]

Two specific problems in the relations between the federal government and state, local, and university and school officials require particular comment. One is the matter of *timing;* the other is the problem of *evaluation.*

Timing. A considerable gap exists between the appropriations procedure in Congress and the planning cycle of both the public schools and the colleges and universities. School districts typically operate on a fiscal year beginning July 1. If they are to plan most effectively, they need to know by early spring what funds will be available to them for commitment on that date. "The typical school district spends 65 to 70 per cent of its funds on salaries, hires new people in March, April, and May, and fits together a pattern of planned class size and program needs in the light of funds which will be available with the opening of school in the fall. The availability of teachers for new assignments and the continuance of teachers in former jobs are both hitched to this planning cycle." [25] Most colleges and universities adhere to a planning cycle which requires even earlier knowledge for its greatest

22. See footnote 18 above.
23. See American Council on Education, *Federal Programs for Higher Education: Needed Next Steps* (Washington, 1969).
24. Former Commission of Education Harold Howe II, quoted in *The Chronicle of Higher Education,* Vol. III, No. 7, December 9, 1968, p. 8.
25. See footnote 20 above.

effectiveness. But the way in which Congress appropriates money could scarcely be better designed to make the job of school and college officials difficult. Too frequently federal funds "are not made available to school [and college] officials until several months of the school year in which they are to be used have elapsed." "Under these circumstances," Representative Carl Perkins of Kentucky, Chairman of the House Committee on Education and Labor in the 91st Congress, reminded his fellow Congressmen in 1969, "we, at the outset, make it extremely difficult—if not impossible—for school administrators to plan and make the most effective use of Federal dollars. We handicap schools in their ability to employ and retain qualified teachers. . . ."[26] It is not that Congress intends an inconvenience. "It is just doing business as it always has." But somehow school officials "must find out in March rather than in November . . . what federal funds will be available when school opens. . . ."[27] President Johnson, in both his February 28, 1967, message to Congress on education and his Budget Message of January 29, 1968, noted the timing problem and called on Congress to "enact education appropriations early enough to allow the nation's schools and colleges to plan effectively." To date, however, all such pleas have been ignored by Congress.

Evaluation. There is an understandable desire on the part of the Bureau of the Budget, the Office of Education, and Congressional committees to have some measure of the value of the programs they generate and administer. Members of Congress have to go before the people for reelection at regular two- or six-year cycles. They have taken positions for or against education bills or appropriation legislation, and when they go back to their constituents, they quite properly want to know how the programs are doing.[28] Nor is it just Congressmen who feel the need. President Nixon's task force on education told him that one of the first tasks "of the new Administration must be to make a[n] . . . appraisal of the effectiveness of the present major fed-

26. *Congressional Record* 115: H1301 (February 27, 1969). See the testimony of school administrators on this point on this and the next two pages.
27. See footnote 20 above.
28. See footnote 18 above.

eral education programs. . . ." But such an appraisal, it went on, should not be held to make unnecessary "a highly important, longer-range requirement, the need for . . . a mechanism for thorough, objective, research-based evaluation of educational programs. . . ." [29] By early 1969, federal officials had begun to worry about the lack of measurable results of expenditures under Title I of the Elementary and Secondary Education Act. There seemed to be some evidence that the investment of national funds had "paid off" in some school districts, the children there doing measurably better than before. But several studies reported little if any marked improvement in other districts. "One such study . . . actually showed 'a slight decline in average pupil achievement' in 132 schools" after federal funds had been utilized.[30] Needless to say, such findings, if replicated by further studies, would have profound effects on the future of federal aid programs.

Besides adjustment in these areas, what else can be done to assure that the national government continues to lend its strength to education in the United States without usurping control from state and local authorities? Former Commissioner Harold Howe's conclusions bear repeating.

. . . there must be mutual understanding between federal officials and those who . . . operate and control education, so that a number of critical problems of common concern may be identified and answered effectively. My list of those problems is neither complete nor arranged by priorities, but it includes at least some matters on which many educators agree:

1) In many communities and states, tax resources for the support of high-quality education at both the school and college levels are inadequate. Ways must be found by which the federal government can sensibly help to bridge the financial gap which creates the quality gap.

2) Inequality of educational opportunity is a problem for a large proportion of our citizens and even more of a problem for our racial and cultural minorities. The federal government must make adequate resources available to educational authorities to help them establish equal opportunities in education for all Americans. In addition, the government has an obligation to see that the rights of

29. See footnote 20 above.

30. A dispatch of the *Washington Post–Los Angeles Times* News Service, *Durham Morning Herald*, January 2, 1969, p. 29.

American citizens as defined by Congress and the courts are as well protected in the schools as elsewhere.

3) The professional and subprofessional manpower to serve education is not available in many places.[31] Local and state educational agencies must be enabled to receive federal support and planning resources in this problem area, since it crosses state boundaries.

4) The growing proportion of Americans seeking education beyond high school or re-education during adult years points to the possibility of greater federal assistance to higher education. Programs which will help new as well as established institutions are called for.

5) The forward planning, research, and development capacities of education need strengthening. The federal government can sponsor research and development activities, but much of the planning for change must be done at the state level. One answer may lie in additional federal programs to help the states do this job better.

Federal action in the field of education does not, of course, preclude the continued active participation of both the states and local school districts; in fact, federal action is based on the premise that the chief burden and responsibility for education will continue to be carried by those jurisdictions. And at the state and local levels, as at the national level, there are a good many serious problems. The chief one at the state level is lack of manpower: "Larger staffs are needed if the state departments are to provide the administrative, regulatory, consultative, and service programs to aid schools. . . ." that are being increasingly required of them. But it is more than a matter of numbers; it is also "a matter of quality. . . ." Low salaries constitute the chief obstacle to hiring top-quality personnel; other obstacles are "the heavy impact of federal aid, politics, long-standing traditions. . . ." [32] The state departments of education and the state superintendents of public instruction are "politically sensitive in all states, but especially so

31. Perhaps nowhere do the manpower deficiencies which have become such a problem in modern American federalism (see Chapter V below) reveal themselves more clearly than in the field of education. "The searching examination of our school system that was stimulated by the launching of the first Sputnik in 1957 revealed serious deficiencies in the training and competence of a dismaying proportion of our classroom teachers. And the problem reaches upwards into the top level of state educational systems." (Stephen K. Bailey, "Coordinating the Great Society," *The Reporter*, March 24, 1966, p. 40).

32. Braddock, "Do the States Have a Place in Education?" *op. cit.*, p. 25.

in some of them." [33] In 1967, the chief state school officer in twenty-nine states was appointed, most commonly by the state board of education or the governor, but in the remaining twenty-one states he was elected by the people. In none of those states are school officers immune from political pressures. The Governor's Study Commission on the Public School System of North Carolina (one of the states where the superintendent is elected) pointed out that in 1968 "Educational leadership must start at the State level if attempts to improve our schools are to be successful."

The State Board of Education should be the policy formation agency for public education. At present, the Board must not only set policy, but it must also assume the administrative responsibility of working with three individual agencies to see that policies are carried out.

What is needed is a "highly qualified administrator appointed by and responsible to the Board rather than [one] obtained through general election. This would assure the Board of having its own administrator charged with carrying out Board policies." [34]

Moreover, "if state departments are to set standards—and to meet standards for their own performance—they must have long-range planning, something difficult to achieve without continuity of leadership at the top," which, under the present circumstances, too many state departments lack.[35]

All of these factors have combined to reduce the capabilities of state departments of education to perform their important functions in the field of education as well as they might. Perhaps as a consequence of this combination of factors, state departments of education are not "always viewed as primary founts of wisdom, expert knowledge, new thinking and educational vision." Rather, universities and colleges, the growing corps of educational talent in Washington, professional teacher associations, specialists in the rapidly developing commercial education industry, accrediting agencies, and urban school districts have come to vie

33. *Ibid.*, p. 26.
34. "A Child Well Taught," The Report of the Governor's Study Commission on the Public School System of North Carolina (Raleigh, 1968), p. 11.
35. *Ibid.*, p. 32.

with state departments for educational leadership. Even so, as Clayton Braddock correctly observes, if a "state lacks a good education climate . . . much of the blame for the shortcoming falls on the heads of state leaders, including those in the state departments of education." [36] In a partial attempt to meet the problem, funds under Title V of the Elementary and Secondary Education Act may be sought for strengthening state departments, thus providing another example of the interrelatedness of governmental concern and support in the area of education.

The main problems at the local level are the overlapping ones of providing an adequate education for inner city (ghetto) children and handling the explosive question of racial integration in local schools (although a good case might also be made for the necessity of strengthening the position of the local superintendent and indeed the local school boards themselves and for a good deal more consolidation of rural school districts so as to make better institutional facilities available).

The states, however, do not bear the major burden of responsibility for public education; rather, the many public school systems at the local level do so. Perhaps no area of government has come under as much fire as have local school districts. As McGeorge Bundy put it recently,

"A most striking example of local need and opportunity is public education . . . Most [public school systems] are very badly run. Especially in our larger cities they have become enmeshed in a tangle of negative powers which makes them extraordinarily resistant to change, and they are currently failing to do the job that this new age demands of them. They do not have the money, the public support, the leadership, the teachers, the buildings, the atmosphere, the energy, or the concept of their meaning that they need. . . . our public school world [must be transformed] from a political system marked by impotence and irresponsibility into one marked by authority, accountability, and much wider community participation." [37]

Alan K. Campbell recently pointed out that "despite the obvious need for more resources in city schools, we are spending less—any way you measure it—in the cities than in the suburbs."

36. Braddock, "Do the States Have a Place in Education?" *op. cit.*
37. McGeorge Bundy, *The Strength of Government* (Cambridge: Harvard Univ. Press, 1968), pp. 58–59.

For the thirty-seven largest U.S. metropolitan areas, the average per capita expenditure for education in the central cities is $82; the same expenditure in the suburbs in $113. On a per student basis, the comparable figures are $449 for the cities and $573 for the suburbs. These figures would not be so startling if the gap between city and suburb appeared to be closing. It is widening however. To compete with the suburbs, central cities must have a resource advantage. Yet, the present system of resource allocation clearly discriminates against the city.[38]

This takes place for several reasons: central cities simply no longer have the available income to support the service requirements of their populations. Not only do higher income citizens move to the suburbs in a well established pattern, but manufacturing is beginning to follow the people to the suburbs. As both higher income residents and industries move outward, the taxable assessed valuation in the central city falls and is no longer able to keep pace with the special problems and needs of the central city school population, to say nothing of other central city needs. Nor does the system of intergovernmental aid help as one might expect. Indeed, Campbell concludes, "It may be that the single greatest failure of the aid system is in the field of education." Ideally under the aid system

aid should flow to areas of greater than average need. Until recently, state and federal aid systems for education worked just that way. It took resources from centers of wealth, the cities, and provided it to the less affluent rural areas. But today, the aid system does not allocate resources relative to need, whether measured as total need or for education alone. Most revealing about the present fiscal system is the failure of aid, either state or federal, to fill the gap left by the unequal distribution of local resources available. For example, state and federal aid supports 27 per cent of public expenditures in central cities, while supporting 29 per cent of those in suburban areas, and 37 per cent of all local expenditures in the rest of the nation. Considered as a proportion of local tax effort, federal and state aid represents only 44 per cent of central-city taxes; the comparable figure for suburbia is 53 per cent, and for the rest of the nation, 74 per cent.

Such disparities create one of the most critical problems in the whole field of education, and of federalism as well. It is obvious

38. Alan K. Campbell, "Inequities of School Finance," *Saturday Review*, January 11, 1969, p. 44.

on the face of it that increased local tax efforts by central cities will not go far toward solving the problem. And to date, states have shown little willingness to provide differential treatment for cities. To be sure, they could adapt aid patterns to existing metropolitan situations and go so far as to adjust local boundaries to make richer tax jurisdictions possible. But state legislatures have done little in this connection, reapportionment having converted a rural bias into a suburban bias. Whether the answer is greater federal aid, and if so, how it is to be granted, remains to be seen. In any case, funds under Title III of the Elementary and Secondary Education Act can be used to provide assistance to specific projects in central city schools, and in April, 1968, the Office of Education created an Office of Urban Education to tackle the problem.

The integration problem is rooted in the simple fact that white and Negro children in many urban schools do not go to school together. The extent of this isolation is easily seen in one of the findings of a study done by the United States Commission on Civil Rights. It points out that

In the Nation's metropolitan areas, where two-thirds of both the Negro and white population now live, it [racial isolation] is most severe. Seventy-five percent of the Negro elementary students in the Nation's cities are in schools with enrollments that are nearly all-Negro (90 per cent or more Negro), while 83 per cent of the white students are in nearly all-white schools. Nearly nine of every ten Negro elementary students in the cities attend majority-Negro schools.[39]

To many, this condition calls for a thorough restructuring of the urban school district system. There are three main arguments for such reform which are well documented and analyzed in the report of the Commission on Civil Rights:

1. There is a moral and legal obligation to fulfil the promise of the Fourteenth Amendment to the American Negro for equal protection of the laws. The circumstances which have produced racial isolation in the school systems are not simply value-free empirical facts. This isolation has grown in large part out of the basic race prejudice of the American society. Housing patterns

39. U.S. Commission on Civil Rights, *Racial Isolation in the Public Schools* (Washington, 1967), p. 199.

and employment opportunities are not free of this underlying bigotry. It should be a major commitment of American society to counteract the effects of such bigotry where it is possible, and it is possible to do so in the school systems of the urban areas.

2. There is a great disparity in quality between the schools in predominantly white areas and the schools in predominantly Negro areas. The Commission on Civil Rights found that the Negro schools had poorer libraries and facilities in general, as well as usually a less qualified teaching staff.[40] This disparity is especially disheartening in view of the traditional commitment of American society to the education of *all* children according to their abilities. With the growth of urban America and the concomitant development of suburbs, there seems to have been a trend for the quality of public education to be correlated directly with the class, income, and race of the parents, to the obvious disadvantage of the urban Negro poor.

3. There is a meaningful link between the racial composition of a school and the achievement and attitudes of the students. The report of the Civil Rights Commission demonstrates that:

(a) Disadvantaged Negro students in schools with a majority of equally disadvantaged white students achieve better than Negro students in school with a majority of equally disadvantaged Negro students.

(b) Differences are even greater when disadvantaged Negro students in school with a majority of disadvantaged Negro students are compared with similarly disadvantaged Negro students in school with a majority of advantaged white students. This difference in achievement for 12th grade students amounts to more than two entire grade levels.

(c) Negroes in predominately Negro schools tend to have lower educational aspirations and more frequently express a sense of inability to influence their futures by their own choices than Negro students who have similar backgrounds attending majority-white schools. Their fellow students are less likely to offer academic stimulation.

(d) Predominately Negro schools generally are regarded by the community as inferior institutions. Negro students in such

40. *Ibid.*, p. 203.

schools are sensitive to such views and often come to share them. This stigma affects the achievement and attitudes of Negro students.[41]

In light of these arguments, the case for reform of the present pupil distribution pattern in urban area schools appears to be strong. Basic problems of racial unrest in the cities may well be traced to the feelings of inferiority and frustration which were early instilled in the urban Negro school child through racial isolation in the educational process.

In some cases—in Providence, Rhode Island, Berkeley, California,[42] White Plains, New York, and Evanston, Illinois, for example—where the ghetto areas are fairly small, it has been possible to deal with the problem of racial isolation quite effectively.[43] There have also been experiments in bussing students, as in Boston, Rochester, Los Angeles, Cincinnati, Great Neck, New York, and Hartford, Connecticut, which required no basic structural changes. The Hartford experiment, which is entirely voluntary as far as both students and participating schools are concerned, is especially interesting in that it busses inner-city children, mostly Negroes, to new, well-equipped, and superbly staffed suburban schools in the Greater Hartford area in an attempt to determine if better personnel, plant, and programs will turn out to be "the significant factor[s] in changing the plight of . . . urban culturally deprived" youngsters.[44] Even if such experiments are successful, the problem will not easily be solved. What may be required is an innovative realignment of school districts in each metropolitan area to eliminate or sharply reduce racial segregation therein. Such a realignment would be a major and time-consuming process.

There are those who argue for a still more drastic remedy. Some, Henry M. Levin reports, "would dismantle the present system of public schools altogether, replacing them with private

41. *Ibid.*, p. 204.
42. See Ray Halpern, "The Berkeley Plan. Tactics for Integration," *Saturday Review*, December 21, 1968, pp. 47–49, *seq.*
43. See the in-depth study of education in the ghetto, *Saturday Review*, January 11, 1969, pp. 33–36.
44. Charles O. Richter and S. Francis Overlan, "Will Urban-Suburban Busing Work?" *Nation's Schools* 80:32 (August 1967); see also M. Buskin, "City-to-Suburb Busing in Hartford," *School Management* 11:67–70 *seq.* October 1967).

schools that would be—in part—publicly financed." This "free market approach" operates on the assumption that "by giving students and their families a choice of schools, and by requiring schools to compete for students, massive increases in educational effectiveness and output would result." [45] The government (presumably local government with state and federal aid) would provide for each school-age child a voucher, which would be redeemable as tuition at an approved school. It might be that some public schools would be retained, to enter into the competition with private schools for students.

Freedom of entry by schools into the market—provided that they met minimum qualifications—would insure efficiency in the production of schooling, and students and their families would be given a market of educational alternatives in place of the present rigid assignment practices. Moreover, such competition would induce innovation and experimentation in that each school would try to obtain competitive advantages over the others. Thus, the operation of the market would provide far more choices and a greater degree of efficiency in the schooling of all students, especially those pupils who are presently confined to slum schools. [46]

Given the lag in the democratic process on the one hand and the complexities of the urban decision-making structure on the other, no such radical innovation seems immediately likely. If, however, the traditional public school system in the United States continues to fail to meet the needs and fulfill the expectations of vast numbers of their clientele, as it has done for many years, and if the states and the national government cannot arrive at a viable alternative, some such proposal may be accepted and implemented in one or more urban centers in the United States.

No discussion of education in the federal system can be concluded without some mention of the larger economic problem involved. As Fred M. Hechinger, education editor of *The New York Times,* has pointed out,

Education is not a commodity that gets cheaper with mass production—indeed, it threatens to become [more expensive] with rising

45. Henry M. Levin, "The Failure of the Public Schools and the Free Market Remedy," *The Urban Review* 2:32–37 (June 1968), reproduced as Reprint 148 by the Brookings Institution (Washington, 1968). The quotations are from the latter, at pp. 1, 2.

46. *Ibid.,* p. 3.

volume unless funds rise in proportion. The cost of knowledge is rising. . . .[47]

Enrollment in all types of educational institutions is growing, although the rate of growth in the elementary grades is slowing down some. The cost accruing from the increase in numbers is aggravated by the general inflationary trend the country is experiencing, the competition of the war in Vietnam, and other defense operations, and of course by the still-developing national commitment to education. How to meet the staggering costs of American education in the future is a perplexing question. In relation to higher education, Alan Pifer, the president of the Carnegie Corporation of New York, which has been closely involved in the national education picture over the years, observed in a somber report early in 1968 that "Whether public or private, most U.S. colleges are in such desperate financial straits that by the year 2000 they will be almost totally dependent on the Federal government for support." [48] The trend, Pifer reasoned, is irreversible. The national government "supplied nearly one-fourth of the $16.8 billion that all colleges spent [in 1967]; by 1975," he predicted, "this may climb to 50 per cent." It is therefore high time, Pifer warned, "for educators in the public and private sectors to stop their selfish factional disputes and get together to help shape new national policies on which federal funding must be based." The nation, he concluded, "can no longer afford the luxury of an unplanned, wasteful, chaotic approach to education in which freedom often means 'freedom to duplicate what others could do better, to perform useless, even meretricious, functions.' " What is called for at the collegiate level is the creation of a "long-range planning center for higher education, drawing heavily on university advisers and given authority to guide federal policy." Its first task, Pifer declared, should be to seek agreement on how federal aid should be distributed.[49]

The economic problem is not of course confined to higher education; it is as severe, if not more so, at the elementary and sec-

47. Fred M. Hechinger, "Education: Monumental Tasks and Problems . . . A Nervous Year," *International Herald Tribune*, January 20–21, 1968, p. 11.
48. Quoted in *Time*, January 26, 1968, p. 75.
49. *Ibid.*

ondary level. There, however, something like what Pifer proposed for higher education has recently come into being, and its proponents predict great things for it. Certainly if it works as hoped it will be a significant development in federalism. This is the Compact for Education, which was signed and became operative in 1966. The idea for the compact came from James B. Conant's book, *Shaping Educational Policy*. Conant, seeking to determine how educational policy below the baccalaureate level was shaped in the United States, "concluded that it wasn't being shaped at all except in a totally unorganized way. [He] felt that education is too important to be left to the haphazard chance of unconnected state and local efforts and too complex to be left to a single guiding hand." He concluded that what was needed was a device by which the states, and through them their local subdivisions, might come together to take the initiative in the development of national education policy. Governor Sanford's Study of the American States undertook the task of bringing a compact for that purpose to fruition, and the interstate agency called for in the compact, named the Educational Commission of the States, was formally organized in June, 1966. It is based in Denver, Colorado; it has a full-time staff and is financed on a formula basis by contributions from its forty-two member states (as of June, 1969).

"The Compact doesn't solve any of the states' problems," Governor Sanford points out. "But it does set up a mechanism whereby the states can begin to seek the massive improvements that must occur if American education is to meet the challenge of the last third of the twentieth century." [50]

The Compact gives the states an office for developing alternatives for policy decisions, which ultimately, and in any event, are to be made by local and state policy-making bodies. It furnishes the states with the best available information. It is a clearing house for ideas, and a forum for sharing experiences, improving performances, and debating goals. The Compact makes it possible for success to feed upon success, as ideas are . . . transmitted across state and regional lines.

Its unique feature is that it joins the political and professional forces in education across the nation to discuss what they can do in part-

50. Sanford, "A New Strategy for State Initiative," *op. cit.*, p. 5.

nership. . . . *Its purpose is to assure a constant confrontation between the political forces which must support education and the educators who must transform new funds into real achievements.*[51]

Although the Commission's concern is not limited to elementary and secondary education, the major focus of its attention is there. And questions of finance, although by no means the only ones discussed, will be central issues at all times. "The Educational Commission," Governor Sanford concludes, "is enabling the states to unite in the resolve to meet their responsibility to the quickening interest of the American people in the pursuit of educational excellence. The Compact for Education places the states in the forefront of that pursuit." [52]

The mere creation of a new agency like the Educational Commission of the States and the planning agency Pifer suggests will not by themselves solve even the problems in education suggested in this case study, to say nothing of many others not discussed here. But the Compact for Education does put a new force at work in both American education and American federalism and points the way to at least a partial solution of some of the problems raised by the intergovernmental nature of American education. Indeed, its presence makes the program area of education unique in America today. It may well come to occupy the role Pifer sees as necessary as it develops and matures and may offer a model to areas outside of education where action in the American system is intergovernmental. As such, it bears a good deal of watching in the years ahead.

51. Terry Sanford, *Storm Over the States* (New York: McGraw Hill, 1967), pp. 117–118.
52. *Ibid.*, p. 119.

V

WEAKNESSES IN STATE
AND LOCAL GOVERNMENT

IT MAY SEEM WRONG to embark on a discussion of state and local government weaknesses without first analyzing the problem of the national government. Admittedly there is a great deal that could be done to improve the national government's functioning, as McGeorge Bundy, for one, has recently made abundantly clear.[1] The weakness of executive power, the relation between the legislative and the executive branches, particularly between the President and the leaders of Congress, the difficulties encountered in coordinating federal programs with one another, the need for extensive reorganization in the executive branch, the difficulties the President encounters in trying to function as chief executive, not to mention the problems of Congress—all these and still more difficulties within the national government suggest themselves at once. Without taking cognizance of their impact on the way the federal system meets the demands made upon it, no one can seriously study the American system of government. But although its faults do have an impact on functional federalism, the national government is nonetheless at present the most effective partner in the federal system. Both the executive and the legislative branches of the national government, if marked too by weaknesses, are characterized by their ability to perform reasonably well and to produce a close approximation in the end of what

1. See Bundy, *The Strength of Government, op. cit.*

the American people want from them. It is the state and local governments in our system which more often miss the mark and so are most in need of improvement. As Representative Henry Reuss of Wisconsin put it, "Two crises in American government [had] become apparent by 1969: our State and local governments are becoming both insolvent and archaic. [They] desperately need money . . . [and] modernizing." They must make "the transition into the last third of the twentieth century." [2]

That the states and their local subdivisions should be the least effective partners in the American federal system is in part the result of changing circumstances beyond their power to alter. Certainly the states started out as the strongest partners, far outdistancing the national government. The first national government, under the Articles of Confederation, was the tool of the states, purposely kept weak and relatively ineffectual so that the states could retain the dominant position in the Union. And for a good many years after the new Constitution went into effect—it was designed, it will be recalled, specifically to strengthen the national government—the states did in fact remain preeminent. They attracted men's loyalties and they performed most of the important governmental functions of the day quite well. Just when—and why—they began to lose ground is hard to pinpoint. Perhaps the liberalization of the suffrage after the turn of the nineteenth century and the general acceptance of the Jacksonian thesis that government was so simple that any man could perform its functions contributed to the decline in the excellence of their performance. Or perhaps it was because there were so many other attractions as the new country opened up that only lesser men, unable to inspire state government to its best efforts, were content to occupy positions there. In any case, a pattern of corruption and abuse in both state and local government was initiated which persisted for many decades. In the process, the states and local governments forfeited their position of preeminence in the Union. The national government did not step forward to fill the vacuum at once. Except during the Civil War, there did not seem to be much need for strong governmental action from any quarter. By the end of the nineteenth century, however, with the beginning

2. *Congressional Record* 115: H159, 158 (January 8, 1969).

of the emergence of the United States as a world power, a more active role at least for the national government began to be indicated. With increasing nationalization of the economy and rapid urbanization on the one hand and Woodrow Wilson's New Freedom, World War I, the Great Depression, and World War II in rapid succession on the other hand, all combining to place ever heavier demands on government, the need for the quick and efficient exertion of national power was increasingly felt.

For the most part, the national government responded to the demand admirably. The states and local governments, unprepared for changing circumstances and unsure what role they might play, continued along the path they had long since made for themselves, "a vicious circle by which mistrust . . . imposed impotence" on them.[3] It was the Depression more than anything else which almost proved their undoing. In Terry Sanford's words,

The depression of the 1930's forced the nation to reach back for all its historic powers in political, wartime, constitutional, and fiscal experiences, and to convert them to massive action across the nation. As a number of emergencies in the 1780's removed the first layer of retained state sovereignty, so the depression of the 1930's peeled off all the other layers right down to the core.

Out of the ordeal of the depression came damaging blows to the states. From the viewpoint of the efficacy of state government, the states lost their confidence, and the people their faith in the states; the news media became cynical, the political scientists became neglectful, and the critics became harsh.

"Is the state the appropriate instrumentality for the discharge of these sovereign functions?" Luther Gulick asked in 1933. "The answer is not a matter of conjecture or delicate appraisal. It is a matter of brutal record. The American State is finished." [4]

To battle the economic disaster and to put America once again on the move fell to the national government, and it is to that gov-

3. Bundy, *The Strength of Government, op. cit.*, p. 78.
4. Sanford, *Storm Over the States, op. cit.*, p. 21. The Gulick quotation is from his article, "Reorganization of the State," *Civil Engineering*, August, 1933, pp. 420–421. Great reliance has been placed in this chapter on the book by Governor Sanford. This is so not only because it is a very good book, which has deservedly received a great deal of attention, but also because Governor Sanford is perhaps the best-informed individual in the nation today on the subject of the states. His book should be read in its entirety in conjunction with the issues raised in this chapter.

ernment's everlasting credit that it met its new responsibilities heroically.

But if what Sanford calls the "weakening of the states" came about in large part because of unalterable circumstances (it is worth noting that national governments nearly everywhere were forced to move to the center of the stage during the Depression—Canada's experience, for example, was very similar to that of the United States in the 1930's), it also resulted from their own actions—or lack of them. Their present plight has been to a considerable degree their own fault.

The states contributed to their own eventual ineffectiveness first by the kind of constitutions they drew up. There was never any question but that a written constitution must be at the base of every state's power, and from the beginning, either by converting their colonial charters into a constitution or by writing a wholly new instrument, constitutions were universally utilized by the states.[5] Generally speaking, however, the states did not follow the style of the new national constitution and content themselves with a broadly stated—and far from all-inclusive—statement of principles. They erred first in terms of length. Louisiana's telephone directory-sized constitution amounts to some 253,830 words, that of Alabama to 106,000, of California, to 82,570, and of Texas to 52,270. These are the worst, but few state constitutions followed the example of the national constitution, which is confined to about six thousand words and can be read in less than twenty minutes. Nor did they heed the injunction of Judge John Parker, long-time chief judge of the Fourth Circuit Court of Appeals, who cautioned that

The purpose of a state constitution is two-fold: (1) to protect the rights of the individual from encroachment by the State; and (2) to provide a framework of government for the State and its subdivisions. It is not the function of a constitution to deal with temporary conditions, but to lay down general principles of government which must be observed amidst changing conditions. It follows, then, that a constitution should not contain elaborate legislative provisions, but should lay down briefly and clearly the fundamental principles upon

5. Thirty-seven state constitutions in effect in 1968 were adopted prior to 1900; only thirteen are products of the twentieth century, and only seven have been written since World War II.

which the government shall proceed, leaving it to the people's representatives to apply these principles through legislation to conditions as they arise.[6]

Rather, they indulged in writing detailed applications of constitutional policy and principle until all distinction between what was truly constitutional in nature and what was merely statutory finally was lost altogether. Thus the Louisiana constitution contains five pages of text describing the powers of East Baton Rouge Parish (county) in connection with acquiring and financing sewerage improvements (Article XIV, section 3); the Delaware constitution specifies step by step the entire judicial procedure to be followed in prosecuting election offenses (Article V, section 8); the Iowa constitution sets the per diem rate of pay for state legislators at $3 (Article III, section 35); the California constitution states that the per mile rate for reimbursing state legislators shall not exceed $.05 a mile (Article IV, section 26); and there is an article in the Illinois constitution dealing with public warehouses (Article XIII). Nor are these examples either the most ridiculous or the most extreme. They merely demonstrate that writers of state constitutions have generally not been able to "forego the temptation to impose their own views as to details of policy and procedure on future generations to which those views may not be relevant." [7]

So written, state constitutions have constantly been before the legislatures and people for amendment, "as problems arise that were not contemplated at the time the constitution was drafted, or as old solutions prove inadequate to governmental problems in their new manifestations." [8] Over the years, the Louisiana constitution has had to be amended some 460 times, that of California, 350, that of Alabama, 260, and that of Texas, 178. And amendments seldom improve the situation. They are not usually comprehensive in scope, most often being directed to the correction of specific defects, and aimed at accomplishing a limited objective so as to arouse the least opposition possible to their adoption. As Grant McConnell observes, state constitutions are generally re-

6. Quoted in *Report of the North Carolina State Constitution Study Commission* (Raleigh, 1968), p. 1.

7. *Ibid.*, p. 3.

8. *Ibid.*

garded today as amendable "as the winds of political fashion shift and circumstances change" and consequently are held far less sacred in the public mind than the national constitution. Even if this suggests a nice theoretical justification for amendment— McConnell points out "that in a very basic sense the spirit of state government may be considerably more majoritarian than its national counterpart" [9]—in practice their susceptibility to fashion frequently makes state constitutions unable to provide for the effective functioning of state government.

State constitutions, in sum, work to slow down the rate at which states can meaningfully adjust to altered circumstances; to render adaptation and change difficult; to inhibit effective performance—in short, to reduce the flexibility and dynamism of state government to the vanishing point. In earlier years, when life moved more slowly and there was less need for governmental involvement at every turn, a cumbersome state constitution made little difference, but today it is one of the prime reasons why the national government has been called on so often when action has been necessary. Rather than supporting and facilitating state action, state constitutions hinder and obstruct it and thereby provide justification for national action.

The constitutional difficulty is greater, moreover, than merely the rigidity imposed on state government. State constitutions, perhaps again in devotion to majoritarianism, reflect a distrust of the very officers of government for which they provide. This also contributes to governmental ineffectiveness. In particular the power of governors to act and to lead is restricted by most state constitutions. Not only are too many of them limited to either two-year terms or to a single four-year term, too often they have to share the executive power with other elected state officials. The argument for electing many executive officers is that it brings government closer to the people. But in practice that simply is not so. The people hardly know that executive officers other than the governor exist, and few can or do keep up with their activities and performances. As a consequence of such diffused executive power, responsibility is confused, policy decisions are

9. McConnell, *Private Power and American Democracy, op. cit.,* pp. 169–170.

difficult to reach, and if reached, to enforce, and effective executive leadership is rendered impossible. The situation is aggravated by constitutional (and statutory) failure to make the governor either the responsible budget officer or the chief planner for state government as a whole. Since no one else can function in those capacities, most states have to do without those essential functions. Moreover, too many constitutions establish a multiplicity of state agencies outside of gubernatorial control, "each of which is effectively accountable only to a narrow constituency consisting of the group or groups most directly and intimately affected by the agency's activities." There is no one to ride herd on them, nor can they be held accountable to the people. "Beyond some point, completely separate . . . agencies which can only be coordinated and made responsible through the direct supervision of the governor's office result in irresponsibility, simply because the governor cannot give any of them sufficient attention." [10]

State legislatures receive no better a break in most state constitutions and laws than the executive branch. Long malapportioned, they continue to be unrepresentative of the people of the states. The one-man one-vote principle enunciated by the U.S. Supreme Court in *Wesberry* v. *Sanders* [11] theoretically requires that a representation ratio exist in each house of each state legislature which would assure that the majority of members of that house were elected by a majority of the people. In practice, even so long after *Baker* v. *Carr* [12] finally opened the way to reapportionment in 1962, the states have been slow to achieve such a ratio. In most states today, a majority of the legislature represents less than a majority of the people. Even so, the contrast with the days before 1962 is startling. "In 1962, representation ranged from a high of 48 per cent in one house and two senates to lows of 12 per cent in three houses and 8 per cent in one senate." [13]

Malrepresentation is not the only difficulty under which state legislatures operate. Permitted by state constitutions to sit only

10. *Ibid.*, p. 185.
11. 376 US 1 (1964).
12. 369 US 186 (1962).
13. The Council of State Governments, *The Book of the States 1968–69* (Chicago: The Council of State Governments, 1968), p. 40.

for restricted periods, poorly paid, denied offices and adequate staff assistance, rigidly confined to delegated powers by strict judicial interpretation of constitutional and statutory provisions, regarded as political way stations on the road to higher office by many of their members, or as rightful bastions of private interests by others, they have failed over the years to provide the centers of creative thinking and positive decision-making expected in a viable theory of federal government. "Few American political institutions today enjoy as little prestige as state legislatures," Frank Trippett concluded.

Many are excessively large, most are malapportioned; they are also restricted constitutionally in their powers to legislate, are poorly organized and often hampered by archaic rules and procedures. Theoretically the states' chief policy-making institutions, they have lost much of the respect and support which the people had in the early days of the republic. Serious efforts to reform state institutions have gone on for over half a century but those directed at legislatures have generally met with the least success. Yet many other problems of state government and of the federal system can be solved only by state legislative action—and this in turn depends on something being done about state legislative powers, organization, and representation. Major surgery is called for if these organs of the body politic are to make their essential contribution to contemporary government.[14]

And the indictment of the legislative branch must be broader than that of the executive branch; for it generally is conceded that most men have sought the gubernatorial office in the belief that they could use it to promote the common weal, whereas it cannot easily be demonstrated that state legislators have had such pure motives. One does not have to subscribe to the strong language of Frank Trippett when he says that "legislatures are inefficient and corrupt, that they procrastinate on public business while habitually kowtowing to private economic interests, that legislators . . . line their own pockets, scratch their own backs and roll their own logs," [15] to make the point that state legislatures are notoriously the preserve of special interests. "Railroads ran many a state for decades. So did power companies. In Montana, Anaconda Copper exercised disproportionate influence; in

14. Frank Trippett, *The States—United They Fell* (Cleveland: World Publishing Co., 1967), p. 2.
15. *Ibid.*, pp. 2–3.

Illinois and Florida, the race tracks; in Wyoming, the cattlemen's association; in Louisiana, the oil companies; and in Connecticut, the drug industry and the insurance companies." [16] Often parading behind the false front of states' rights to forestall national action in areas of special concern to them, these special interests have been able to prevent state legislative action as well by working to maintain paralyzing constitutional and legal restrictions on state legislatures.

Nor do state courts emerge unscathed from an examination of the role of the states. As suggested earlier, they have been inclined to take a narrow view of state power under state constitutions and to insist on having word-for-word authorization for any and all state actions. Thus while the state constitutions are devoid of "necessary and proper" clauses, the courts have not sought to find other ways to facilitate state action for change. Rather, they too have contributed their share to state inaction.

Succinctly put, the case against the states is that where action has been required they have too often been inactive; where change has been demanded, they have offered the *status quo;* where imagination and innovation have been needed, they have seldom come up with satisfactory alternatives. The states, students have agreed, are indecisive, antiquated, timid, and ineffective, unwilling to face their problems, unresponsive, and not really interested in taking action when action is required. It is the existence of just such defects that accounts for the title of Governor Sanford's book, *Storm Over the States,* and that leads many to believe that the states have outlived their usefulness in the American constitutional system.

In part, the states' deficiencies stem, as we have seen, from the constitutional and legal heritage of the past. But in larger measure they exist because citizens have not seen fit to alter the conditions which cause such deficiencies in the first place. Certainly since the turn of this century, the need for reforms in state government has been pointed out to the American people frequently and with appalling examples. But they have been reluctant to act, or if they have acted, they have done so slowly and only partially. This has been the case for several reasons: the natural op-

16. Sanford, *Storm Over the States, op. cit.,* p. 33.

position to change always encountered among human beings, the reputation for dullness state government has acquired over the years and the consequent failure of people to become excited about involvement in it, the counter pressures of special interests, both in the private sector and within state government itself, and the generally prevailing negative image of state government which the press and the nation's educational institutions have perpetuated. Others see additional reasons. The people generally have believed since the nation's earliest days that decentralization, weak state government, and something called "local autonomy" are positive goods. They continue to believe this without giving adequate thought to the changed times or to the effects of their beliefs on the efficacy of the governmental process. Theirs is an automatic response which, once learned, is difficult to reach and change when circumstances warrant, even if there were adequate leadership to that end.

Where one might expect to find such leadership—in the press and in political parties, in educational institutions and in state administration itself—one too often looks in vain. The press gives too little and too shallow attention to state government in general, often assigning junior reporters to the subject or relying on wire services or the handouts of state agencies for their information. Understandably, it is the graft, the nepotism, the corruption, the conflicts of interest, which attract attention, rather than the less spectacular but far more common and important body of positive governmental accomplishments. Thus the press only serves to reinforce the public misunderstanding of—indeed, its aversion to—state government as a whole.

Political parties in the states usually are not broadly representative of the people. There is a dominance of one-party states, or, put another way, there is a widespread absence of "effective party competition" in the states. The "general picture is [one] of a disorganized and atomized politics."[17] What the late V. O. Key pointed out in his book, *Southern Politics*, applies with almost no exceptions to American state politics as a whole:

Not only does a disorganized politics make impossible a competition between recognizable groups for power. It probably has a far-reach-

17. McConnell, *Private Power and American Democracy, op. cit.*, p. 175.

ing influence on the kinds of individual leaders thrown into power and also on the manner in which they utilize their authority once they are in office. . . . Factional fluidity and discontinuity probably make a government especially disposed toward favoritism . . . A pulverized politics decentralizes power to county leaders and county officials. . . . In a granulated political structure of this kind with thousands of points of authority there is no point at which accountability can be enforced.[18]

Key might have added that in such a system there is no point at which strong and forceful leadership can emerge either. Although some students take exception, many agree with Key that these conclusions have general validity. State politics do not provide opportunities for corrective action in the government; rather, they contribute to stability and to the continued acceptance of the *status quo*.

Educational institutions have been no more helpful. In both their research and teaching programs, they have by and large neglected the states in favor of both the other partners in the federal system. While a good many colleges and universities have focused attention on the national government, and a smaller number more recently on urban governments, those which have featured attention on problems of state government, either within their curricula or in some research or training program, are few and far between. State government remains a subject to which virtually no academic attention is paid, with the result that each new generation of potential leaders remains as ignorant as the last about both the problems and the opportunities therein.[19]

Where all this really hurts, as John P. Wheeler, Jr., has pointed out, is the damage these facts do to that bit of "the folklore of federalism" which "projects the states as laboratories of experimentation." It has been tradition—the conventional wisdom, in Galbraith's terminology—that the states, independent of external control as they are, lead the way in the United States, vying with each other to produce new and novel solutions to public problems, which can then be adopted by other states or by the Congress of the United States as needed. History does show some examples of the states trying "the new, on their own, without ei-

18. V. O. Key, *Southern Politics* (New York: Knopf, 1950), p. 304.
19. See for instance McConnell, *Private Power and American Democracy, op. cit.*, pp. 176–177.

ther the federal carrot or the federal stick.[20] Yet the sum total is less than convincing that this has been a meaningful function of the states." Indeed, concludes Wheeler, the states "have not proved themselves laboratories of experimentation, seeking knowledge and experience to be shared cooperatively. Rather, their efforts have too often been aimed at closing each other in, or, at best, at a kind of economic one-upmanship. Identity of long-run interests has played second fiddle to short-term politics. Even where issues have had strong state implications, states [have] seem[ed] willing to pass the most troublesome ones (and thus the most exciting ones) to the federal level, avoiding the necessity of energetic involvement with them. . . ."[21] For instance, there is general agreement that the states have long avoided the many-sided metropolitan area problem. Yet, as Senator Joseph D. Tydings of Maryland has said, it is likely that it will be on their record in dealing with that problem that "the states will stand or fall." "Already," Tydings observed, "vast federal sums for city improvement and rehabilitation flow directly from Washington to the cities without touching base in the Governor's mansion or state house. This trend is likely to continue and accelerate unless the states become more meaningful partners."[22] Other areas the states have avoided can easily be listed; it is as if the states had foresworn their own importance in the federal system.

Yet the states are important. They perform vital and intimate functions for the American people, functions, it should be noted, which the national government would have a hard time undertaking by itself. The states first of all administer justice for most of us most of the time. Most crimes are state crimes and most civil cases arise in state courts. The states plan, construct (to be sure with a great deal of federal aid), and maintain most highways and roads. Police, health, welfare, education, safety are all primarily state functions (many of them, to be sure, carried on with a good deal of federal money). So are such things as registration of births,

20. Wheeler cites as examples unemployment compensation, hail insurance, and industrial regulation.

21. John P. Wheeler, Jr., "A Great Partnership," *National Civic Review* 56:191, 192 (April 1967).

22. Joseph D. Tydings, "Reform is Possible," *National Civic Review* 56:11–12 (January 1967).

occupational examination and licensing, marriage and divorce, the disposal of bodies, and the administration of estates. If the charge be made that government is ever with us, in the United States at least it applies today as it always has with greater pertinence to state governments than to the national government. Even in a country as small as the Netherlands, the national government cedes the right to carry on many of the same functions to provinces and municipalities. If the national government of a nation as compact and homogeneous as Holland finds it necessary to employ lesser units of government for effective service to the people, how much more that must be the case in the United States—and this quite apart from the fact that the states in the United States exist independently of the national government in any case and exercise these functions quite apart from national government authorization. The states (and their local subdivisions) play both a necessary and a rightful role in American government, a role which has not diminished in significance despite the greater attention paid to and the urgency of the national government's role in American life. Evidence of the states' relevance is to be found in the increasing expenditures of state and local governments and in the far larger number of state and local employees today than even a few years ago.

Therefore one suggestion made for reform need not detain us long here. That is that the first step in strengthening the federal system is to abolish the states altogether or at least to redraw their boundaries to make them into more viable economic and social—if not political—units. On just how this might be done there is no agreement. Whether it *could* be done is doubtful. For the conventional wisdom about government in the United States includes belief "in the merit of the states as autonomous units of government . . . [embodying] the virtues of decentralization and smallness in an overly complex world. Occasionally, they appear virtuous just because, unlike the federal government, they do not deal with foreign policy or foreign aid and because they have almost nothing to do with national defense and cannot formulate or carry out a monetary policy. The most persistent and strongly held belief in the virtue of the states, however, is based upon a feeling that they are closer to the people and that power in their hands represents self government more than does power in the federal government. . . ." [23] Belief may not accord with practice, but it compels respect. Even if the states are not perfect, the difficulties encountered in attempting to make basic alterations would daunt all but the foolhardy. Discussion of remedies, instead, must be based on the states as they are.

In any case, the drastic step of redrawing state boundary lines is not necessary. Though it may appear that the states are living on the fiction of their power rather than on the fact of it, that they are content to watch the initiative in American government be taken by the national government and increasingly by their own municipal creations, that they are, as the late Senator Everett M. Dirksen of Illinois once put it, resigned to becoming of interest only to Rand-McNally, a number of signs indicate that the appearance may no longer be the whole reality.

State constitutional revision is becoming widely recognized as necessary. By 1967, indeed, the *National Civic Review* was able to note editorially that "state constitutional revision is receiving more attention than ever, with both political and civic leaders agreeing that restrictive detail is intolerable in a dynamic society." [24] Even before then, several states had undertaken general revisions of their constitutions, and a number of others had instituted a process of revision by stages. In the elections of 1968, voters in Florida adopted a revised constitution (except for the judicial article) and those in Hawaii a wholly new constitution, and voters in Arkansas, Illinois, and New Mexico authorized the calling of full-fledged constitutional conventions in 1969. The voters of Tennessee approved the calling of a limited convention in 1969, and those in Massachusetts approved placing the question of calling a convention on the ballot in 1970. In Indiana, the state Constitutional Revision Commission submitted twenty proposals amending the Indiana constitution to the legislature for its consideration during 1969. So remedial action at the very base of state government is being taken, and, as state legislatures are made more representative of the people, there is a good likelihood that

23. McConnell, *Private Power and American Democracy, op. cit.*, p. 167.
24. "Rising Tide in the States," *National Civic Review* 56:184 (April 1967).

constitutional revision will become an impelling objective in every state. Recently a National Council for Revision of State Constitutions was established to assist the states in achieving that objective.

The mere recognition of the worthiness of constitutional revision, however, does not assure united efforts toward achieving it. The revised and modernized constitutions that have been proposed to the voters of Kentucky, Maryland, Rhode Island, and New York in recent years have been rejected. In New York the proposed revision was defeated by nearly a three-to-one margin. The reasons for its defeat in May, 1968, are instructive, for with variations they probably account also for the defeats of revision in the other states. It appears, first of all, that the new constitution was opposed by New York City, where Mayor John V. Lindsay declared that it offered "pitifully little" toward helping the city solve its problems. Moreover, revision was offered as a package rather than as a series of independent propositions; the voters had to take all of it, or none. Thirdly, it failed to swing party support strongly behind it; only one Democratic leader campaigned at all enthusiastically for it. Finally, it involved a religious issue in that it proposed equal educational support for parochial and public schools and thus aroused a good deal of organized opposition on the part of Protestant and Jewish groups. Despite much publicity, the campaign for the new constitution did not succeed in persuading the people. In New York, as elsewhere, constitutional reform has yet to become a popular cause. Revision too often reflects the results of contest between groups and parties for high political stakes rather than popular commitment to good government. Thus the efforts of constitutional reformers are continually frustrated, and the battle for constitutional improvement continues.

In the meantime, piecemeal improvements are being made, including the strengthening of the governor's position in a number of states. There is no single pattern to this, but several examples will indicate the range of actions taken: [25]

25. As reported in "Action by the Legislatures," *State Government* 39:271–274 (Autumn 1966) and "Action by the Legislatures," *State Government* 40: 65–70 (Winter 1968).

ARIZONA: created a Budget Department with a full-time director to review departmental requests for funds and assist the governor in developing a budget to submit to the legislature.

COLORADO: created an Office of Planning Coordinator, responsible to the governor.

HAWAII: gave the governor funds to coordinate all federal aid programs operating in the state.

IDAHO: created an Office of Coordinator of Federal-aid Programs to enable the governor and the executive branch to take advantage of them more effectively.

MISSOURI: provided the governor with power to submit reorganization plans to the legislature, subject to a sixty-day legislative veto.

UTAH: authorized the governor to reorganize the state executive branch.

In recent years improvements have also been made in state administration. Arizona set up a strict code of ethics for both elected state officials and public employees. Delaware adopted the merit system for all state employees. Kentucky strengthened its administrative procedures for interstate cooperation. Realistic salary increases were voted for state employees in Delaware, Massachusetts, Michigan, and New York. New Mexico created a Department of Automated Data Processing and South Dakota authorized the establishment of a data processing revolving fund and the development of a data processing system to bring the advantages of new techniques to state government. In Virginia an Office of Administration was created in the Governor's Office to supervise the divisions of budget, personnel, and planning. And in Idaho a Department of Administrative Services was set up to handle housekeeping functions, prepare the state budget, and operate communications facilities. The Colorado legislature made an appropriation for a study of the reorganization of the executive department into no more than twenty departments and agencies, as called for in a recent constitutional amendment. Connecticut established a state Department of Personnel. The first stage of reorganizing the Utah executive branch began with the establishment of three coordinating councils, and in Wisconsin the executive department was streamlined by reducing the number of units from eighty-four to twenty-eight.

Similarly, the states have at long last begun to look at legislative procedures and to devise ways of improving them. In just the last few years,

ARIZONA: established a code of ethics for legislators.

CALIFORNIA: enacted a code of ethics for legislators and amended its constitution to provide for annual legislative sessions of unlimited scope and length.

DELAWARE: created a Legislative Council to assist members of the legislature in conducting research.

IDAHO: created a Legislative Budget and Fiscal Committee to provide constant review of state spending.

IOWA: created ethics committees in both houses of the legislature to establish rules for the conduct of both legislators and lobbyists.

KANSAS: adopted an amendment to its constitution establishing regular unrestricted annual sessions of the legislature and permitting a two-thirds vote of each house to prolong a session past the 60-day limit.

KENTUCKY: established an Office of Legislative Auditor.

UTAH: provided for the establishment of a Joint Legislative Operations Committee and a full-time legal adviser to the legislature.

WYOMING: passed a law permitting the Joint Ways and Means Committee of the legislature to meet for up to 20 days between sessions.

All these illustrations demonstrate, as Senator Tydings suggested in an article by that name, that "Reform Is Possible" and indeed that it is taking place. Nor is it necessary for the states to bear the whole burden of their modernization themselves. Legislation was introduced in the 91st Congress to provide federal grants-in-aid to the states over a three-year period to enable them to take steps toward improvement.[26]

The necessity of revitalizing the states so that they can more effectively perform their functions and work in conjunction with the other governments in the federal system to satisfy the full range of the people's needs evidently has yet to be fully under-

26. HR 2519, 91st Congress, 1st Session.

stood, however, in as much as a great many plans for action fail to be implemented. As the national president of the League of Women Voters of the United States observed,

Many studies are being made and much time, money and talent are being invested in plans for improving the capabilities of state government. But some of the finest plans in the world . . . gather dust on the shelf after the hue and cry accompanying their unveiling has died away. . . . most ideas, however good they may be, must have some pushers and shovers or they do not get off the ground. "Spontaneous movements" and the "people" rising up to demand reform are more likely the results of plain, hard, organized work.[27]

Fortunately for those who are involved in that work, a number of blueprints for action have been drawn up, most recently by the Committee for Economic Development in its statement on *Modernizing State Government*. The Committee's recommendations called for six major steps:

1. Constitutional revision stressing the repeal of limitations on constructive legislative and executive action and the elimination of matters more appropriate for legislative and executive action.

2. Reconstruction of state legislatures to include no more than 100 members who serve four-year terms, are paid salaries commensurate with their responsibilities, and are so organized and staffed as to make effective policy-making possible.

3. Development of the governor as a true chief executive with salary, responsibility, and staff suited to his new functions.

4. Modernization of state court systems into a single statewide system served by judges appointed for long terms.

5. Structuring of party politics so as to foster two-party competition and active citizen participation.

6. Full exploitation of the possibilities of interstate cooperation in solving problems shared by two or more states.

At least these corrections are imperative, the Committee concluded, "if the states are to be more than administrative instrumentalities of decision-makers at other levels." [28] "State govern-

27. Julia Davis Stuart, "Following Through," *National Civic Review* 56: 14–15 (January 1967).

28. Committee for Economic Development, *Modernizing State Government* (New York: Committee for Economic Development, 1967), summarized in "For Stronger States," *National Civic Review* (July 1967), pp. 378–384, 423.

ments are unquestionably on trial today," Governor Daniel J. Evans of Washington declared in his second inaugural address. They must be willing to pay the price of change if they wish to continue to bear their share of the responsibility of governing in the federal system. If there has been progress in that direction, there is still a good way to go.

The problem of government other than at the national level in the American federal system does not stop with the problem of state government.

American institutions of local government are under severe and increasing strain. Well designed, by and large, to meet the simpler needs of earlier times, they are poorly suited to cope with the new problems imposed on [them] by the complex conditions of modern life. Adaptation to change has been so slow, so limited, and so reluctant that the future role—even the continued viability—of these institutions is now in grave doubt.[29]

The problem posed by poor local government, indeed, has come to be viewed by the public as one of the top dozen domestic problems facing the United States, and many of the other major problems so viewed are a direct consequence of it.[30]

The problem of local government is partly one of numbers: there are simply too many units for the purposes of modern gov-

---

29. The opening paragraph of the Committee for Economic Development's report, *Modernizing Local Government* (New York: Committee for Economic Development, 1966), p. 5.

30. A release by the American Institute of Public Opinion (the Gallup Poll), February 28, 1968, reported in the *International Herald Tribune*, February 29, 1968, p. 3. The entire list of problems in the order of their importance as ranked by the respondees to the question, "What do you think is the most important problem facing this country today?" were as follows:

1—Crime and lawlessness
2—Education: crowded schools, poor quality of education
3—Transportation, parking, traffic
4—High taxes
5—Unemployment
6—Lack of community service programs
7—High cost of living
8—Racial problems
9—Slums, overcrowded housing
10—Poor local government
11—Sanitation: garbage, sewage
12—Lack of cultural, recreational facilities
13—Lack of religion, ethics

ernment and effective governmental service. It is also a matter of size: very few units of local government are large enough to cover a meaningful area, and they both overlap and compete with each other senselessly. It is a matter of purpose: although cities and counties are multipurpose units, special districts, which are the most rapidly proliferating units, are for the most part single-purpose units which add to the complexity of local government much more than they help by fulfilling that purpose effectively. It is, moreover, a problem of administration: coordinating mechanisms between the many local units in an area are weak or nonexistent, administrative concepts and procedures are often antiquated, and personnel systems are in many cases still rooted in politics. It is a problem of personnel: the municipal civil service nationwide is of a lower caliber generally than the federal or state civil services, and the quality of municipal representation is not high. It is a problem of leadership: except in the larger cities, policy-making and long-range planning are weakened by the almost total lack of provision for strong executive leadership. Multiple and divided executive power is the norm in local government. Thus weakened, the executive is no match for the pressure groups which so often dominate urban politics. Finally, it is a problem of popular control: municipal politics has long been characterized by demands for ethnic representation, and so for "balanced political tickets," and by local political bosses, whose power reflects the notorious fact that public interest in local affairs never runs high, despite the hallowed tradition in America to the contrary. At best that interest is sporadic. "Confusion from the many-layered system, profusion of elective officers without policy significance, [the] increasing mobility of the population," and demographic trends that are making cities the ultimate refuge of the disadvantaged all contribute to disinterest.[31]

But chiefly it is a problem of power: states have been niggardly in their grants of power to local units of government, and even under "home rule," local governments seldom have enough

31. *Modernizing Local Government, op. cit.,* p. 13. An excellent case study on all these points as they are revealed in one city is given in the *Final Report of the Fargo* (*N. Dakota*) *Mayor's Task Force on City Government* (1966), reproduced in its entirety in *Congressional Record* 113: S1178–1181 (January 31, 1967).

legal authority to cope with urgent community needs. Indeed, if there is a single point at which the indictment of the states is strongest, it is with regard to the way they have shackled local governments, rendering them too weak and inept to accomplish the purposes for which they were originally created. In a perceptive study of state restrictions on local governments, the Advisory Commission on Intergovernmental Relations found that not only have traditions and the natural conservatism of the law worked to retain state restrictions on local governments, but also that the states have taken positive action over the years to maintain their control. In any case, today local governments are forced to operate under a mass of express statutory and constitutional restrictions, which, if originally designed "to protect the people from local officials and local officials from the State," [32] by now comprise a straitjacket which immobilizes local governments in the face of rapid change and development. Summarized briefly, the Commission's findings are as follows:

1. Constitutions restrict local governments directly by specifying the method governing the way local power shall be exercised and by defining the extent of that power.

2. State constitutional provisions prevent or make extremely difficult the decrease of numbers of local governments or the increase in their size, either or both of which are necessary to enable them to adjust to changing area demands.

3. State constitutions prescribe and restrict the election of local governing bodies and the selection of management personnel.

4. State constitutions frequently make it impossible for local governments to perform desirable functions for their citizens.

5. Constitutional restrictions on municipal officials and personnel are found in provisions requiring the use of the long ballot, fixing terms of appointed officials, requiring officials and personnel to be residents of the jurisdiction which employs them, setting local salaries, and prescribing methods of personnel administration.

32. *Modernizing Local Government, op. cit.,* p. 33. See also House Report No. 1270, 90th Congress, 2d Session, *Unshackling Local Government* (revised). 24th Report by the Committee on Government Operations.

Nor is all the fault constitutional. State legislatures constantly interfere with local government. Statutory restrictions are both direct and indirect. The most debilitating indirect limitations are those which relate to geographical and substantive jurisdiction, keeping local units too numerous and too small to provide adequate services in the areas they serve and limiting what they can do and how they can do it unrealistically and unnecessarily. The universal application of Dillon's rule—that no local power exists unless it is expressly delegated or clearly implied in a state constitution or statute—has resulted in such a strict construction of local powers by the courts that they obtain no relief from that quarter. As a consequence they find themselves literally frozen in an anachronistic system designed in the nineteenth century. Even city attorneys do not know what the city can do, state constitutions and statutes are so "rife with procedural and methodological restrictions upon substantive functional powers."

Concluding its study, the Commission commented, "We are convinced that the American federal system in general, and the initiative and self-reliance of local government in particular, would be greatly strengthened by loosening many of the existing bonds upon local government." As it is, "the adequate and sound development of local government functions [is] retarded and repressed," if not paralyzed or killed.[33]

Local units themselves do not come off scot free in any assessment of how they got into their current predicament. "The nation's courthouses and city halls," comments the Committee for Economic Development, "have often seemed to lack the vision and dedication . . . to diagnose conditions, devise solutions, and make vigorous response" to demands made on them. "New functions needed to meet new situations are neglected by most local units and old functions are conducted without the benefit of new techniques. By default, initiatives have commonly been left to more resourceful federal forces." Vested interests and the fear of change have paralyzed local officials just when they might have

33. All of these remarks are from Advisory Commission on Intergovernmental Relations, *State Constitutional and Statutory Restrictions Upon the Structure, Functions, and Personnel Powers of Local Government* (Washington, 1962), pp. 23–59. The direct quotations are from pp. 33 and 63.

been expected to come up with new ideas for resolving the difficulties facing them.[34]

Those difficulties are both numerous and increasing. The list of urban woes includes, besides the fundamental problems posed by the concentration of racial minorities there, grave problems of transportation, including airports, mass transit, highways, congestion, and parking; a crisis in water supply and sewage disposal; rapidly multiplying needs for educational, recreational, and cultural facilities; the deterioration of the urban landscape (one article describing urban ugliness is entitled "The Great Gas Station Dilemma"); the critical problem of urban violence and crime; unmet housing needs and ever more rapidly deteriorating slum areas; problems in connection with employees of urban governments, including police-community problems and the grievances of underpaid and overworked teachers, firemen, and other municipal employees; the difficulty of meeting the need for open space near urban areas; and the need to find new and more meaningful ways to remove some of the inner-city/suburban tension which inhibits much urban action, and to involve a majority of urban citizens in the decision-making process. But the difficulties facing urban governments are more than a compound of urban problems. As President Nixon put it in one of his campaign statements:

The problems of our cities are, of course, much broader and much more complex than those of jobs or schools, poverty or race. They are the problems of human concentration, with all the abrasive frictions that occur when many people of diverse backgrounds occupy a small place. Increasingly, they are the problems of the physical environment we all share—congested streets, fouled air, and polluted water. And they are the problems of the future. When we look toward the year 2000, we see that the population of our cities will have doubled; this means that we will need as much *new* city by then as we have *old* city today.[35]

Luther Gulick has described urban problems as the discontent of millions of human beings, dissatisfied with urban life in gen-

34. *Modernizing Local Government, op. cit.,* p. 9.
35. Statement by Richard M. Nixon, "Problems of the Cities," submitted to the Republican National Convention Committee on Resolutions, August 1, 1968. Mimeographed.

eral. Their dissatisfaction has both economic and psychological aspects. Economic resources for public purposes are always limited, and the post-war years have witnessed unprecedented demands in the United States for all kinds of urban facilities and amenities. These demands will continue and in all likelihood increase. But they come at a time when governments in urban areas have still not solved the problems created by yesterday's and today's population. Millions of urban Americans live in substandard housing. Schools are overcrowded. Traffic congestion is rampant. There is a large backlog of need in every sector. The strain on municipal finances is aggravated by the current tight money market and skyrocketing interest rates. In the face of all this, there is hardly a city in the nation that has the economic resources to solve its present problems, let alone those just over the horizon.

Nor can urban governments count on the kind of "moral" support that might be expected. The ties that bind the modern metropolitan community are not those that bound the typical rural community of the last century. Though there often is a certain degree of neighborhood consciousness, and even of loyalty, too often it does not extend to the unit as a whole. The mobility of American urban residents is remarkable. Roughly 20 per cent of them move every year, from one urban center to another. Even more than their parents, the rising generation of voters will be mobile. People constantly on the move have less time to become involved, or even interested in politics, at least on the state and local levels, and frequently find themselves deprived of the right to vote in state and local elections. The result is an apathy and noninvolvement that strikes at the heart of the concept of local self-government and at the ability of local governments to meet today's needs, to say nothing of tomorrow's.

Yet local governments remain as necessary as they always have been. They perform the basic protective and service activities that enable us to live together in modern urban society. They patrol the streets, guard our homes, protect us from dishonest shopkeepers and restauranteurs, gather our garbage, remove our mountains of rubbish, do away with sewage and industrial waste, seek to prevent and put out fires, supply us with water and often with public transportation, provide recreational facilities and such cultural and educational amenities as libraries and museums, and of course are the main proprietors of kindergartens, elementary and secondary schools, and, increasingly, junior colleges and even universities. There is no complete listing of all the functions being performed by American local governments today; they vary widely from state to state and the range of functions is very great indeed. Although many urban functions are handled satisfactorily by individual units of local government, a good many now require cooperation to provide adequate protection or service over an entire metropolitan area. Increasingly, the states find themselves faced with the necessity of assisting or assuming these urban responsibilities—though they are slow to act on the necessity! Even so, the share of the total governmental responsibility assigned to local units in the United States remains a great one, one which neither the states nor the national government conceivably could fill themselves. If, in the face of rapidly mounting problems, local units are not discharging their responsibilities well, the answer lies in improving the opportunities for satisfactory response rather than in finding alternative sources of power and action.

In one sense, remedial action was initiated by the first federal grant-in-aid to help local governments meet the demands made upon them. Without doubt, a great many local needs were met adequately for the first time in consequence of federal aid. But federal-aid programs have been palliatives, relieving the symptoms without getting at the basic difficulties. Only the states and the local units themselves can act to get at these. Nor has federal aid always relieved the symptoms. "Local governments have . . . problems in knowing just what Federal aid is available to them . . . there is now no truly effective policy for sorting out overlapping . . . Federal-aid programs . . . Towns, cities, and small villages . . . have no real clearing place where they can know immediately what aid is there for them, how they can become eligible for [it] and how they may apply for it." [36] Thus federal aid is not as useful as it appears to be. Moreover, it is argued, federal-aid programs take the initiative away from local

36. The words of Representative Richard D. McCarthy, *Congressional Record* 113: A558 (February 8, 1967).

units and substitute for it the policy choices of the national government. Thus, "local governments tend to become administrative mechanisms for implementation of national policies, rather than dynamic centers of authority in their own right." [37]

That such charges are valid cannot be wholly demonstrated. But they beggar the main point in any case, for while the national government can help (as it did in 1968 by providing most of the financing for an Urban Institute, which is developing a program of basic and applied research into the ills of the nation's cities), basically it is the states which must take action remedial to local governments. And they can do that only with the understanding support of the people. Fortunately, what the states can do has been expertly laid down by the Committee for Economic Development in its report on *Modernizing Local Government*. The Committee calls for "major changes consistent with [three basic] criteria: massive county consolidations to conform with logical geographic and economic boundaries; structural modernization and professional staffing for all local units; and severe reduction in the overlapping layers of local government." [38] Its proposals are nationwide in scope and apply to both urban and rural communities. They define broad objectives, rather than forming a blueprint for any state or locality to adopt in detail. They recognize that as generalizations they cannot apply to every situation; instead, they imply the need for specific study of each local government and the tailoring of recommendations to meet special conditions. The recommendations of the Committee for Economic Development are as follows:

1. The number of local governments in the United States, now about 80,000, should be reduced by at least 80 per cent.
2. The number of overlapping layers of local government found in most states should be severely curtailed.
3. Popular election should be confined to members of the policy-making body, and to the chief executive in those governments where the "strong mayor" form is preferred to the "council-manager" plan.
4. Each local unit should have a single chief executive, either elected by the people or appointed by the local legislative body, with all administrative agencies and personnel fully responsible to him; election of department heads should be halted.

37. *Modernizing Local Government, op. cit.,* p. 9.
38. *Ibid.,* p. 13.

5. Personnel practices based on merit and professional competence should replace the personal or partisan "spoils" systems found in most counties and many other local units.

6. County modernization should be pressed with special vigor, since counties—everywhere except in New England—have high but undeveloped potential for solving the problems of rural, urban, and most metropolitan communities.

7. Once modernized, local governments should be entrusted with broad legal powers permitting them to plan, finance, and execute programs suited to the special needs, interests, and desires of their citizens.

8. The fifty state constitutions should be revamped—either by legislative amendment or through constitutional conventions concentrating on local government modernization—to provide for boundary revisions, extensions of legal authority, and elimination of needless overlapping layers.

9. The terms and conditions of federal—and state—grants-in-aid should be revised to encourage the changes recommended [above].[39]

Obviously action on the CED recommendations, even if undertaken forthwith, would take considerable time to complete. In the meantime, there are a number of interim steps the states can take to help relieve the plight of their local subdivisions. It has been suggested, for example, that the states establish offices of local affairs to help local governments find solutions to intergovernmental problems, to conduct research, to study local government needs and to recommend action to meet them, to serve as a clearinghouse of information about local government problems and proposed solutions, and to advise the governor and the legislature on how to coordinate local activities and services. In 1966, the Advisory Commission on Intergovernmental Relations prepared a model bill designed to serve as a guide to state legislatures in setting up such offices, and already about a dozen states have acted along these lines.[40]

The establishment of a state office of local affairs is not the only interim action the states can take. Governors in several states have appointed assistants to advise them on local affairs; Maryland has created a Municiple Technical Advisory Service; and in

39. *Ibid.,* pp. 13–16; the explanatory paragraph following each recommendation has been omitted.

40. See Appendix 1, State Agencies and Activities for Local Affairs, in House Report No. 1270, 90th Congress, 2d Session, *op. cit.*

North Carolina the state university's Institute of Local Government has been conspicuous in its assistance to local units of government. The states could also act to encourage coordination of local planning. A major gap exists because of the absence in most states of governmental machinery and authority to develop and execute areawide development plans. Filling this gap will require state action and local initiative, but the primary responsibility rests with the states.

To make such recommendations is one thing; to see them carried out is quite another. The size of the proposed action is staggering. "The kind of sweeping reform the CED advocates would require revamping most of the fifty state constitutions—and though CED doesn't say so right out, would probably meet stern resistance from at least two quarters: the state governments, which might feel threatened by the considerably stronger counties which would emerge under the CED plan, and, of course, the local government units, most of which would disappear—and many of their personnel with them, at least in the official sense." [41] CED predicts that the process of reform may take a decade in some states, but that would seem to be an extremely optimistic expectation. Considering the force of long tradition that has to be overcome, a more realistic hope might be another generation.

As one of the members of the CED Research and Policy Committee took pains to point out, such an indictment of local government should not be read as an absolute denial of their utility. For even as they are structured and operate today, "Many units of local government are doing an outstanding job of meeting the needs of their communities." [42] The need is to make it possible for all units of local government to do so.

41. Carnegie Corporation of New York, *Carnegie Quarterly*, Vol. 14, No. 4 (Fall 1966), p. 5.
42. See the statement of Mr. George Russell, *Modernizing Local Government*, *op. cit.*, p. 65.

VI

THE PROBLEM OF GOVERNING
METROPOLITAN AREAS

THERE IS GENERAL CONSENSUS among students of government in the United States that the effective government of metropolitan areas poses one of the most serious challenges America has ever faced on the domestic front. Governing metropolitan areas is one aspect of what has come to be called the "metropolitan area problem," that compound of problems which is caused by the extremely rapid concentration of population in a relatively small number of the nation's urban areas. "The concentration of the American people in metropolitan areas is evident from the fact that 113 million persons—nearly two-thirds of the entire population—lived in the 212 areas classified as metropolitan in 1960, and these areas accounted for 84 per cent of the nation's total population increase during the 1950–60 decade." [1] The pace of concentration has continued since the last census, and it is estimated that by 1980 three-fourths of the population of the United States will be living in metropolitan areas. Indeed, if population forecasts are accurate, nearly thirty-five million people will be added to those

1. *Metropolitan America: Challenge to Federalism.* A Report of the Advisory Commission on Intergovernmental Relations, Committee on Government Operations, House of Representatives. Committee Print. 89th Congress, 2nd Session (1966), p. v. This report provides the best single study of the problem posed in this chapter. As the footnotes show, it has been used extensively here and should be read in its entirety by students seriously interested in the issues presented in this chapter.

areas in the next fifteen years alone. This is the equivalent of the total present population of the New York, Chicago, Los Angeles, Philadelphia, Detroit, and Baltimore metropolitan areas. Between now and the end of the century, more than 80 per cent of all population increase in the United States will take place in metropolitan areas.

With the growing concentration of people in a limited number of areas came industrial and commercial development, as well as the concentration of social, cultural, and educational resources and facilities, until it is not far from the truth to assert that the focal point of American life in the mid-twentieth century is those same few metropolitan areas. The United States has become, in short, a metropolitan—some would say even megalopolitan—nation, and the development is likely to be an irreversible one.

The influx of population and industry to urban centers in the quantity which is involved here poses tremendous problems to metropolitan governments in terms of the new and more sophisticated services and facilities required. As President Johnson put it in his 1965 message to Congress on cities:

Our new city dwellers will need homes and schools and public services. By 1975, we will need over 2 million new homes a year. We will need schools for 10 million additional children, welfare and health facilities for 5 million more people over the age of 60, transportation facilities for the daily movement of 200 million people, and more than 80 million automobiles.

In the remainder of this century—in less than forty years—urban population will double, city land will double, and we will have to build in our cities as much as all that we have built since the first colonist arrived on these shores. It is as if we had 40 years to rebuild the entire urban United States.

But demands for new services are only the smallest part of the metropolitan problem. They come on top of unmet demands by those who were already in the nation's metropolitan areas when the influx accelerated after World War II. The Depression first and then World War II resulted inevitably in delay and postponement in renewing old facilities and constructing an adequate number of new ones for the existing urban population, to say nothing of providing facilities for new millions. Unfortunately, many of the newcomers to metropolitan areas were from lower income groups and racial minority groups whose needs as they moved off of farms or from smaller towns into the great urban centers were disproportionately high. As they came, they crowded into those areas which were available to them, in most cases areas already entering into economic and physical decline, and so exacerbated an already serious problem. Some of the new population was accommodated in jerry-built extensions of existing urban areas, as suburb after suburb began to spring up in response to population pressure. Too often, the problems which had plagued the central city dweller—poor planning and zoning, inadequate educational and recreational facilities, crowded streets and overextended means of transportation, insufficient water supply and water and air pollution, confusion and ugliness—followed the newcomers to the suburbs as well. Everywhere, metropolitan America was becoming, if not the necropolis Lewis Mumford described in his *The City in History*, at least overcrowded, rundown, poorly serviced, and unsatisfactory in meeting the basic needs of modern man.

Moreover, for a large percentage of the people in them, they became merely temporary stopping places, which added a new dimension to American life. Mobility has become the chief characteristic of the metropolis. People are constantly moving from city to suburb and from suburb to city or from suburb to suburb and from city to city. "Today, one out of five families changes residence every year, and it is a common pattern for a married couple to start off in a small apartment, move to the suburbs when the children arrive, shift from suburb to suburb as income rises, and then move back into the city after the children are grown. . . ."[2] Not only does such mobility virtually "nationalize" metropolitan problems (Los Angeles thus has a vital interest in the kind of education and services its new arrivals have been accustomed to and will demand), it also works a great hardship on the viability and strength of local government. Who are the constituents of today's metropolitan areas? The old belief in the sanctity of local government is undermined, if not washed away, when the people come to regard local units as mere way stations,

2. *Time*, February 9, 1968, p. 30.

temporary stops en route to somewhere else in a never-ending cycle of movement.

The many sides of the metropolitan problem attracted attention and consideration early, but proposals for remedy never amounted to much, for not only were the economic costs involved in meeting the crisis tremendous, but the governmental and administrative arrangements available to meet it were—and remain—totally inadequate. It is just here that the division of power which is the hallmark of the American federal system presents its sharpest challenge to the continued development and progress of the American people. For at the root of many parts of the metropolitan problem is "the failure of governmental institutions to come to grips with the growing interdependence of people and communities within metropolitan areas." [3] Traditionally, units of local government in the United States were created as separate entities and each was in fact isolated and remote from its nearest neighbors. Over the years they took no account of the fact that

As urban settlement [spread] across lines of local jurisdiction, the cities and suburbs together come to comprise a single, integrated area for living and working. People look for housing and employment within a broad region circumscribed more by the convenience of commuting and by personal preferences than by local government boundaries . . . Metropolitan areas are integrated in other ways as well. Local communities share many kinds of natural resources used for urban living . . . [and] many man-made facilities that cut across local boundaries. These forms of interaction, together with the metropolitan character of housing and employment, create a broad area of common interest. The optimum use of shared facilities and resources calls for a high level of cooperation and for coordinated action by interdependent communities.[4]

That is precisely the problem. The required amount of cooperation or coordinated action is not forthcoming under the present system of fragmented local government. As urbanization developed, new local units were created at the request of a group of local residents, exactly as they had been since the beginning of the nation. Adopting a latitudinarian policy toward incorporation of local units, state governments made no plan to guide local units

3. *Metropolitan America: Challenge to Federalism, op. cit.,* p. 5.
4. *Ibid.,* pp. 5–6.

in the creation of new ones or to require amalgamation of new local units and existing units, even when they were adjacent to one another. Instead, they yielded to local pressures and created new independent units virtually on demand. Nor were any requirements for cooperation and/or coordination imposed on local units. By the decade of the 1960's, the situation verged on the ridiculous, if not the macabre. The integration of metropolitan areas in other ways was not being paralleled by the integration of units of local government. Quite the contrary. As Tables 6.1 and 6.2 show, the 1967 Census of Governments listed 20,703 independent units of government within the then 227 Standard Metropolitan Statistical Areas (SMSA), an increase of 2,261 over the 1962 Census, and one-quarter of all local governments in the United States. Nowhere, as Tables 6.1 and 6.3 show, was the proliferation of local governments in metropolitan areas more evident than in the proportion of the nation's special districts in such areas. The average number of units per SMSA was 91. The Chicago area was in the lead with 1,113 local governments, Philadelphia had 876 local units, Pittsburgh, 704, and ten other major metropolitan areas had between 261 and 551. Indeed, these thirteen areas with the most units of local government included nine of the twenty-four SMSA's with over 1,000,000 population and together accounted for 6,033 local governmental units, or about one in thirteen of the national total. Another sixteen SMSA's reported between 200 and 250 units of local government.

The significance of these numbers is that the pattern of local government in metropolitan areas is already unbelievably complex and is becoming more so. "The typical metropolitan resident is a citizen of . . . [many] overlapping governments [all of] which adopt and enforce laws, regulate activities, and provide services. Lines of responsibility in the public business are unclear, and coordination is difficult." [5] As the Advisory Commission on Intergovernmental Relations concluded,

Fragmentation may appear to bring government "closer to the people," but it compounds the difficulties of achieving coordination within metropolitan areas. Political responsibility for government performance is divided to the point of obscurity. Public control of

5. *Ibid.,* p. 24.

government policies tends to break down when citizens have to deal
with a network of independent governments, each responsible for
highly specialized activities. Even where good channels are developed for registering public concern, each government is so circumscribed in its powers and in the area of its jurisdiction that important metropolitan action is virtually impossible for local
governments to undertake.[6]

Obviously cities could not act to relieve the situation by
themselves because their legal powers expired at the city limits,
where only too often a rival city waited to exert its powers in its
own way. In any case, cities have always been regarded in the
United States as severely limited units of government, constituting merely municipal corporations, whose powers and attributes
are wholly subject to the determination of state legislatures. Nor
were counties any better able to act. County governments have
never been accorded power over the cities set up within them but
have been viewed chiefly as devices for extending state power in
certain areas to the people. Powerless to act except within the
most limited ways, cities and counties could do little else than
drift with the tide toward governmental chaos.

The states, of course, had it in their power all the time to act
in response to the growing problem. Indeed, "because the states
set the ground rules for local government, it is difficult for state
government to dodge the accusing finger of municipal havoc.
Among other failures, the states have been slow to cede to the
cities adequate powers to tax, zone surrounding areas, regulate
housing, provide or require mass transportation, and acquire open
space. The states control the municipal dividing lines, and there is
not logic, rhyme, or reason in the present crosshatch patterns of
local government." [7]

But for a variety of reasons—including long and continuing
domination of state legislatures by rural majorities with little or
no interest in urban problems; vested interests on the part of local
officeholders; the relatively poor quality of the municipal civil
service; the local roots of political parties; sheer inertia; fear of
judicial restriction as a consequence of the almost universal lack
of a clear constitutional mandate for action; conservatism; and
failure to understand how rapidly the problem was developing—

6. *Ibid.*, p. 7.
7. Sanford, *Storm Over the States, op. cit.*, p. 24.

TABLE 6.1 *Number of Local Governmental Units in the United States, 1967*

Type of government	US	Within SMSA's	Outside SMSA's	Per cent in SMSA's
All local governments	81,248	20,702	60,545	25.5
School districts	21,782	5,018	16,764	23.0
Counties	3,049	404	2,645	13.3
Municipalities	18,048	4,977	13,071	27.6
Townships	17,105	3,255	13,850	19.0
Special districts	21,264	7,049	14,215	33.1

TABLE 6.2 *Number of Local Governmental Units in SMSA's, 1967*

SMSA Size group (1960 population)	No. of SMSA's	Population 1960	Local governments 1967
All	227	118,108,000	20,703
1,000,000 plus	24	61,598,000	7,367
500,000–1 million	32	22,012,000	3,878
300,000–500,000	30	11,359,000	2,734
200,000–300,000	40	10,083,000	2,919
100,000–200,000	74	10,848,000	3,123
50,000–90,000	27	2,209,000	682

TABLE 6.3 *Kinds of Special Districts in SMSA's, 1967*

Type of special district	Per cent in SMSA's
Natural resources	19.5
Cemeteries	10.2
Fire protection	37.7
Highways	25.2
Hospitals	19.6
Housing and urban renewal	33.4
Libraries	32.0
Parks and recreation	49.8
School buildings	61.5
Sewerage	63.1
Urban water supply	45.0
Other single function districts	38.7
Multiple function districts	62.0

the states were slow to take remedial action. The result was the creation of a kind of vacuum, into which almost inevitably and without any preconceived plan or direction the national government began to move as, from the 1930's on, despairing mayor after despairing mayor journeyed to Washington to seek relief for specific urban problems. Washington's response was hearty. The forces of politics being what they are, at first Congress and later on presidents began to realize that votes followed action in behalf of the nation's large urban areas. Program after program was enacted, and grants-in-aid, subsidies, research activities, and direct federal relations with cities were all employed in the process. But all this was done on an *ad hoc* basis, with no effective coordination between programs, and very likely some of the national government's actions only succeeded in making the over-all problem worse.[8]

But if the national government became deeply involved in attacking bits and pieces of the metropolitan area problem, it did not help solve the central problem, fragmentation of government in metropolitan areas. Not only did its programs for the most part deal with existing units (only recently have requirements for an integrated community or area-wide approach been inserted in program legislation), but for a while at least the programs contributed to a comforting feeling at the state level that the problem was being taken care of and that nothing was required there. In the meantime, a great many metropolitan needs went unmet, and, blithely ignorant of the consequences, state legislatures readily responded to pleas of distressed citizens with the creation of special districts. Thus a multitude of these mini-governments came into being: water and sewage-disposal districts, districts to establish and maintain port facilities, housing and airport districts, transportation districts, and a bewildering variety of other special uni-purpose districts began to join the older school districts (the prototype after which the later special districts were modeled), to compound further the metropolitan governmental picture. The Los Angeles area alone came to have 350 special districts; along with Los Angeles County, 76 incorporated municipalities,

and 100 school districts.[9] Table 6.3 lists the most common types
of special districts and shows what percentage of each type is
found in the Standard Metropolitan Statistical Area grouping.
By 1967 a local official, describing the chaotic world of local
government, could observe that "In Park Forest, Ill., for instance,
a citizen . . . is governed by two counties, three townships, five
school districts, a forest-preserve district, a mosquito-abatement
district, and . . . his own village board of trustees." [10] And the
Park Forest citizen could count himself lucky at that. In almost
every metropolitan area—those in the South, developing a bit
later, have for a variety of reasons [11] been less afflicted than
those in other regions—there is both a hodgepodge of governmental units, confusing to the citizen and ineffective in operation, and
a uniform failure on the part of all the governments involved to
provide the kinds of action needed to make metropolitan life tol-
erable. Luther Gulick has commented on the inadequacy of the
various units of government in meeting the problems of metropolitan development. "There are three kinds of governmental
failures involved in the big, bursting urban regions," he observes:

The *first shortage,* and the most obvious, is *service* failure. . . . The
second shortage is seldom recognized but is, in fact, far more serious. This is the failure in virtually every city, and in all metropolitan areas, to work out any *comprehensive community program for
general development* and for tackling the major social and economic
problems of the foreseeable future . . . The *third shortage* is the lack
of *region-wide democratic machinery for teamwork,* for thinking
about and dealing with the common problems of the metropolitan
area.[12]

Although there is no arguing Gulick's conclusions, little
has been done so far to reverse the process. In many states,
W. Brooke Graves points out, "there is not even permissive legis-

9. The subject of special district governments is covered by John C.
Bollens, *Special District Governments in the United States* (Berkeley: Univ.
of California Press, 1957).
10. Franklin H. Ornstein, "Local Government is a Farce," *Saturday
Evening Post,* December 2, 1967, p. 10.
11. See Robert H. Connery and Richard H. Leach, "Southern Metropolis: Challenge to Government," *The Journal of Politics* 26:60–81 (February 1964), reprinted in Avery Leiserson, ed., *The American South
in the 1960's* (New York: Praeger, 1964).
12. Gulick, *The Metropolitan Problem and American Ideas, op. cit.,*
pp. 120–123.

lation under which communities volunteering to cooperate with neighboring communities may do so . . . The need for joint action on the one hand, and the desire of each local unit to preserve both its geographical integrity and its legal powers on the other, present a troublesome dilemma indeed. Although they are interacting and interdependent, and although there are large areas of potential cooperation, the municipalities . . . counties [and special districts] that comprise metropolitan areas have not yet found a generally acceptable solution for areawide policy determination and uniform enforcement." [13] Nor have either the states or the national government found their proper role in bringing such a situation about. By 1968, the Advisory Commission on Intergovernmental Relations had become so pessimistic it concluded that because of the metropolitan area problem the federal system itself was on the brink of destruction. The abdication or inability of city governments, of the states, and of the national government, singly or in combination, to hold back the deterioration of urban life, it warned, raises fearful prospects for the future. "The manner of meeting these challenges," the Commission declared, "will largely determine the fate of the American political system; it will determine if we can maintain a form of government marked by partnership and wholesome competition among National, State, and local levels, or if instead—in the face of threatened anarchy—we must sacrifice political diversity as the price of the authoritative action required for the nation's survival." [14]

Fortunately, there are exceptions to the prevailing condition.[15] Most of them have been made within the existing framework of metropolitan government, with no attempt at widening the area of legal jurisdiction to make it coequal with the metropolis itself. Devices that have been employed with some success include:

1. AREAWIDE PLANNING. "A national survey of metropolitan

---

13. Graves, *American Intergovernmental Relations, op. cit.,* pp. 634–635. The section on "Metropolitan Regionalism" on p. 622 ff and the bibliography to Chapter XVIII are both worth careful attention.
14. Advisory Commission on Intergovernmental Relations, *Ninth Annual Report* (Washington, 1968), p. 14.
15. The following material is condensed from *Metropolitan America: Challenge to Federalism, op. cit.*

planning agencies in 1964 indicated that 150 of the 216 standard metropolitan statistical areas recognized at that time had some form of metropolitan planning," and a good many more have acquired some since. Most of these planning agencies cover an area approximately equal to the SMSA.[16] In the largest metropolitan areas, metropolitan planning has become a function of combined city-county agencies or county agencies alone. While such agencies provide considerable useful research and advice, however, the main problem is still how to translate plans into action. Only a handful of metropolitan planning agencies are given powers that enable them to put their plans into operation.

2. EXTRATERRITORIAL POWERS TO CENTRAL CITIES. State legislatures have occasionally permitted cities to go beyond their own boundaries to provide specific services to over-the-line residents (water, sewage disposal, milk and meat inspection, for example) and to regulate subdivisions in adjacent *unincorporated* territory. Few states, however, permit extraterritorial planning, zoning, or subdivision control by central cities in *incorporated* areas adjacent to them, and of course it is not possible for one state to extend such authority unilaterally across its own boundaries. Moreover, such extraterritorial powers are widely regarded as undemocratic, in that they deny residents of fringe areas a voice in determining their own affairs. At best, the device is a useful interim step.

3. INTERGOVERNMENTAL AGREEMENTS. Especially in California, where the city of Lakewood early was permitted to contract for most of its services with Los Angeles County, but to some extent elsewhere, local governments have agreed, formally and informally, either to conduct an activity cooperatively with one or more other local units or to contract for its performance by another local unit. Water supply, police protection, and fire-fighting services are common subjects of agreements, though some provide for such services as purchasing and personnel administration. Permission of state legislatures has been regarded as necessary, but voter approval has not. Intergovernmental agreements make possible economies of scale and do not require adjustments

16. Standard Metropolitan Statistical Area, the term used by the Bureau of the Census to describe conglomerate urban units.

of boundaries or of existing structures of local government. They depend upon a mutuality of interests, however, and generally are voluntary and temporary. Their use also raises questions with regard to the principle of control of local interests by local citizens, and their utility is largely limited to metropolitan areas within the jurisdiction of single states.

4. METROPOLITAN COUNCILS. In a fairly large number of metropolitan areas, the elected public officials from the governmental units in the area voluntarily [17] come together in a variety of guises "to seek a better understanding among the governments and officials in the area, to develop a consensus regarding metropolitan needs, and to promote coordinated action in solving their problems." [18] Since these groups are informal, their interests can cross state lines, and they generally have been concerned with all the problems of the area, rather than with only one or a few. Often they have received outside financial help, frequently from foundations, and thus can afford a staff. They have been found extremely useful in creating an awareness of problems and in providing the climate necessary for a successful attack on them. Constituted as they are, however, they function only as discussion and study units, depending for implementation of their recommendations upon the participating governments.

Other devices have been developed which do require the reorganization of traditional units of government and of the relations between them in the federal arrangement. None of them has been universally accepted, any more than have the experiments which do not require structural alteration. Described briefly, those devices are the following:

5. URBAN COUNTIES. County government has generally been regarded as rural in coverage and orientation, affecting cities chiefly by its involvement in elections, law enforcement, and the judicial function. Recently, however, several states [19] have

17. The oldest, the Supervisors Inter-County Committee in the Detroit area, created in 1954, was given legal status by the Michigan legislature in 1957. California has passed general enabling legislation for such councils.
18. Samuel Humes, "Organization for Metropolitan Cooperation," *Public Management* 44:106 (May 1962).
19. Rhode Island never had counties, and Connecticut recently abolished them. In Louisiana, parishes are much the same as counties elsewhere.

strengthened their counties by giving them responsibility for a significant number of urban services throughout all or part of their jurisdiction. The most common services so reassigned are police protection, street construction, libraries, and parks and recreation. In some cases zoning has been made a county function. Dade County, Florida, is the best example of the strengthened county to date. The reorganization of county government to give it authority to solve metropolitan area problems in general, however, is hindered both by the fact that political parties are rooted in county organizations and resist attempts to alter the *status quo,* and by state constitutional and legal restrictions which limit the role counties can play in providing urban services, to say nothing of providing for effective urban government. Whether they could do the latter, backward as they have been in adopting modern administrative and organizational techniques, is a serious question. In any case, many of the most important metropolitan areas in the United States cover more than one county, so that at best the device has only limited utility.

6. TRANSFER OF FUNCTIONS TO STATE GOVERNMENT. The states have always had the power to handle whatever functions of government they wish; neither counties nor cities have any inherent rights in this regard. Thus while the transfer of an urban function to a state executive agency better to provide for metropolitan areas appears innovative, it has always been a possibility. In any event, transfer of a local function to the state usually involves more a shift in the respective responsibilities of the units of government than full state assumption of the particular function. Such shifts have taken place mainly in the areas of highway planning and construction, traffic control, mass transit, air pollution control, and water supply, but the states have also extended their responsibilities for environmental sanitation and crime control. The transfer of urban functions to the state is especially appropriate where metropolitan areas make up much of a state and where the state is a small one. It also has the advantages of ease of accomplishment, economy of scale, and avoidance of duplication. On the other hand, it obviously undermines local responsibility and authority and weakens local units still further as viable units of self-government. In states with sizable non-urban areas, it per-

mits decisions on metropolitan matters to be made by representatives from non-metropolitan parts of the state.

7. METROPOLITAN SPECIAL DISTRICTS. Mention has already been made of the propensity of state legislatures in recent decades to create limited-purpose special districts as independent units of government to perform one or more functions through part or all of a metropolitan area.[20] Usually the governing bodies of the districts consist in part at least of officers of the state and/or the local governments within them, serving *ex officio*. Special districts offer the advantage of freedom from the fiscal limitations under which other local units of government labor and make it possible to create an area commensurate with the problem to be handled. On the other hand, their single-mindedness inhibits the development of a coordinated approach to metropolitan problem-solving; their proliferation complicates and confuses the local governmental picture still further, increasing the difficulties of voter control and leading to duplication of effort; and their concern to be self-supporting tends to become a preoccupation, to the detriment of their harmonious relations with other governmental units in the area.

8. ANNEXATION. Annexation is a process provided for by state law to permit a city to absorb adjacent, usually unincorporated, territory. Until about 1900 it was the most common method of adjusting urban boundaries to changing population movements. After that time, as suburban areas around central cities were themselves incorporated as independent municipalities, or as they organized to persuade state legislatures to give them a voice— effectively a veto—in annexation procedures, the device became less and less useful. Today unless the central city is lucky enough to be surrounded by a great deal of unincorporated territory, as a number of western and southern cities have been, annexation is no longer a useful antidote to fragmentation of governmental units in metropolitan areas.

9. CONSOLIDATION. This procedure is the joining together of two or more cities, one usually larger than the other, to create a

20. Special districts are not created solely in response to urban or metropolitan needs. A common kind of district is thus the irrigation district, and many others are primarily concerned with functions in rural and sparsely settled areas of the states concerned.

new unit of government with inclusive boundaries. It was ordinarily imposed on the units involved by special legislation, but when restrictions came to be placed on the power of state legislatures to enact special legislation, and local loyalties and political ties had developed and rigidified, the use of consolidation diminished. It is rarely used today, except for small villages and towns. The consolidation of Newport News and Warwick, Virginia, to form the new city of Newport News is the only major consolidation in recent years.

City-county consolidation may involve the merger of all the cities in a county with the government of the county; the partial merger of the cities in terms of some functions, but the retention of the county for other functions; the unification of some but not all the municipalities with the county government; or the consolidation of two or more counties and the municipalities and other local units of government within them. It too is done by legislative act, often with majority approvals required in the units affected. Like municipal consolidation, city-county consolidation was used much more in the last century than it is today. The consolidation of the city of Nashville and Davidson County, Tennessee, constitutes the only important recent exception.

Consolidation has the advantage of providing the larger base needed for attacking area-wide problems, but its use is handicapped by the fact that less than half the states authorize it, and even when they do, enabling legislation is ordinarily required. Nor is it popular with the people of the localities involved. Local electorates turned city-county consolidations down in at least six instances between 1955 and 1965, and local office holders can be counted on to oppose such a change. Even more important, unless the new boundaries are excessively generous, consolidation only offers temporary or partial relief until the metropolitan area so encompassed grows beyond the new borders.

10. FEDERATION. The so-called "federal" approach to governing metropolitan areas involves the division of governmental functions in the metropolitan area between two levels, area-wide functions being granted to an over-all governmental unit whose boundaries coincide with the metropolitan area, local functions being given to existing (sometimes reconstituted) municipalities.

The Advisory Commission on Intergovernmental Relations concluded that

> The assignment of each governmental function to its appropriate level . . . facilitates optimum handling of each function, from the point of view of most effective planning, decision, and scale of operation. Retention of the identities of local governments preserves the focus of local civic pride, interest, and participation. It also encourages diversity and experimentation in government performance.[21]

Because it requires complete redrafting of local governments, approval by the electorates involved, and usually even a constitutional amendment, federation is not easily accomplished, however. In Canada, where it has been put into effect in Toronto and Winnipeg by act of the provincial legislatures alone, these difficulties have not hindered its use. In the United States, despite many proposals and enthusiastic recommendations, it has not been adopted in any metropolitan area to date.

These ten devices do not exhaust the list. Professor Roscoe Martin has listed fifteen ways which have been developed to overcome some of the difficulties of fragmentation, and other ways are being developed right along.[22] The problem of governing metropolitan areas has thus not been wholly neglected. There are already in existence enough diverse approaches to permit a good deal of adjustment to the prevailing metropolitan condition, at least on the part of local governments. Indeed, it is to them that most of the credit for the exploration leading to the devices which are now available should be given. While not all local units in all metropolitan areas have exerted themselves to find solutions, and while some have resisted any change, local governments have been at the forefront in what progress there has been. The impediments to progress are elsewhere.

First and foremost, the states provide barriers to action. As indicated earlier, state restrictions on local government have too often kept local units hamstrung, unable to experiment and innovate, confined to outmoded forms and procedures. Somehow the

21. Advisory Commission on Intergovernmental Relations, *Alternative Approaches to Government Reorganization in Metropolitan Areas.* Report A-111 (June, 1962), p. 79.
22. See Roscoe C. Martin, "Action in Metropolis, I," *National Civic Review* 52: 302-307, 316 (June 1963).

states must be persuaded to remove those restrictions and take instead an active and positive role in facilitating the adjustment of local governments to the metropolitan age. Specifically, there is agreement that the states should revise their approach to local government, permitting a maximum degree of local self-determination as to forms and functions of government. This could be done generally, as it is in New Jersey under the Faulkner Act, by authorizing a number of optional forms of government among which local units could choose as dictated by their peculiar needs and desires. Second, there is agreement that the states should review their policies of incorporation with a view toward developing a rationale for creating new units of local government and so reversing the trend toward increased fragmentation. Third, the states can grant advance standing authority to local units of government to work in collaboration with each other on area-wide problems. Fourth, the states can assume some of the functions which have traditionally been entrusted to local units and can do so on an across-the-board basis, so as to assure that area-wide needs will be met. "In the case of planning, construction, and administration of a metropolitan transportation system, sewage collection and treatment system, or air pollution control system," as well as in providing sufficiently broad land-use planning, "state action is frequently the only positive alternative."[23] Moreover, the states can provide a wide variety of technical services and assistance to units of local government to help them adjust to their new role in metropolitan government, perhaps most effectively by creating a state department or office of local affairs to serve as the focal point of such activities. Finally, the states can both raise the antiquated tax and debt limits on local governments so that they are better able to finance the services they need to perform, and also increase the amount of financial assistance they make available to local units of government.

These and other options are open to the states. Whether they will be able to act on them depends in large measure on the public's response to the metropolitan crisis and on the pressure it ex-

23. David B. Walker and Albert J. Richter, "The States' Role in Meeting the Urban Crisis: Positive or Negative," *Metropolitan Viewpoints*, Vol. II, No. 2 (May 1967), p. 2. The entire article is worth reading and is drawn on heavily in these pages.

erts on state leadership to initiate reform. Unfortunately, as the Advisory Commission on Intergovernmental Relations observed, "reorganization proposals face a largely apathetic public," [24] and state political leaders have not sought to do more than their constituencies' bidding. ". . . the public has a negative image of state government," Terry Sanford has noted. In all honesty, he comments, "state government has become less interesting to most people than the space race, the cold war, sports, movie stars, air crashes, Congress, and hallucinogenic drugs." Perhaps, Sanford suggests, an intensive public relations drive to portray states in a better light is called for.[25] Something like this may indeed be necessary to secure the kind of state action required for metropolitan reorganization as well as for reform of state government generally.

But the states are not alone in their slowness to move. Certainly political parties have not made the contribution they might have. They have failed conspicuously to embrace the cause of effective metropolitan government. Their roots are in existing structures—in central cities, in the suburbs, in surrounding counties—and although both major parties deplore the urban crisis and have suggested a variety of palliatives to counteract it, neither party has developed a plan of metropolitan government reform and presented it to the voters. Nor has the press, broadly defined, been more helpful in this connection. A good many exposés of metropolitan ills have been made, some of them much to the point, and a number of metropolitan daily newspapers and their related radio and television stations have supported specific proposals when they have been made. For the most part, however, neither newspapers nor radio and television have accepted the responsibility of mounting a campaign of civic education and presenting positive alternatives to the people or have urged the people to see to it that one or more of them is adopted by state legislatures.

Pressure groups have been active over the years in urging a variety of stands on urban and metropolitan matters. But their concerns, too, have been fragmented. Most groups are concerned

24. *Metropolitan America: Challenge to Federalism, op. cit.,* p. 108.
25. Sanford, *Storm Over the States, op. cit.,* pp. 47, 50.

with only a small part of the area's life. Though the Chamber of Commerce, labor unions, real estate boards, utility groups, and others have taken positions on many urban issues, they often disagree with one another; central-city and suburban groups take opposing sides; and a number of groups—labor unions, taxpayers, neighborhood-improvement organizations, and racial groups—do not appear with any consistency on the same side of a single question. They also lack the basic requirements for exerting effective influence: "an adequate institutional base, legal authority, direct relationships with the metropolitan constituency, and established processes for considering and resolving issues as they emerge." Like political parties and the press, "these organizations [seldom] ask the citizen to think about the total city, to dream about the full potentialities of his urban existence. Rather the focus is upon . . . [a] special issue . . . dear to the hearts of [the] groups [concerned]." [26]

Two parties in the federal process have been active in developing a basis for change in the metropolitan situation. Universities and foundations comprise one force that has been at the forefront of the advance toward improvement. Even before World War II research into metropolitan government was of concern to universities and foundations, and in later years the attention they have devoted to the subject can be demonstrated by reference to any bibliography on metropolitan areas and to the credits given in many of the forewords to the sources of support. The same forces have not been as effective in reaching the public and persuading it of the need for action and change, however. The other active element has been the national government. Not everything the national government has done to meet demands of local units for aid has contributed to the solution of the over-all problem of metropolitan government; indeed, in some ways, by continuing to work with existing local units of government and by failing to coordinate its own programs and to require earlier unification of planning by supplicant local units, it has aggravated the problem of governing metropolitan areas. Nevertheless, particularly since the creation of the Department of Housing and Urban Develop-

26. Webb S. Fiser, *Mastery of the Metropolis* (Englewood Cliffs, New Jersey: Prentice-Hall, 1962), pp. 5–6, 8.

ment in 1965, it has tackled the problem head-on. In the words of Robert C. Weaver, former Secretary of Housing and Urban Development,

Before our grants can be made, it must be shown that the area has a metropolitan-wide comprehensive planning and programming operation which provides an adequate basis for determining the location, financing and scheduling of the public facilities and land development needed for sound growth. Moreover, there must be adequate governmental administrative arrangements for the execution of all such development in full accordance with the plan.[27]

But all federal programs affecting metropolitan growth and development—directed, that is, toward solving individual metropolitan area problems—are not under the aegis of the Department of Housing and Urban Development, and neither Congress nor the executive leadership have required coordination between departments or that other departments follow the example of Housing and Urban Development. "Less than one-quarter of the Federal [urban development] programs encourage broader areas of planning or administration than a single local government. . . . nearly one-quarter of the programs have provisions which tend to discourage joint participation."[28] Obviously, there is much more to be done by the national government, but it has at least shown a partial awareness of the problem and has begun to act accordingly.

This is not the place to suggest detailed solutions to the problem posed here. The purpose of the discussion has been, rather, to delineate the problem and attempt to give some idea both of its dimensions and seriousness and also of what is involved in getting a solution underway. Hopefully it has become obvious that implied here is an issue of fundamental importance for the future of the American federal system, the resolution of which will involve all the parties to the federal process. Local governments, which will likely remain chiefly responsible for tackling the hard problems of the exploding metropolis, have not yet reached the absolute limits of effective action and must be persuaded to do all they can to cope with the problem. State governments, which

27. Robert C. Weaver, "Creative Federalism and Metropolitan Development," *Metropolitan Viewpoints*, Vol. I, No. 1 (August 1966), p. 2.
28. *Metropolitan America: Challenge to Federalism, op. cit.*, p. 138.

have so far played the role of observer, if that, have to take a hard look at their relation to the local governments of their creation and re-examine their own role in governing a rapidly urbanizing America. The national government too must analyze its contribution to the existing situation and strive to find ways to offer the maximum degree of help to state and local governments as they work toward a rationalized system of metropolitan government. Parties and pressure groups, the mass media, universities and research organizations, and industrial and commercial elements in the private sector all have their work cut out for them too. The Advisory Commission on Intergovernmental Relations has found that "It is necessary to consider not only the tangible problems that require solution, but also an equitable allocation of responsibilities within the federal system. The political philosophy of federalism needs to be extended and applied to metropolitan affairs," even as it has to other problems in the past.[29]

There is no easy way to begin to tackle the deficiencies of metropolitan government. As the Advisory Commission concludes:

Poor coordination and conflicts of interest among governments often block effective action to deal with metropolitan problems. Changes in the structure of government within metropolitan areas, and innovation in relations between the Federal government, the States, and local communities are needed to overcome these obstacles. The complex federal system of the United States, however, is rich in possibilities for adaptation to meet the changing circumstances [brought about by] metropolitan growth. With sufficient imagination and effort . . . ingenuity, sensitivity . . . and leadership . . . the resources of the federal system can be brought effectively to bear on the urban problems that challenge our age, just as previous generations found ways of adapting the federal system to other national challenges.[30]

Luther Gulick asks "How to Get Going" in reorganizing and adjusting metropolitan governments to handle their jobs adequately and answers by saying that "the initiative for action must . . . come from the broadest constituency involved," namely, the national government, and that the "only political leadership which can really start the ball rolling" is the President of the

29. *Ibid.*, pp. 9–10.
30. *Ibid.*, pp. 11, 168.

United States. After having "set his own house in order, making explicit his commitment to rationalizing federal programs as they hit metropolitan areas . . . he should personally sit down with the governors, the mayors, and the county executives of each major area . . . and join in working out an agreed assignment of duties as to the jobs that need doing, especially the joint assignment of developing for each area a program toward defined goals." Gulick estimates that, with the help of a staff financed largely by the federal government, this phase would take about two years. Once such a plan were evolved, the three units would work together to carry out their assignments. Such a methodology would indeed be "creative federalism." This "teamwork machinery," Gulick concludes, provides the only effective answer to the basic question of how satisfactory metropolitan government can evolve.[31]

But of course political reorganization alone will not be enough. "Creating a more desirable urban environment depends upon a combination of private and governmental action . . . The greater part of the character of our cities," Webb Fiser points out, "is the result of private action . . . . [of] the architectural taste of merchants and bankers, the imagination of realtors and builders, the sensitivity of architects and engineers, the thoughtfulness of industrialists, the resources and good taste of educational institutions, the richness of religious expression, the pride of homeowners, the habits of renters, the depth and breadth of our cultural strivings, and countless other private manifestations of our values and desires . . . We need a way to bring the various private and public perspectives [together] to bear upon decision making."[32] "Building a solid base to move forward in a democratic society means convincing a substantial majority" of the necessity for action.[33] In so building, each of these groups has an important role to play.

Perhaps there is, as Professor Fiser believes, a parallel in the experience of the Founding Fathers which is of value here.

The problems under the Articles of Confederation had become so many and fundamental that there was no way out except by a thor-

31. Gulick, *The Metropolitan Problem and American Ideas, op. cit.*, pp. 149, 147.
32. Fiser, *The Mastery of the Metropolis, op. cit.*, pp. 5-6.
33. *Ibid.*, pp. 86-87.

ough reappraisal of the whole matter of government . . . We too are now confronted with problems demanding far greater governmental authority than is now available for coping with them . . . In similar circumstances our forefathers made the bold decision to create a governmental authority commensurate with the new problems . . . We are confronted with a similar situation, but have not yet had the wisdom to approach it in a systematic way . . . It is time that we raised the basic question of how we can get an institutional framework which will make it possible to treat the metropolitan region as a coherent whole.[34]

34. *Ibid.*, pp. 3–4.

VII

THE PROBLEM OF
ADMINISTRATION

FOR A GENERATION OR MORE, administration has been recognized in
the United States as the heart of the modern problem of government, central to the service of a free people. Basic to the successful functioning of "the future American democracy," the late
Leonard D. White wrote in 1948, "is a sound administrative system, able to discharge with competence and integrity the tasks
laid upon it by the people." [1] Yet for many years before that it
was virtually dismissed as an unimportant detail. The Constitution, for example, is silent on administrative matters, and so few
were the programs of government to be administered in the early
days that it hardly seemed worthwhile devoting time and attention to it. Thus the United States built up a "loose-jointed, easy-
going, somewhat irresponsible system of administration" [2] under
which it was still functioning when the terrible strain of war and
depression had to be endured in the twentieth century. Somehow
the system held up well enough so that the crisis was surmounted,
and even well enough so that White could write shortly after
World War II, "The present system is far in advance of that
which sufficed in 1925." "But," he went on, "its improvement has
no more than kept pace with the added responsibilities heaped

1. Leonard D. White, *Introduction to the Study of Public Administration* (New York: Macmillan, 1955), p. xii.
2. *Ibid.*, p. xiv.

upon it. We have gained, but whether we have gained relatively to the work to be done is an open question." [3]

Since World War II, further responsibilities have been placed on the administrative system, as under both Democratic and Republican leadership the concept of the welfare state has been developed and broadened in response to the demands of the times. Over 60 million people have been added to the population; the gross national product has more than tripled; Americans have crowded into urban centers in unprecedented numbers, and have come to enjoy higher living standards and the benefits of modern science and technology; and in the process they have demanded more from their governments in terms of education and public welfare, job opportunities, transportation facilities, housing, pollution control, equal rights, and the elimination of poverty. The response of the national government to all these demands was a rapid proliferation of grant-in-aid programs, in the implementation of which all levels of government have been involved. In 1946, state and local governments spent a total of $11 billion on satisfying public needs, and they had a combined debt of $16 billion. By 1966, state and local governments, with the aid of the national government, were spending some $85 billion for the same purposes and had incurred a total debt of about $100 billion. This represents an increase of over 500 per cent in state and local outlays in the twenty-year interval, most of which was due to the mushrooming joint programs made possible by the categorical grant-in-aid. The impact on the national government was just as great. In 1946, the federal government spent $894 million to help the states and localities with their public programs. By Fiscal 1970, expenditures for that purpose had risen to approximately $25 billion and involved more than 500 separate federal categorical grant-in-aid programs, which were administered by over 150 departments in Washington and over 400 federal offices in the field.

There were project grants and formula grants; incentive grants and multi-functional grants. Some went through the States, others directly to local governments and agencies. Some were conditioned on cost-sharing and planning requirements; some were not. All com-

3. *Ibid.*, p. xii.

bined to provide a barrage of complicated standards, regulations, and planning requirements which were straining the patience of State and local officials.[4]

More new programs involving appropriations of federal aid were initiated by the 85th through the 89th Congresses than by all the previous sessions of Congress since the beginning of the Republic. The 89th Congress (1965–1966) alone passed no fewer than 136 major domestic bills, including seventeen new resource development programs, seventeen new educational programs, twenty-one new health programs, fifteen new economic development programs, twelve new programs on city problems, and four for manpower training. By 1969, there were all told fifty different programs for vocational and job training, thirty-five programs for housing, sixty-two for community facilities, and twenty-eight for recreation, as well as countless others in a great variety of fields.

As then Vice President Humphrey pointed out in 1967, "this rapid increase in grant programs has created new stresses and produced new suspicions in federalism's already overburdened administrative network. Many of the difficulties are simply the natural by-product of an effort to translate legislative objectives into administrative attainments. Some relate to our failure to relate old to new programs effectively . . . Some stem from our effort to achieve higher, more uniform levels of performance in certain program areas, and this always causes difficulties. Some result from our deep concern in meeting diverse needs of whole regions, age [and economic] groups . . . while relying on the . . . traditional narrow categorical program approach in achieving legislative implementation." [5] President Nixon in a message to Congress accompanying a draft of an act to consolidate grants in April, 1969, echoed Humphrey's refrain:

Under our present fragmented system, each one of a group of closely related categorical grants is encumbered with its own individual array of administrative and technical requirements. This unnecessarily complicates the planning process; it discourages comprehensive planning; it requires multiple applications, and multiple bookkeep-

4. *Congressional Record* 115: S4479 (May 1, 1969).
5. Hubert H. Humphrey, "A More Perfect Union," *National Civic Review* 56: 323–324 (June 1967).

ing, both by the Federal agencies and by State and local governments.[6]

One result of such a system in operation was the creation of a "management muddle," which by the mid-sixties had become one of the basic problems of the federal system.[7] Part of the trouble lies in the nature of administration itself. So rapid an acceleration of governmental activity, even in the best of circumstances, would involve serious management problems. Administration is far from an exact science. Rather, "it is a dynamic art, taking the human and physical resources available in a system . . . and bending them to the achievement of some required end." [8] It is the capacity, Brooks Adams wrote, "of coordinating many, and often conflicting, social energies in a single organism, so adroitly that they shall operate as a unit." [9] It is a social accomplishment, not an automatic process. Perfection of administration is never possible. However well conceived, and operated under optimum conditions, it will encounter difficulties.

In the United States, operating conditions are never optimal. The national government, first of all, creates problems in the way it conceives and handles its part of the program load. Congress "enacts too many narrow . . . grant programs with stringent guidelines, unnecessary requirements, and burdensome reporting procedures. These lead to waste motion and ineffective administration. . . ." Too often, in response to both bureaucratic and outside pressures, programs are divided and subdivided among different departments and agencies. Moreover, Congress creates programs for the most part individually, in isolation from other on-going or developing programs, rather than following a comprehensive, over-all plan of program development. Thus, from the outset, "Federal programs are uncoordinated, leading to

6. Quoted in *Congressional Record* 115: H3221 (April 30, 1969). See *Congressional Record* 115: S4478–4480 (May 1, 1969) for the full text of the proposed act.

7. See Senator Edmund S. Muskie, "The Challenge of Creative Federalism," *Saturday Review*, June 25, 1966, pp. 12–15. See also his speech to the Committee of 39 Annual Awards Dinner, Wilmington, Delaware, May 26, 1966, reprinted in *Congressional Record* 112: 11498–11500 (June 2, 1966).

8. White, *Introduction to the Study of Public Administration, op. cit.*, p. 2.

9. Adams, quoted in *ibid.*

overlapping, duplication, triplication, conflicting goals, cross purposes, lack of consistency, and loss of direction." [10] Drawn up
without administrative considerations having been taken into account, they constitute an administrative maze once they are put
into operation.

Nor does Congress stop there, for it not only establishes the
legal bases of programs, it exercises continuing supervision and
control over their execution as well. In the routine administration
of their jobs, federal administrators are never allowed to forget
the presence of Congress.[11] Once it has created a program and
assigned its administration to a unit, Congress is always free to
rearrange, reorganize, and reassign functions and to specify what
administrative methods and practices shall be used. Administrators
quickly become conscious of the possibility of Congressional interference and adjust themselves to it. The extensive interference
by recent Congresses with the functioning of the Office of
Economic Opportunity is an excellent case in point. The propensity of Congress to exert its power over administration is not
confined to intergovernmental programs, but many of the members of Congress seem to take a special interest in them because
they still distrust those programs as departures from their own
views of federalism.

Under the best of circumstances, the President would have
difficulty administering the programs as chief executive. There is
little he can do about Congress's role but recognize and accept it.
Not only are there too many units of administration for him to
ride herd on effectively, but some of the most important of them
were made independent of the President by Congress at the outset. More important, the President and his immediate subordinates
are amateur administrative leaders, whose power varies with time
and circumstances; those who staff the departments, agencies,
bureaus, and boards are professionals, responsible in the long run,
they are aware, not so much to the chief executive as to their
own agency heads and to their sense of professional duty and to
Congress. David Brinkley once remarked that

10. Sanford, *Storm Over the States, op. cit.,* p. 159.
11. See the perceptive paragraphs about "The Administrator as Politician" in Grodzins, *The American System, op. cit.,* pp. 270–274.

an old-line government agency is a hissing, clanking machine without an off switch. It has a comfortable sense of its own permanence, knowing it was here before the President arrived and will be here when he is gone, still doing precisely what it was doing before he came.[12]

Because this is true about old-line agencies, presidents are prone to recommend and establish new agencies to carry on new programs, hopeful that they will be more amenable to control. Thus they make their own contribution to the administrative maze.

Nor has the Bureau of the Budget, which in other management areas is of great assistance to the President, been able to provide leadership in bringing about administrative coordination. Perhaps recognizing the entrenched attitudes of most federal personnel, the Bureau has been content to exercise its considerable influence elsewhere.

The Bureau can hardly be blamed. For there is no doubt that there is always a tendency toward isolation and rigidity in administrative agencies: isolation, because each is likely to think primarily of its own mission and to ignore supplementary or complementary programs in sister agencies; rigidity, because it is easier to concentrate on the job at hand if procedures are known and fixed. In many cases, both the existing administrative structure and the program were the result of a lobby's successful effort, and having accomplished its objective, the lobby exerts pressure on Congress to resist any subsequent change. Civil service rules also make for rigidity, inasmuch as jobs are tied to specific positions for the administration of given programs. To attempt to change all this usually proves difficult, if not impossible.

To bring the problem down to essentials, it is chiefly one of middle management, that group of administrative officials, including bureau chiefs, division and section heads, and front-line supervisors, which directs and controls the performance of government business within the scope of the law, and of policies and procedures established by top management. "Middle management takes over the production job, program planning and the direction of operations; the establishment of . . . standards and their

12. David Brinkley, "Leading from Strength: LBJ in Action," *Atlantic Monthly*, February 1965, p. 52.

enforcement; the provision of personnel . . . ; the supervision of
the rank and file; the coordination of operations; the maintenance
of morale; and constant regard to improvement of operations.
These are matters vital to good administration, calling for skill,
fidelity, and capacity for leadership." [13] By and large, middle
management consists of specialists, who in their own agencies and
offices form a relatively homogenous group directed toward the
accomplishment of a single task or at most a series of closely related tasks. "As such, [they constitute a] highly stable organization unit that reorganization plans may shift around, but rarely
abolish. . . . Stability based on tenure; professionalism based on
technical training, experience, and program goals; and a narrow
functionalism based on the relatively homogenous program mandates of the bureau and division—these are the usual traits
of middle management found in the lexicon of public administration experts." Such executives, "with a strong functional, professional, and status-quo orientation, are not likely to approach broad
questions of a multifunctional, interlevel, interagency, or coordinating nature with any great enthusiasm or concern." [14]

The difficulties are great enough within Washington itself.
They are compounded in the field. Indeed, Stephen K. Bailey declared recently, if the "barriers to effective administration seem
nearly insurmountable in Washington, they grow even more so
away from Washington. Between the nation's capital and the
ninety per cent of Federal employees who work in other parts of
the country [there is] a lack of co-operation and [an] absence of
effective coordination [that] threaten[s] the very base of program
effectiveness." [15]

Finally, it should be remembered that the programs under discussion here are intergovernmental programs; state and local governments are involved in their implementation as well as the national government. In President Johnson's words, "The problems
of managing many of our more important new programs are in-

13. White, *Introduction to the Study of Public Administration, op. cit.,*
p. 89.
14. *The Federal System as Seen by Federal Aid Officials, op. cit.,*
pp. 93–94.
15. Stephen K. Bailey, "Co-ordinating the Great Society," *The Reporter,* March 24, 1966, p. 40. See also Bailey's remarks on "Managing the
Federal Government," in *Agenda for the Nation* (Washington, D.C.: The
Brookings Institution, 1968), pp. 301–321.

tensified by their intergovernmental character." [16] The process of administration is a single one, whether it is entrusted to federal, state, municipal, or county governments. Unfortunately, many state constitutions and statutes have not been brought up to date in recognition of that fact. Nor have state and local administrative procedures been generally as adjusted to modern administrative techniques as have those in Washington. To make matters worse, state and local administrations are confused by the extensive fragmentation of federal grants-in-aid and by what they consider the "red tape" of the federal bureaucrats which in many cases they feel frustrates comprehensive development of plans to tackle area-wide problems.

Indeed, the necessity for intergovernmental cooperation in program development and execution gives rise to a great many opportunities for administrative mismanagement. Most federal grant-in-aid programs require that state enabling legislation be enacted, a responsible state agency designated, and a state plan developed and submitted for approval. At the same time, the Congressional legislation entrusts responsibility for the federal part of the program to a particular department or agency, which then interprets the basic legislation for itself in the detailed procedures, standards, regulations, and guidelines which it draws up for the implementation of each particular program. Even though representatives of the federal agency work with state and local officials in the implementation of the legislation, as officials of the U.S. Public Health Service have in the development of state plans for hospital construction under the Hill-Burton Act (the Hospital Survey and Construction Act of 1946), for example, there is no guarantee that state desires and federal requirements will effortlessly gibe with each other. Indeed, some of the worst intergovernmental snarls develop as the result of conflict between them. Often, either the basic grant legislation or the agency guidelines will require action by the state or local subdivision which it did not plan on or of which it does not approve. Thus the Hill-Burton Act required all hospitals built under the act to be licensed by the state in which it was built, even though in 1946, when the act was passed, thirty-seven states had no licensing procedures. And the impact of the desegregation guidelines

16. Budget Message to Congress, January 29, 1968.

on state and local educational agencies has already been referred to.[17] Nor have dependability and consistency, two necessities of successful administration, always been parts of the intergovernmental operation. Congress is notoriously fickle in appropriating funds for on-going programs. Often the expected amount is cut, as it was in three successive years in Hill-Burton appropriations, or new programs are imposed with no warning, so that state and local long-range planning is made extremely difficult. And of course operations under federal grants are subject to personnel and financial requirements which occasionally generate a good deal of opposition and hostility.

Most of the difficulties just described have existed a long time and in connection with the administration of all governmental programs. They alone are enough to have caused the management muddle. But that muddle has become much more severe due to the very rapidity with which government programs have been created in recent years. Not only have so many programs been forthcoming that they threaten to bury administrators at all levels under an avalanche of work, but program has followed upon program so closely that those they were designed to aid cannot be sure just what is on the statute books to help them meet public problems. There is a growing concern among city administrators, in whose jurisdictions are concentrated most of the problems recent programs were designed to meet, that "they may not be aware of all the opportunities" available to them to participate in federal programs. As a result, local participation in federal-aid programs is essentially haphazard; there is no guarantee at all that assistance goes where it is most needed. "Local officials, lacking large staffs, are often bewildered by the mass of Federal programs which confront them, uninformed about the Federal funds and projects they might obtain, and ill-equipped to determine which available Federal programs best meet their community needs. In short, we are faced with a crisis in communication." [18] To make things worse, just at the time people are demanding better domestic public services which are more effectively administered, the drain on the economy by military and defense-related commit-

17. See Chapter IV above.
18. The words of Senator Edward Kennedy, *Congressional Record* 112: 18099 (August 10, 1966).

ments is accentuated, "making the problem of public administration on the home front [even] more acute." [19]

Concerned about the snowballing of the management problem, the Senate subcommittee on intergovernmental relations undertook in 1963, as part of its continuing study of federalism, a study of the mounting administrative crisis. The findings of that study provide the best summary of the current problem available. They reveal the existence of

substantial competing and overlapping of programs at all three levels [of government]—sometimes as a direct result of legislation and sometimes as a result of "empire building." [They showed] that too many federal officials, particularly in the middle management level, were not interested in, and, in fact, were hostile to, coordinating programs within and between their departments, and were reluctant to encourage coordination and planning among their state and local counterparts.

Standpattism, or the rigid defense of traditional practices, procedures, and principles is a theme [constantly found]. . . .

At the same time, federal . . . officials complained that . . . they found a variety of archaic state constitutional and legal restrictions that continue to block effective application of federal aid programs, and hamstring state and local administrators in developing their own programs.

In short, we found conflict between professional administrators at the Federal level and . . . administrators at State and local levels, between line agency officials and elected policy-makers at all levels, between administrators of one aid program and those of another, between specialized middle-management officials and generalists in the top management category, and between standpat bureau heads and innovators seeking to strengthen the decision-making process at all levels.[20]

What is needed, the study concluded,[21] is "the modernization of our administrative machinery and better working relationships between Federal, State and local governments." Without both

19. The words of Senator Edmund S. Muskie, undated press release, 1966, p. 2.

20. Muskie, "The Challenge of Creative Federalism," *op. cit.; The Federal System as Seen by Federal Aid Officials, op. cit.;* Muskie, Speech for Delivery on the Floor of the Senate, March 25, 1966. Mimeo release, p. B3.

21. Former Governor Terry Sanford of North Carolina comes to almost the same conclusions in *Storm Over the States, op. cit.,* especially pp. 72–74, 80–81.

being accomplished, and accomplished quickly, the nation is "headed for trouble . . . If we do not pull the Federal Establishment together and develop a more positive attitude of helping State and local governments meet their increasing public needs . . ." the functional utility of the federal system may be paralyzed. "Our programs are only as good as the machinery that carries them out. At the moment, that machinery" is in serious disrepair.[22]

It is not, fortunately, as if repair must be started from scratch. A number of improvements in federal administrative machinery were made in the latter days of the New Deal in response to the recommendations of President Roosevelt's Committee on Administrative Management. A major contribution of the Committee was its stress on the need for presidential authority over the entire federal establishment and its influence in getting provisions made in 1939 for staff assistance to the President in carrying out his administrative responsibilities. The present Executive Office of the President was the product of the Committee's original recommendation. The Committee's recommendation of a single civil service administrator, responsible to the President, to serve as a personnel resource man for the President, was substantially achieved by President Roosevelt who asked one of his staff assistants to act as liaison officer for personnel and by later presidents who have utilized the chairmen of the Civil Service Commission in that capacity. The Committee also emphasized the need for constant attention to reorganization within the executive branch, an emphasis which was first converted into operating procedure in the Economy Act of 1932 and subsequently embodied in the Reorganization Act of 1949, granting the President power to impose reorganization plans which would become effective if they were not disapproved by both houses of Congress within sixty days. That act, which had been renewed a number of times, was allowed to lapse in 1968, and President Nixon's first message to Congress was an urgent plea for its resumption and extension. Public Law 91–5, signed March 27, 1969, gave the President what he asked for through April 1, 1971. President Roosevelt's Committee also addressed itself to the need to bring the indepen-

22. *Congressional Record* 112: 12611 (June 15, 1966).

dent regulatory commissions under the ultimate supervision of the President, by placing each within one of the then ten Cabinet departments, and by creating two new departments, public works and public welfare. Although these recommendations were not adopted, the Committee's "report and . . . accompanying documents were outstanding contributions to an understanding of the federal administrative system and to the underlying theory of administration." [23] Right after World War II, Congress passed the Administrative Procedure Act of 1946, which regulates the internal procedures of federal regulatory agencies. The act requires that publicity be given to agency operations and rules and provides in detail for hearing procedures. Broad standards for judicial review of agency actions are also set forth. In quick succession in the fifties, the first Hoover Commission and the Kestnbaum Commission offered further suggestions for the "substantial reconstruction of many aspects of our system" of administration, some of which, including the creation of a Department of Defense, the assignment of the National Security Council to the Executive Office of the President, the creation of a Cabinet-level Department of Health, Education and Welfare, the centralization of authority in department heads, the development of a centralized federal procurement system, and the establishment of the Advisory Commission on Intergovernmental Relations, were subsequently acted upon. To many of their suggestions, however, including many concerned with the intergovernmental aspects of administration, Congress turned a deaf ear or was only partially responsive, so that the over-all problem remained and became more severe as the administrative work load increased sharply with the new needs of post-war America. The creation in 1964 of a permanent Administrative Conference of the United States to replace earlier temporary commissions established by Presidents Eisenhower and Kennedy helped alleviate the situation, and through their work and the use of the President's reorganization power a good deal of other adjustment and change had been introduced by the time the subcommittee sounded the warning bell.

The Advisory Commission on Intergovernmental Relations had, for its part since its creation in 1959, made a great many rec-

23. White, *Introduction to the Study of Public Administration, op. cit.,* p. 176.

ommendations for the improvement of administration, particularly but not solely at the state and local level, and the record of their adoption was surprisingly good. But the core of the problem had barely begun to be tackled.

President Johnson was made painfully aware of the problem, and he tried to speed up the process of administrative reform during his administration. He designated the Vice President and the Director of the Office of Emergency Planning in the Executive Office of the President to act as his liaison with mayors and governors respectively and ordered the Bureau of the Budget to review the areas in which basic consolidations of overlapping grant-in-aid programs could be achieved. He issued a memorandum on coordination for development planning and signed an executive order assigning the Secretary of Housing and Urban Development the responsibility of convening special working groups composed of appropriate federal agencies involved in urban development to see how cooperation and consistency among them might be achieved.[24] Acting under his general endorsement, a number of departments and agencies embarked on actions of their own: the Department of Health, Education and Welfare established an intergovernmental relations staff under its Director of Field Coordination to maintain direct and continuing contact with governors and local executives and with their national organizations, and the Department of Housing and Urban Development established procedures to improve federal-state coordination in the designation of development-planning districts, and for area-wide planning agencies to comment on applications for specific grants that might affect the orderly development of their metropolitan areas. Finally, in November 1966, the President issued a memorandum calling on all federal officials to take steps to insure closer cooperation among federal, state, and local officials in the management of the federal aid programs coming under their jurisdiction. "To the fullest practical extent," the President noted,

I want you to take steps to afford representation of the chief executives of state and local government the opportunity to advise and

24. These actions are described in some detail in an address by Harold Seidman, Assistant Director of the Bureau of the Budget, delivered to the National Legislative Conference, September 19, 1966, reprinted in *Congressional Record* 112: 22113–22114 (September 19, 1966).

consult in the development and execution of programs which directly affect the conduct of state and local affairs. I believe these arrangements will greatly strengthen the federal system at all levels. Our objective is to make certain that vital new federal assistance programs are made workable at the point of impact. I am asking the Director of the Bureau of the Budget to work with you, with the advisory Commission on Intergovernmental Relations, and with other public interest groups representing state and local government in developing useful and productive arrangements to help carry out this policy.

Subsequently a Budget Bureau circular (No. A85) established a procedure for direct consultation between federal agencies and representatives of chief executives of state and local governments and for use of the Advisory Commission on Intergovernmental Relations as a liaison for consultation about proposed federal rules, regulations, standards, procedures, and guidelines for the administration of federal grants.

President Nixon went even further within the first month of his administration by combining the functions previously exercised by the Office of Emergency Planning and the Vice President's Office and creating by executive order [25] an Office of Intergovernmental Relations under the direct supervision of the Vice President. The new office, the President said, "will seek to strengthen existing channels of communication and to create new channels among all levels of government." [26]

Specifically, the Vice President was directed to act as the President's liaison with state and local officials, encourage and assist maximum cooperation among federal departments and agencies and state and local governments, help to make the executive branch of the national government "more sensitive, receptive and responsive" to the views and wishes of state and local officials, serve as the focal point of federal efforts to resolve conflicts in relations with state and local officials, work closely with the Advisory Commission on Intergovernmental Relations, and inform the Urban Affairs Council on general intergovernmental issues that might affect its work. In addition, the office was charged with assisting the Vice President in carrying out his duties under

25. Executive Order 11455, February 14, 1969. The text is given in *Federal Register*, Vol. 34, No. 33, pp. 2299–2300, February 18, 1969.
26. Quoted in *Durham Morning Herald*, February 15, 1969, p. 3A.

the order, serving as a clearinghouse for the prompt handling and resolution of problems brought to its attention, identifying and reporting on intergovernmental problems, developing ways and means of strengthening intra-federal procedures as they relate to intergovernmental activities, staying in close touch with federal departments and agencies in the area, and reviewing procedures those agencies utilize in working with state and local officials with an eye to strengthening them.

Nixon also has evidenced his concern for good administrative management in his creation of an Urban Affairs Council to do in domestic affairs what the National Security Council is empowered to do in foreign affairs, namely, coordinate programs and provide a forum for the discussion of interdepartmental problems that cut across jurisdictions. And to provide the same kind of opportunity at the local level, he reorganized the field office of five departments—Health, Education and Welfare, Housing and Urban Development, Labor, Office of Economic Opportunity, and Small Business Administration—so that they all have the same boundaries and common regional headquarters.

But potentially one of the most important developments as it affects administration in the federal system is the passage of the Intergovernmental Cooperation Act of 1968, which grew out of the investigations of the Senate subcommittee on intergovernmental relations. President Johnson called for passage of such an act by Congress in his 1967 Budget Speech, it won the support of all four national groups which represent state and local governments—the National League of Cities, the National Association of Counties, the Council of State Governments, and the United States Conference of Mayors—and it was endorsed by the Advisory Commission on Intergovernmental Relations. It was passed by the 90th Congress and became Public Law 90–577 on October 16, 1968. As enacted, the bill has been hailed as "the first major step in bringing some order to the confused state of contemporary Federal-state-local relations." It

revamps procedures affecting the distribution of Federal grant funds to the States, authorizes Federal departments and agencies to provide specialized and technical services to other jurisdictions on a reimbursable basis, mandates a coordinated intergovernmental policy for the administration of development assistance grants which policy includes incorporation of systematic planning required under separate federal grant-in-aid programs into comprehensive local and areawide development planning, establishes uniform policies and procedures with respect to the acquisition and disposal of urban land and seeks to ensure the consistency of such land transactions with the zoning and land use practices of the local governments involved, and strengthens congressional oversight over grant programs for which no expiration date was provided.

By its passage, some of the impediments to the effective operation of the federal system have been removed.[27]

But other impediments remained, and to get at them, Representative L. H. Fountain, the Chairman of the House subcommittee on intergovernmental relations, offered to the 91st Congress a number of amendments, including requirement of simplified and standardized accounting, auditing, and reporting procedures for federal assistance programs, the consolidation of federal assistance programs in the same functional areas, and simplification of the funding of joint interdepartmental programs. Representative Florence Dwyer, urging passage of the bill incorporating those amendments, remarked that it was "in essence . . . a good management bill, in that [it] seek[s] to overcome antiquated and ineffective techniques of public administration" so as to adapt American federalism "to the rapidly changing needs of our time."[28]

But even the enactment of this legislation, which should tighten up program management and other administrative procedures in the grant system, is not by itself enough. The large number of grant programs, which the subcommittee on intergovernmental relations found to be one of the major causes of confusion at the state and local levels, must be considerably reduced. To accomplish that objective, President Nixon has recommended passage of a grant consolidation act, which

would be patterned in part after procedures used successfully for the past 20 years to reorganize Executive Branch functions. It would give the President power to initiate consolidation of closely related

27. Representative L. H. Fountain, *Congressional Record* 115: H1109 (February 20, 1969).
28. *Congressional Record* 115: H1111 (February 20, 1969).

Federal assistance programs, and to place consolidated programs under the jurisdiction of a single agency. However, it would give either House of Congress the right to veto a proposed consolidation within 60 days, and it would establish stringent safeguards against possible abuse.[29]

Passage of the grant consolidation act, the President concluded, would "not be a substitute for other reforms necessary in order to improve the delivery of Federal services, but it would be an essential element. It would be another vital step in the administrative reforms undertaken already . . . [whose aims are] to help make more certain the delivery and more manageable the administration of a growing complex of Federal programs, at a time when the problems they address increasingly cross the old jurisdictional lines of departments and agencies."[30] The proposed legislation was at once heralded by leaders in both houses of Congress and stands an excellent chance of final passage.

An additional suggestion for improvement in intergovernmental administration, offered by Senator Edward Kennedy to the 89th Congress, was that a computerized information system be designed which would both enable states and localities to participate more effectively in federal aid programs by providing full information about their availability and also allow the Congress and the President to have a better measure of state and local needs and performance in those programs. As Senator Kennedy sees it, his idea would get at the need "to build an effective communications system between local, State, and Federal levels of government."[31]

It is not, as Professor Stephen K. Bailey has pointed out, merely that recent legislative enactments have created more complex administrative problems than ever before. That of course is true. It is also that basic problems of coordination and effective operation have long been neglected in the United States, and time has suddenly caught up with us. To be sure, Professor Bailey remarks, "It is easy—and politically popular—to overstate the administrative difficulties" facing the federal system today. ". . . ad-

---

29. *Message from the President of the United States,* House Document No. 91-112, *Congressional Record* 115: H3221 (April 30, 1969).
30. *Ibid.*
31. *Congressional Record* 112: 18908 (August 10, 1966).

ministrative tidiness is not the be-all and the end-all of government . . . Nonetheless, the dangers are real and the need
for new administrative machinery and methods correspondingly
urgent. Federal programs must be more effectively related to
each other and must complement state and local programs without the sacrifice of initiative [and] experimentation," [32] and other
administrative improvements must be made, or the federal system
as a device to serve the people of the United States will lose its
vitality and viability.

Organization and coordination are only part of the problem,
however. More serious, because effective personnel can make
even creaking devices for coordination function smoothly, is the
manpower crisis which now faces the entire federal system.
". . . the weakest link" in the chain of federal-state-local administration, President Johnson once said, "is the emerging shortage
of professional manpower." Within the national government itself, a shortage of professional and high-grade technical and administrative personnel is affecting all operating units, so much so
that the Brookings Institution concluded that the national
government had before it a recruitment problem of major proportions. "Its demand for technical experts and able administrators is steadily increasing . . . Unless there is a sharp drop in the
total size of the federal service, to replace personnel who retire,
resign or die in office, 300,000 new civilian recruits are needed
every year. . . ." [33] These figures are generally regarded as minimal. In addition, because of the changing nature of the federal
service, jobs are becoming more and more technical, requiring
specialized training. "With each passing year we will need to recruit a high percentage of college graduates in relation to our
total hiring—with increased emphasis on getting the Ph.D.," a
member of the Civil Service Commission testified before Congress.[34] Present estimates are that as many as 15,000 new employees will have to be recruited from professional ranks every
year into the indefinite future. Increasing specialization offers no

32. Bailey, "Coordinating the Great Society," *op. cit.*, p. 41.
33. *What Americans Think of the Federal Service*. Brookings Research
Report No. 19 (Washington, 1964), p. 1.
34. Robert E. Hampton, quoted in *Congressional Record* 110: 11522
(May 26, 1964).

alternative.

The problem is not merely one of filling existing and new positions. It is also one of providing trained people to administer new programs in areas where the national government has had no prior experience to guide it. Recent Congresses have placed huge responsibilities in the area of metropolitan planning and development on the new Department of Housing and Urban Development, and especially sensitive duties in connection with civil rights on the Department of Justice. There is not only a good deal of resentment and suspicion to overcome as the national government develops its programs in those areas; some of those programs were long overdue and were enacted as last resorts to fill voids long felt in American society. It is therefore essential to move rapidly and imaginatively to get them into full operation. So the need is for quality personnel as well as for an increase in over-all numbers. Under these circumstances, manning the executive branch becomes a more difficult task than it ever has been before, and it requires more attention than has so far been devoted to it.

The problem of recruitment at the federal level can be met in part by salaries more nearly competitive with those in the private sector of American life. (In the Federal Salary Act of 1962 the principle that federal salary rates at all levels of employment shall be comparable with salary rates in private employment was made law, and Congress has adjusted salary scales upward almost annually since the law was enacted.) It can also be met by more aggressive recruiting, by the introduction of manpower forecasting and analyses of labor needs into the recruiting process, and by experimenting with new sources of personnel services. Contracting out for services might be utilized beyond the research area, to which it is virtually limited now, on the pattern of contracting for buildings and facilities which has become standard federal practice. The need for additional employees can be met also by improved personnel management services up and down the line. Government employment centers might be developed in the larger metropolitan areas, to bring jobs to where the people are, and more attention could be paid to full career development within the federal service. But the special committee appointed by the prestigious Committee for Economic Development to study the recruitment problem came to the conclusion that the mere development of better personnel techniques would not meet the need without the simultaneous development of what it called "commanding incentives": opportunities for employees to improve their talents while on the job, good prospects for promotion, and a variety of chances for personal growth, creativity, and innovation. Such incentives, the Committee concluded, are virtually nonexistent in the government today. Indeed, the government has lagged far behind business in planning opportunities for the growth and development of its employees.

The creation of a Civil Service Academy to help fill the growing need for properly trained civil servants at the national level has been suggested many times. Just as the government maintains academies for training military and naval leaders, it is argued, it might establish and maintain a federal civil service academy to prepare young people for posts of civilian administrative leadership. Suggestions have also been made for an annual performance review of every key official by agency selection boards who would be concerned both with promotion potentials and with corrective measures for failures in performance and growth.

But all these problems in connection with federal personnel fade in comparison with the difficulties encountered at the state and local level. Thus President Johnson observed in his 1967 Quality of Government Address:

. . . nowhere is the magnitude of government manpower [need] greater, and the accompanying challenge more critical, than at the State and local levels. Consider the following:

> Between 1955 and 1965 employment in State and local governments increased from 4.7 million to 7.7 million, or four times the rate of growth of employment in the economy as a whole.

> By 1975, State and local government will grow to more than 11 million.

> Each year, from now through 1975, State and local governments will have to recruit at least one-quarter of a million new administrative, technical, and professional employees, not including teachers, to maintain and develop their programs.

A breakdown of state and local employees by occupational categories reveals that from 1957 to 1965, the number of full-time State and local highway workers rose by 24 per cent. Employment in police protection increased by 30 per cent, and in public health and hospitals by 41 per cent. The number of full-time public employees in education soared by 60 per cent, and those in public welfare, by 62 per cent. Much of this massive growth in State and local employment can be attributed to the population explosion and the demand for expanded services generated by it. The physical and social problems stemming from urbanization and suburbanization, however, have been other key factors in developing greater needs for police, fire, housing, sanitation, welfare, and other public services. In addition, one of the by-products of our affluent society is the rise in popular expectations with respect to governmental services. To put it more bluntly, the American citizenry is not willing to settle for the level and quality of services that were provided three, or even two, decades ago.[35]

As is the case with the federal civil service, the problem at the state and local level is one not merely of numbers but of quality as well. State and local administration is "lacking in quality and experience, unimaginative, and too subject to negative political and bureaucratic pressures" to provide the kind of administration that is required today. "Confronted with urban congestion, slums, water pollution, air pollution, juvenile delinquency, social tension, and chronic unemployment, public administrators today must be professionals in every sense of the word. Yet . . . too often [state and local officers] are not, mainly because of . . . antiquated, patronage-oriented personnel systems which hinder the hiring and keeping of good people."

. . . unfavorable working conditions, low pay, excessively bureaucratic rules and procedures discourage both prospective employees and careerists. Personnel development programs, including opportunities for job mobility, in-service training, and educational leave [are] unknown, except in some of the larger jurisdictions. [There is] a noticeable lack of effective merit systems, which results in the loading of some agencies with unprofessional, uninspiring, and often unfit personnel. Finally, responsible administrators [complain] that inflexible rules and regulations—dictating whom, when, and how they could hire, promote, or fire—frustrate their efforts to develop effective staff support.[36]

35. Remarks of Senator Edmund S. Muskie on introducing the Intergovernmental Personnel Act of 1966. Mimeo. No date. Pp. 2–3.
36. Muskie, "The Challenge of Creative Federalism," *op. cit.*, pp. 12–13.

The indictment is not recent. Leonard D. White noted in 1955 that he was "driven to the conclusion that the states have been slow in adopting the merit system, either formally or informally," and though he acknowledged that there had been considerable progress in the cities, he concluded that "in the great metropolitan areas, standards of performance [were] not infrequently low." "Civil service commissioners [were] sometimes politicians first and officials second." In such metropolitan centers as Chicago, New York, Philadelphia, Pittsburgh, Cleveland, Minneapolis, and Seattle were "being fought out the most difficult battles between spoils and merit, with the patronage system well entrenched and in command of almost impregnable defences." And in counties, "the patronage system still maintain[ed] almost complete sway." Indeed, White's survey of the scene showed that there were two powerful systems of personnel administration in the United States, "each irreconcilable with the other," and so virtually at war: the one used by the national government, based on merit, and the one used by state and local government, based on patronage.[37] Professor Charles Adrian has made it abundantly clear in his writings that conflict in the federal system does not grow out of the relations between different levels and units of government as such, but results whenever the administrative personnel at a particular level for a particular function are not fully professionalized, and those at another level dealing with the same function are. This is unfortunately the case across the board in most of the grant-in-aid programs presently in effect in the United States. In very few does federal legislation require the operation of a merit system for participation.

This battle has been raging for more than seventy years. Great gains have been made by the merit system in those years, greater than is usually realized. The basic conditions of government are such that the eventual triumph of the merit system seems inevitable. The ever-increasing technological aspects of governmental operations; the greatly intensified social responsibility of government, making the risk of administrative failure equivalent to the risk of social catastrophe; the emerging professional point of view in many branches of administration; and the expansion of civil service unions intent on protecting their own interests by the steady application of the merit

37. White, *Introduction to the Study of Public Administration, op. cit.*, pp. 314–316.

system—these and other circumstances forecast the certain destruction of patronage in due course of time.[38]

The question is, is there enough time? As early as 1964, W. Brooke Graves observed in his definitive book, *American Intergovernmental Relations*, that the "response of the state political organizations to the urgent need for sound systems of public personel administration in modern government has been pitifully slow and inadequate."[39] The situation is no better in the cities, where vacancies are numerous, young professionals have little interest in municipal employment, there are serious shortages in certain key occupations, the selection system is slow and inflexible, employee morale is often indifferent, salaries in some jobs lag behind those paid by other employers, and employee training is insufficient.

What is the answer? The forces at work at the state and local levels are so firmly entrenched that the possibility of early internal remedial action seems remote. Indeed, it is very likely that decision-makers at state and local levels of government are even less "fully aware of the critical nature of the manpower gap" than are those at the federal level, and "that long-range planning in this area is in its infancy."[40] Equally remote seems the solution suggested by the Municipal Manpower Commission, which pointed to the failure of the nation's institutions of higher education to provide adequate opportunities for training in the public service and challenged them to come up with realistic and suitable educational programs for governing tomorrow's cities.[41]

To meet the emergency, therefore, it has been widely proposed that the national government come to the assistance of state and local governments in the field of personnel administration, as it has in so many other fields of need. Since the success of the grant-in-aid programs is a primary objective of the national government, but one which it can achieve only if state and local governments have the administrative competence and efficiency to

38. *Ibid.*, pp. 315–316.
39. Graves, *American Intergovernmental Relations, op. cit.*, p. 195.
40. The conclusion of Senator Muskie in Remarks on Introducing the Intergovernmental Personnel Act, *op. cit.*, p. 5
41. The Commission's report, published in 1962 by McGraw-Hill, New York, was entitled *Governmental Manpower for Tomorrow's Cities.*

carry out their portion of each program, it would seem clearly within the federal field of power to extend help. If this be accepted, there are a number of ways it can do so.

Over twenty-five years ago, when Leonard D. White was a member of the United States Civil Service Commission, he suggested the possibility of some sort of federal-state-local cooperation in personnel administration:

Why should Federal, State, and local agencies, all recruiting, examining, and hiring new employees for necessary common types of work, all in the same geographical area, compete with one another and duplicate one another's efforts? Tests . . . are fairly well standardized. Why shouldn't there be *one* place . . . where tests are given and scored, eligible lists compiled, and eligibles certified therefrom to *any* government appointing officer . . . Federal, State, or local—having . . . vacancies to be filled? The costs would be greatly reduced because overlapping and duplication would be eliminated. There are many common types of employment for which such cooperation should now be possible. . . .[42]

And since the work of government at all levels has come increasingly to be concerned with the same programs, another possibility is an interchange of civil servants among levels of government, but chiefly between the federal government and those of state and local units. In 1954 the Sixth American Assembly, which devoted its attention to the federal civil service, included in its final report the recommendation that "The Federal Service . . . should be open[ed] to interchange with other fields of American life—business, trade unions, universities, the professions, *State and local governments*. Such exchanges benefit both the Federal Service and these groups, and our society is the richer."[43] The Public Health Service Act does contain authority for the Secretary of Health, Education and Welfare to place federal officers for periods of up to two years in state and local health agencies upon the request of those agencies, and the Department of Agriculture has similar authority on a limited scale. With these as precedents, the Council of State Governments incorporated in its annual *Suggested State Legislation* a proposal to

42. White, quoted in Graves, *American Intergovernmental Relations*, *op. cit.*, p. 196.
43. Quoted in *ibid.*, p. 197. Italics supplied.

enact general permissive statutes allowing state and local departments and agencies to participate in employee interchange programs, and the same suggestion has been made to Congress.

Training is also a field where the possibilities of intergovernmental cooperation are many. The national government already has extensive cooperative training programs among its own departments and agencies, which cooperate in some states with local units of government. The Federal Bureau of Investigation for some time has trained state and local law-enforcement officers,[44] the Food and Drug Administration in the Department of Health, Education and Welfare trains state and local enforcement officers in that field, and similar arrangements are in effect in a number of other agencies. A further step toward developing intergovernmental facilities for training would be to re-enact the provisions for federal financial assistance to state programs of personnel training that were in effect from 1937 to 1945 under the George-Deen Act, a vocational education act. Another would be support for and extension of the principle incorporated in Title VIII of the 1964 amendments to the National Housing Act, authorizing matching funds to the states for advanced training and fellowship programs. As Dr. Graves points out, "the barriers to Federal-State-local cooperation in this area have as yet scarcely been cracked." [45]

In an attempt to provide an across-the-board approach to replace the partial and piecemeal attempts to solve the government personnel problem of previous years, President Johnson recommended the consideration and adoption by Congress of an Intergovernmental Personnel Act in his special message on the quality of American government in March 1967, and a bill to that end was submitted to the 90th Congress. A similar proposal was submitted to the 91st Congress and seemed assured of consideration and eventual enactment.[46] In its declaration of policy, the bill de-

44. Under President Johnson's proposed crime control legislation offered to Congress in 1968, additional funds would be made available for federal help in training state and local police officers.

45. Graves, *American Intergovernmental Relations, op. cit.,* p. 199.

46. S. 3408 in the 90th Congress, S. 11 in the 91st Congress. See the statement to the subcommittee on intergovernmental relations by Donald C. Stone, Dean, Graduate School of Public and International Affairs, University of Pittsburgh, *Congressional Record* 115: S934–936 (January 27, 1969).

clares that the quality of public service at all levels of government can be improved by the further development of the merit system of personnel administration and finds that federal "financial and technical assistance to state and local governments for strengthening their personnel systems" in a manner consistent with the following principles would be in the national interest:

1. recruiting, selecting, and advancing on the basis of ability, knowledge, and skill;

2. equitable and adequate compensation;

3. training to assure high-quality performance;

4. retaining employees on the basis of adequacy of performance;

5. nondiscrimination with regard to political affiliation, race, national origin, religion, or sex;

6. protection from coercion for partisan political purposes and prohibition of use of official authority to interfere with or affect an election or nomination to office.

Specifically, the bill would make it possible:

1. to develop through intergovernmental cooperation policies and standards for the administration of programs for the improvement of state and local personnel administration and training;

2. to authorize federal agencies to admit state and local government officials and employees, particularly in administrative, professional, and technical occupations, to federal training programs;

3. to authorize federal agencies administering grant-in-aid programs to provide special training for state and local government officials or employees who have responsibilities related to those programs, and to permit state and local governments to use federal funds to establish training courses or to pay educational expenses for officials and employees who have responsibilities related to grant-in-aid programs;

4. to assist state and local governments through grants to improve their systems of personnel administration;

5. to authorize grants to state and local governments for the development and implementation of approved employee-training plans and for government service fellowships for selected em-

ployees for university-level graduate study;

6. to authorize the Civil Service Commission to join with state and local governments, upon request, in cooperative recruitment and examination activities and to provide technical advice and assistance;

7. to give the consent in advance of Congress to interstate compacts designed to improve personnel administration and to provide training for state and local government employees;

8. to authorize the temporary interchange of federal, state, and local personnel.

The passage of this act would not solve all the manpower problems faced by state and local governments. In certain professional fields, there will be a shortage for many years in both government and private employment. But its terms are geared to meeting the personnel needs for specific intergovernmental programs currently of great importance in the United States, and its passage would help equip personnel administration in the states and localities to handle more effectively their assignments in the joint programs currently in force to meet the needs of the American people.

But though the federal government can help, it cannot carry the burden of reform by itself. If the partnership concept has any validity as it applies to the functioning of American government, the states and local governments must act simultaneously to attack the problem outlined here. Clearly, former Vice President Humphrey declared, the "states and localities must assume their full share of the burden of upgrading intergovernmental administration and equipping themselves for mounting management responsibilities. . . . [they] must launch their own attack on . . . the short supply of fully professional personnel." "Public administration in a federal system," Humphrey continued, "is never a simple task. A certain amount of inefficiency is always a by-product of a system that takes pride in its diversity and steadfastly adheres to the decentralized principles of its constitutional and political life. Our goal, then, must be less friction, less conflict, less duplication, and all within the context of a partnership that is fully collaborative." [47]

47. Humphrey, "A More Perfect Union," *op. cit.*, p. 328.

Nor is that all. Part of the difficulty lies in the fact that just at the time that new demands arise for governmental personnel, and for changes in administration which only they are likely to bring about, heavy demands are also being made by the private, industrial, and educational sectors in American life. American colleges and universities have not kept an adequate supply of new personnel coming, nor have they delved as deeply as they might into the research side of administration. Thus government at all levels shares the administrative and personnel problem with the private sector; both groups are faced with finding solutions at the same time. It has only recently been recognized that adequate liaison and coordination must be provided somehow between government at all levels and commercial, industrial, and educational units in the private sector if solutions satisfactory to both sides are to be devised.

This entire discussion has been based on the assumption that the grant-in-aid device will continue to be used into the indefinite future. There is of course the option of abandoning it. But, although there have been many complaints against it, the grant-in-aid remains the most acceptable means so far found to translate nationally accepted goals into action programs. It has made a tremendous contribution to the capacity of state and local governments to cope with the problems of modern society; if those units of government gripe some, they are likely unwilling to give up the grant-in-aid system in exchange for something else of unknown problems and effects. Assuming, then, that the grant-in-aid remains a part of the American scene, the emphasis in American administration will remain intergovernmental. For the grant-in-aid involves joint action and the utilization of governmental manpower at all levels. In that very fact lies its great challenge. Its effective use is predicated on intergovernmental cooperation, and it is painfully evident that that can come about only if the management and manpower arrangements of all levels of government are compatible and if each is capable of bearing its full share of the load. In the final analysis, this is why management and manpower constitute a crisis in contemporary federalism.[48]

48. A paraphrase of a paragraph in Senator Muskie's Remarks on Introducing the Intergovernmental Personnel Act, *op. cit.,* p. 1.

VIII

THE PROBLEM OF
FINANCES

AMERICAN FEDERALISM was probably foreordained to have financial problems. As Albert Lepawsky wrote in 1940, "The primary difficulty about administering—let alone planning—American public revenues is the fact that the American tax dollar is spent three ways. . . . No single level of government may be called the controlling revenue authority of the country."[1] The states and their local subdivisions, even in colonial days, had been permitted to tax independently of any central authority, and by 1787 their "right" to do so was unassailable. The framers of the Constitution did not attempt to question it. Nor did they take up the problem of distributing revenue between the new national government and the states, although that question was a central reason for holding the Constitutional Convention in the first place. The Articles of Confederation had failed miserably to provide a source of revenue for the national government independent of the states, and the states had proved reluctant to grant money voluntarily, despite the many requisitions submitted by Congress. As a result, the national government was hard pressed for operating funds from the outset and had to resort to borrowing. But the states had not only been penurious with the national government, they

---

1. Albert Lepawsky, "America's Tax Dollar—A Key Problem in Governmental Reconstruction," *Annals of the American Academy of Political and Social Science* 207:185 (January 1940).

had also entered into a fiscal competition with each other which threatened to Balkanize the young nation. The urgency of the Philadelphia Convention was in large part due to the financial crisis which was rapidly developing as a consequence of both these forces in late 1786 and early 1787.

Most of the delegates to the Convention were convinced that the states should no longer function as intermediary between the people of the United States and the national government, and that the national government should have tax sources of its own. Thus the very first power listed in Article I, section 8, of the new Constitution was an almost unlimited [2] grant of power to Congress "to lay and collect taxes, duties, imposts, and excises. . . ." Elsewhere the framers of the Constitution placed limitations on the states' power to tax, but these were not onerous.[3] Nowhere, however, did they broach the subject of the relation between the new national and the old state powers to tax. As the Constitution came from the framers, it left the power to tax as a concurrent power to be shared by the two main levels of government, but gave no specific directions as to how that sharing might be accomplished.

For a good many years that lack did not make much difference. The national government began at once to levy a tariff and a number of excise taxes, and these, with the increasing income from the sale of public lands, provided sufficient revenue.[4] The states for their part turned to the use of direct taxes, chiefly taxes on real property. They allocated some of their taxing power to their local units, and all three levels managed to get along with no great amount of difficulty. Federal aid began to be extended to state projects quite early,[5] and for the most part a happy sort of

2. Article I, section 9, required direct taxes, if levied, to be laid "in proportion to the census" and forbade the imposition of any taxes or duties on exports. Indirect taxes were also required to be uniform.

3. Article I, section 10, denies state power to "lay any imposts or duties on imports or exports" or "to lay any duty of tonnage," save with the consent of Congress.

4. The Federalist Congress did adopt a direct tax on dwelling houses, land, and slaves in 1798, but it was scrapped by the first Jefferson Administration. The same taxes were reintroduced during the War of 1812 but were dropped in 1817.

5. See Daniel Elazar, *The American Partnership, op. cit.*, for a detailed discussion of this development.

fiscal balance seemed to have been achieved. Conflicts were settled early in accordance with the principles of a series of decisions by the Supreme Court under John Marshall, which, working from the premise of national supremacy, unequivocably declared the immunity of the national government and its instrumentalities from state taxation.[6] The doctrine was later made reciprocal and extended to local governments as well. The early conflicts were not particularly sharp ones, however, for the national government did not assume many functions that required great expenditures (with the exception of the Civil War) and so did not often compete with the states for available sources of revenue.

Looking back, the period from 1789 to 1913 seems idyllic. For the purposes of government which the people then considered to be desirable and necessary, sufficient income (although some of the states tended to live beyond tax revenues and borrowed heavily, a few to the point of bankruptcy) combined with a spirit of implicit cooperation made the fiscal problem negligible. That period ended abruptly in the first years of the Wilson Administration, however, first with the passage of the Sixteenth Amendment, enabling the national government to tax directly without having to meet the requirement of apportionment among the states, and then with the first use of the grant-in-aid, in which the national government proposed a program (in this case establishing an agricultural extension service) and offered large grants to states willing to participate. The income tax, which was levied almost at once after the amendment was ratified, provided "a readily expandable source of revenue which, as World War I demonstrated, could funnel billions into the national Treasury," and before long "public opinion and official thinking seized upon [the conditional grant] as a basis for new social and economic programs" combining national money with state and local needs.[7]

6. *McCulloch* v. *Maryland* 4 Wheaton 316 (1819), *Osborn* v. *Bank of the United States* 9 Wheaton 738 (1824), and *Weston* v. *Charleston* 2 Peters 449 (1829). Marshall, it should be noted, was not the originator of the doctrine of intergovernmental immunity. Article IV of the Northwest Ordinance of 1787 specified that no state might impose a tax on lands which were United States property.

7. Grodzins, *The American System, op. cit.,* pp. 42–43.

Although the twenties were not a propitious time for governmental activity of any sort, the lesson was not forgotten, and it was brought to bear at once in fighting the Depression and mounting the New Deal.

The happy fiscal balance of the nineteenth century was destroyed not only by the radical shift of fiscal and program powers to the national government as a result of the income tax and the categorical grant-in-aid, but also by the devastating effects of the great depression. The fiscal resources of both state and local governments quickly proved inadequate to meet the exigencies of the time. (It should be pointed out that the states contributed to the catastrophe by having long denied themselves and their local subdivisions flexibility in fiscal matters, imposing a whole set of inhibiting constitutional and legal restrictions on the power to tax and borrow.) The national government had to step in and fill the breach. It did so at first hesitantly, apologetically, avowedly on a temporary basis, but when under Franklin Roosevelt and subsequent presidents it became evident that national programs of recovery and reform could be achieved only by a large degree of nationalization of financial direction and control, the national government acted overtly and directly. One of the most impressive changes in the United States' history is the shift in fiscal balance thus brought about.

The essence of the problem today, as for the past generation and more, is what Walter W. Heller has called a "fiscal mismatch." John Kenneth Galbraith describes it in these words:

Given the tax structure, the revenues of all levels of government grow with the growth of the economy . . . However . . . [the] revenues of the federal government, because of its heavy reliance on income taxes, increase more than proportionately with private economic growth . . . In the States and localities . . . tax revenues—this is especially true of the General Property Tax—increase less than proportionately with increased private production. Budgeting too is far more closely circumscribed than in the case of the federal government—only the monetary authority [i.e., the national government] enjoys the pleasant privilege of underwriting its own loans. Because of this, increased services for states and localities regularly pose the question of more revenues and more taxes . . . One consequence is that the federal government remains under constant pressure to use its superior revenue position to help redress the balance at the lower levels of government.[8]

The difficulty is that the national government has access to high-yield revenue sources which are unfortunately expended largely on defense and defense-related activities, while state and local governments, with much less tax potential, are expected to provide more and more services for the American people. The problem looks different depending on which level does the viewing. The national government sees the major problem as weak and indifferent state and local governments who are not spending what is available to them so as to receive the most for each expended dollar; the states see themselves caught between exorbitantly high demands for tax revenues for national purposes on the one hand and increasingly strident cries for additional revenues from hard-pressed cities on the other, leaving the states little leeway in the middle; while local governments feel themselves at the bottom of the fiscal totem pole, restricted by stringent state requirements and seeing federal aid diverted to state capitals and not directed to meet their needs. However it is viewed, the focal point is that there has been a long sustained intergovernmental conflict in the fiscal arena.[9]

A number of factors affect that conflict. Without making an attempt to put them in any order of priority, six such factors must be discussed.

1. The conflict is more apparent than real, in that the three levels of government are fighting over what appear to be limited tax resources. Nothing could be farther from the truth. "The first thing we can do," David Walker has declared "is to recognize our potential capacity to finance all our governmental needs. With an economy producing at [its present] rate . . . , with forecasts that will reach $1 trillion by 1976, none of us should doubt that the dollars are there." [10] The difficulty

8. John Kenneth Galbraith, *The Affluent Society*, A Mentor Book (New York: New American Library, 1958), pp. 206–207.
9. See George F. Break, *Intergovernmental Fiscal Relations in the United States* (Washington: The Brookings Institution, 1967).
10. David B. Walker, "Cooperative Federalism: Intergovernmental Fiscal Aspects," an address before the Annual Meeting of the National Association of State Budget Officers, Honolulu, September 7, 1966, quoted

stems from the conception most Americans in both public and private life hold about the over-all taxing and spending power of government in this country. Part of the American conventional wisdom is that governments' share of the gross national product is necessarily strictly limited, that most of the increase in the general prosperity of the nation should flow directly into private hands and remain there. It therefore seems an anomaly to have government plead lack of funds as the reason for not acting, or for acting in only partial response to a large number of public needs, in the midst of the affluent society Galbraith describes so well. It is as if national wealth must be protected at all costs against government if that wealth is not to be sacrificed. Needless to say, the several levels of government which must share the limited amount made available to all of them inevitably quarrel among themselves as to who gets what and how much, and the very size of the national government seems to give it the advantage in the struggle, making it necessary to place it under special restraints so that it will not gobble up the prize all by itself.

This is but another way of saying that Americans have first and foremost "an abiding faith in the virtues of economy, thrift and individual responsibility. . . ." They are notoriously suspicious of government and distrust it particularly as a spending agency. They profess much to prefer self-reliance (though what self-reliance consists of in today's world is never carefully spelled out). "I, as a citizen," Governor Ronald Reagan of California commented in an interview early in 1968, "still have a great deal of faith that government can't possibly match that great body of citizenry out there as to genius and ability and power to get things done, if you just mobilize them and turn them loose on a problem." [11] Reagan speaks for many Americans who, even though faced with rising demands and needs for public expenditure, remain reluctant to open the public purse and continue to insist on "minimum budgets with no frill." The result is a "deep-

---

in *Congressional Record* 112:26517 (October 19, 1966). Mr. Walker was at that time staff director of the subcommittee on intergovernmental relations of the Senate Committee on Government Operations.

11. Governor Ronald Reagan in an interview with James Reston, quoted in the *International Herald Tribune*, March 5, 1968, p. 3.

seated schizoid condition" in the American people.[12] They have turned over to their governments a large number of functions in recent years, which they expect to be carried out in an exemplary manner (and criticize if they are not). But they have not altered their basic attitudes toward government spending and so continually fail to provide adequate resources on which those governments may draw. Perhaps reluctance to pay taxes has not reached the proportions in the United States it did in post-war France, where the Poujadist party won a number of seats in the National Assembly on an out-and-out platform of refusal to pay taxes, but it has a deep root in the American past and still affects both public and private thinking about taxes. Thus there is, William G. Colman has concluded, "an increasing gap between public service needs and the willingness of local and especially State political leadership and the voters at large to impose the taxes necessary to support the new services." [13]

2. A second factor affecting today's fiscal mismatch involves basic philosophies of government. On the one side, proponents of national action argue that the general welfare clause, attached to the constitutional power to lay and collect taxes,[14] amounts to a separate and broad authorization for the national government to spend money to meet the social and economic needs existing in the nation. Certainly pressure groups and both major political parties have embraced the idea at various times in our history, especially in recent years, and the Supreme Court has put its imprimatur on the theory as well. It did so as early as 1923, when in *Massachusetts* v. *Mellon* [15] it declined to take a case testing the validity of an early grant to the states in the area of child wel-

12. The earlier quotation in this paragraph and the last one are from Frederick C. Mosher and Orville F. Poland, *The Costs of American Government: Facts, Trends, Myths* (New York: Dodd Mead, 1964), p. 2.

13. William G. Colman, "Creative Federalism: The Facts of Life," an address delivered to the Conference on Public Administration, University of Oregon, September 7, 1966, reprinted in *Congressional Record* 112: 23738-23740 (September 30, 1966), p. 23738. Colman is executive director of the Advisory Commission on Intergovernmental Relations.

14. The other two parts of the attached phrase, "to pay the debts of the United States" and "to provide for the common defense," seem to be more limited in scope and have not been much in contest over the years.

15. 262 US 447 (1923).

fare. In 1937, in *Helvering* v. *Davis*,[16] the Court went on to say that the discretion as to how to spend for the general welfare

belongs to Congress. . . . Nor is the concept of the general welfare static. Needs that were narrow or parochial a century ago may be interwoven in our day with the well-being of the nation. What is critical or urgent changes with the times.

In this view, the national government is under no disability at all as it seeks ways to spend the money it collects so as to benefit the American people. But if this so-called "liberal interpretation" of the general welfare clause has won wide acceptance, there has always been a cry from the other side that except for certain clearly national programs, where national power is conceded, the national government is limited in the role it may play to enhance the general welfare by the necessity of yielding to the states altogether in some areas—education and the relation between the races are prime examples—and of sharing with the states most other responsibilities for the public good. According to this view, federalism involves both a reserved area for independent state action—or inaction, if that be the will of the states—and "a large degree of acquiescence in local values upon measures supported by the nation. There have been no sadder examples of this than the racial discrimination exercised in federal programs in the South." [17] This "conservative" or "states' rights" position denies the old adage that he who pays the piper calls the tune and tends to freeze the program possibilities of the national government into a mold out of some indefinite past. With this view held by a sizable majority of members of Congress (and often a majority and sometimes chairmen of the key Congressional committees), as well as many state leaders, some leading industrialists, and a few presidential hopefuls, all of them constantly at work to convert their belief into practice, conflict in the fiscal arena is inevitable.

3. From the point of view of state and local governments, the present fiscal crisis in American federalism arises, ironically, out of the very grant-in-aid programs the national government has developed to assist them. Real help has been received and acknowledged with gratitude by state and local officials. But the use

16. 301 US 619 (1937), at 641.
17. McConnell, *Private Power & American Democracy, op. cit.,* p. 358.

of grants-in-aid raises two different sets of problems for state and local units. An increasing percentage of grant-in-aid programs go beyond helping states and local units carry on their own programs to offering support for new activities the national government suggests be added. Here the states and local units are given unpleasant alternatives: either ignore the availability of the new funds and so appear blind to the needs they were designed to help alleviate (needs, it should be noted, of which most state and local officials are only too well aware in their own jurisdictions—no one accuses the national government of dreaming up "pie in the sky" programs), or accept them and be placed in an even tighter financial squeeze than before by having to find somewhere the matching funds conditional to the grant. Since most state and local budgets are devised with little or no flexibility, this is often a most difficult thing to accomplish.

There is a second problem: William G. Colman notes that state and local units have "been helped but in an increasingly inefficient fashion by Federal functional grant-in-aid programs . . . [which] bring with them severe problems of fiscal equity and administrative management. The grants are disbursed under widely varying formulas that bear no apparently logical relationship to one another. Also, the sheer number of these grants is making coordination at Federal, State, and local levels increasingly difficult." [18] The products of a score or more Congressional committees (and behind them hundreds of diverse pressures and interests), the many grants-in-aid do not stand together as a "program" but rather are offered separately, with the result that each seems as imperative and attractive as the next. Not only is discriminating choice difficult, but once some have been chosen, the disparities in their terms constitute a growing irritant to administrators up and down the line. No single method of administration satisfies them all, which adds to the burden state and local units already labor under in carrying out their duties.

4. A fourth factor affecting the problem of fiscal federalism is the competition for and conflict over tax sources that has marked the recent fiscal scene. Somehow it came to be an article of faith early in United States history that a limited number

18. *Ibid.*

of tax possibilities were available to all governments. Since then that number has been increased, but only after a considerable struggle to win acceptance. Taxes first must meet the generally recognized "rules" of the revenue game: that only taxes which are based on ability to pay are permissible, that taxes ought to hit those similarly situated equally, that ease and economy of collection and administration should be taken into account, and that only those taxes which can be levied in ways convenient for the taxpayer, which involve as little uncertainty and ill effect as possible, and which do not burden him unduly, may be employed. They also must take into account modern economic theory, which holds that taxation beyond a certain level exerts a repressive effect on national economic health, so that tax *reduction* emerges as a positive good, a goal constantly to be striven for if the nation's prosperity is to be maintained and developed. Moreover, since it is felt that the number of tax possibilities are limited, care must be taken to divide them among the several levels of government so that none will be without a major tax source. Thus the general property tax is held not to be available to either the national government or the states in deference to the tax requirements of local government; the sales tax has been preempted by the states, though some local use of sales taxes is tolerated; and it is generally conceded by the other two levels that the national government has claim to the major share of the personal income tax.

But these are only generalizations. In fact, taxes are most often enacted, not in response to the dictates of any widely accepted canons of tax "science," but as the result of irresistible political and economic pressures. It is not possible to isolate taxation from politics and the functioning of pressure groups. Moreover, tax "policies" are developed independently, in splendid isolation from each other, so that competition is virtually inevitable, despite the rough allocation of sources.

Experience . . . [has] demonstrated an extreme lack of coordination between national and state fiscal policies . . . From 1930 [on], organized efforts at fiscal coordination multiplied . . . Yet, except for some state use of national tax administration facilities, some interstate exchange of reports and information, and a certain amount of working cooperation between national and state tax officers, no important measure of fiscal coordination was achieved before World War II.[19]

Some improvement has been made since the war, but there is still a long way to go to bring about any semblance of an integrated tax system in the United States.

The strong competition between the national government and the states is far from the only competition. If states share a general feeling of competency to conduct certain programs to meet public need, they rival one another in the drive to finance them. For many years, states have competed with one another for tax advantages. "[A] fact of life for State and local government," William Colman has observed, "is an acute sensitivity to tax competition for business and industry. Although the importance of tax differentials to business success is grossly exaggerated, the impact of the competitive tax argument on legislatures and local governing boards can hardly be overstated. Fear of losing business to another State or city haunts every political leader, and spokesmen for business have become very skilled in exploiting his fears." [20] Moreover, the whole matter of taxing nonresidents has been productive of conflict since mobility came to be one of the leading characteristics of modern American life.

There is also a great deal of state-local conflict in the tax field, growing out of the fact that the rules of local taxation are set by the state governments. This conflict is especially sharp between the governments of rapidly growing urban municipalities and state governments. The plight of the American city does not need to be described in detail here. Suffice it to say that the needs for new and expanded services are heavy and increasing. To meet most of them, vast amounts of money are required. But the states have been slow to yield to municipal demands for more tax sources. They have neither granted significantly large new tax or borrowing authority nor developed large-scale state aid programs to relieve local distress. In some cases, when the state has permitted an expansion of municipal nonproperty taxes, it has followed by cutting down on the amount of state aid tendered. Far too in-

19. Grodzins, *The American System, op. cit.,* p. 55.
20. Colman, "Creative Federalism," *op. cit.,* p. 23739.

frequently have states developed any kind of rational approach to local fiscal problems; instead, they have dealt with them, as with most problems, including their own budgets, on an *ad hoc,* sporadic, and unplanned basis. By now, the municipal-state tax conflict is a given in American political life.

Finally, there is interlocal tax conflict, at least to the extent that rural areas look askance at the rising demands on state and county revenue sources made by urban units of government. They tend to unite in state legislatures, where they have long been dominant, to keep the status quo or at least to slow down the ability of urban units to adjust to changing conditions. The result is that the fiscal crisis is most severe just where the needs are the greatest. Despite the fact that there may be as much as 80 per cent of the taxable wealth, business activity, and income tax collection in the nation's metropolitan areas, the amounts made available to the admittedly fragmented local government units by penurious and rural-oriented state legislatures meet a fraction of their needs. "Inevitably there has to be a transferral of tax funds across jurisdictional lines to meet the problems that demand solution" in the nation's metropolitan areas. "The transferring and enforcing agency can be either the State or the Federal government. The decision as to which it shall be, or whether by partnership, rests with the State government" [21]—specifically, with the state legislatures.

Local governments may have the least enviable position of all in the federal system, and their lowly position is nowhere better revealed than in the fiscal area. As Mayor Lindsay of New York has explained it, "Many expenses are mandated on [New York City,] without consultation, by the Federal and state governments." [22] While in a strict sense no federal expenses are mandated on a local unit, in another sense Lindsay is entirely correct. New York City, for example, is a little Washington—and not so little at that—in terms of the number of federal offices, agencies, and installations there. For the most part they were located in the city without its urging and without prior arrangements for sharing the additional city expenses incident thereto.

21. *Ibid.,* p. 23738.
22. Quoted in *The New York Times,* February 3, 1967, p. 19.

Those federal offices are concentrated in New York below For-
ty-Second Street, a congested area where the city is already hard
put to preserve some semblance of order. In addition to having to
supply parking and/or transit for the thousands of federal employees, as well as citizen access to their offices, the city must
provide water and trash-collection services, protect property, and
perform the myriad other services it offers its own residents. Nor
is New York exceptional in this regard: many localities are the
seats of federal activities, and though the national government has
provided in some cases for special aid to these "impacted" areas,
generally no provisions are made to help bear the burdens thus
imposed. States have always regarded local units of government
as extensions of themselves and have required them to perform
what are essentially state functions at local expense. Municipal
courts provide one example, the function of testing weights and
measures another. To some extent the states may regard their re-
mission of the property tax and their permission to utilize other
taxes as sufficient recompense for local performance of state duties. But there is basic truth in Mayor Lindsay's assertion that the
states have been niggardly in providing help to local units of government for the functions they perform in lieu of the states
themselves.

5. Certainly the fiscal crisis in the federal system cannot be
considered apart from the failure of governmental units at all levels to come fully to grips with their own tax problems. Critics
have long pointed out the difficulties resulting from the way revenues and expenditures are dealt with in the national legislative
process. United in the budget presented to Congress by the President, they are quickly torn apart and confided to jealously separate committees and subcommittees in both Houses of Congress.
Some of the hardest lobbying in Washington is done before each
individual enclave, and every opportunity is used to take advantage of the natural rivalry between committees and the two
Houses to reap the largest private advantage. In the process, all
semblance of a coherent financial plan for the nation in the coming year is lost.

Moreover, through the years, federal tax laws have become
voluminous; the Internal Revenue Code of 1954, as amended, is

the basic law today, running over 1,100 closely printed pages. Some of its sentences run over 1,000 words. When John Brooks did a study of the income tax for *The New Yorker*, he concluded that the code is phrased "in the sort of jargon that stuns the mind and disheartens the spirit. . . . One of the most marked traits of the Code . . . is its complexity. . . ."[23] It is also marked by inequities and loopholes, giving advantage to some taxpayers over others. Tax revision has become of basic importance both to fair administration and to the most effective functioning of the federal tax system. In the course of that revision, consideration might well be given to a number of types of taxes not used now by the national government, among them the turnover or gross receipts tax, the sales tax at several or all stages of production and distribution, the value-added tax, the commodity tax, an investment tax, and a tax on personal expenditures rather than on personal income.[24]

For the states and local governments, the situation is even worse. The budgetary process is even less systematized at those levels; the chief executive often lacks effective budgetary powers altogether, and the legislative bodies are equally, if not more, divided and subject to lobbying. And in tax administration, most states and local governments are far behind the national government. For it cannot be argued successfully that federal taxes are poorly administered. On the contrary, tax collection is one of the most efficient parts of the entire national government operation. Not so with the states, and less so certainly with local governments. Tax administration at both levels suffers from the general deficiencies encountered in administration there. Moreover, state and local taxes tend to defy systematization. Both levels have used a scatter-gun approach, grabbing for revenue wherever it might be, rather than developing any over-all concept of taxation. Some taxes are imposed because they are traditional; others are used or avoided as virtually dictated by pressure groups; seldom do legislatures coordinate and present taxes as a part of governing policy of the state or local unit; often no clear picture of their expected

23. John Brooks, "The Tax," *The New Yorker*, April 10, 1965, p. 72.
24. See for a discussion of the possibilities The Tax Foundation, *Reconstructing the Federal Tax System: A Guide to the Issues* (New York, 1964).

yield is held by anyone in the legislature, to say nothing of those in the state administration.

As suggested earlier, state and local units share the national government's aversion to leaving the safety of familiar tax paths. It is a brave political leader indeed who is willing to recommend either higher rates or new taxes to his constituency. Thus, though early in 1967 "Mayor [John] Lindsay and his top fiscal aides expressed determination . . . to fight for more state aid in an all-out effort to avoid new taxes or make [the] deep cuts in services" which would otherwise be necessary, the city budget director described added revenues the city might obtain from such action as "distasteful choices," to be avoided if possible.[25] But even more than the national government, cities have failed to utilize the full potential of the taxes already available to them. The New York City budget director told a *New York Times* reporter, in discussing the 1967 city budget, that "the city had the power to levy certain taxes it had not chosen so far to invoke. These include an overnight parking charge and an auto use tax." The budget director dismissed them as "bits and pieces" unlikely to solve the city's fiscal problem and likely to anger the citizens.[26] If cities do not even utilize what taxing power is available to them, they will hardly be imaginative about alternatives.

Finally, of course, it must be recognized that the very heavy burden of federal taxation "is a major roadblock to increased state and local revenues, probably the most serious obstacle of all. Against the background of high federal tax rates, even the most marginal rise in state and local levies is likely to seem onerous and to arouse intense opposition." [27]

It is necessary to refer to some figures in order to see the full dimensions of the fiscal crisis in American federalism.[28] Tables 8.1 and 8.2 are mostly self-explanatory. They reveal that ever since the end of World War II state and local spending have been in-

25. Charles G. Bennett, reporting in *The New York Times*, February 3, 1967, p. 19.
26. Quoted in *ibid*.
27. "The Financial Dilemma of American Federalism," a study published in the September 1966 *Morgan Guaranty Survey*, reprinted in *Congressional Record* 112: A5045–5047 (September 30, 1966).
28. For the fullest set of statistics concerning state and local finances,

TABLE 8.1 *State and Local Government Expenditures (millions of dollars)*

	1950	1965	Per cent increase 1950–1965
Education	7,177	28,971	303.7
Highways	3,803	12,221	221.4
Welfare	2,940	6,315	114.8
Health and hospitals	1,748	5,361	206.7
Police, fire, and sanitation	2,098	6,215	196.2
Conservation and recreation	974	2,834	190.0
Interest on debt	458	2,490	443.7
Debt repayments	1,250	5,040	303.2
Utility and liquor store costs	2,739	7,058	157.7
Housing and urban renewal	452	1,250	176.5
Other *	4,072	14,805	263.6
Total	27,711	92,560	234.0

* *Other* includes outlays for purposes such as libraries, administration, contributions to retirement funds not included elsewhere, *etc.*

creasing at the rate of 8 to 9 per cent a year. Between 1950 and 1965 alone, as Table 8.1 indicates, state and local expenditures rose over 230 per cent, reflecting not only a desire to catch up on numerous programs postponed because of the Depression and then World War II, but also an increase in population and a shift in the population's age distribution in the direction of youthful and elderly persons (the two age groups which require the costliest public services). The problem is exacerbated by the fact that modern Americans demand more and better public services of their state and local governments. Their children in greater numbers undertake longer courses of study in the public schools; more police service is needed for a crowded and mobile urban population; streets need widening and narrow two-lane roads replacing to accommodate modern cars and trucks; public health services must be expanded and they cost more due to population

see Advisory Commission on Intergovernmental Relations, *State and Local Finances. Significant Features 1966 to 1969.* An Information Reprint, M43 (Washington, 1968).

TABLE 8.2 *State and Local Government*
Receipts (millions of dollars)

	1950	1965	Per cent increase 1950–1965
Taxes	15,914	51,578	224.1
Individual income	788	4,090	419.0
Corporation income	593	1,929	225.3
Sales and gross receipts	5,154	17,118	232.1
Property	7,349	22,918	211.8
Other	2,030	5,521	172.0
Charges and miscellaneous	2,511	11,735	367.3
Utility and liquor store receipts	2,712	6,355	134.3
Federal aid	2,486	11,029	343.6
Long-term debt issues	3,838	11,249	193.1
Increase in short-term debt	250	614	145.6
Total	*27,711*	*92,560*	*234.0*

SOURCE: Adapted from United States Commerce Department figures, given in *Congressional Record* 112:A5046, September 30, 1966.

growth, urbanization, and advances in medical knowledge; as people move in ever greater numbers to urban centers, vast improvements and additions to community public facilities such as parks, libraries, and water supply are urgently needed. As all these and more service needs have been met in recent years, state and local government has become the nation's largest growth industry. The rise in state and local expenditures has been impressive, measured by any standard. Those expenditures have risen faster than has the gross national product, and far faster than federal spending. Even so, the backlog of unmet needs continues to increase.

Moreover, as demands intensified, unit costs rose. The cost of equipment and construction skyrocketed. Salaries of state and local employees had to be raised and raised again to keep them competitive in the job market. As a result of all this, total state and local spending seems likely to amount to $130 billion in 1970.[29]

29. Colman, "Creative Federalism." *op. cit.*

The difficulties are compounded on the revenue side. State and local governments, taken collectively (there is, of course, a wide variation from state to state and from local government to local government), have made great efforts to raise their tax income. State and local tax revenues rose 224 per cent between 1950 and 1965 (see Table 8.2), and during the decade 1957–1967 state and local governments increased their general revenues from $38.2 billion to $91.6 billion, or 113 per cent. But expenditures keep rising even faster. By conservative estimate, a gap of $15 billion between revenues and expenditures may have developed by 1970. The likelihood of state and local governments filling it by increased taxation is bleak. To keep raising property, sales, and other consumer taxes is not only unpopular but poor economic and social policy. All states are plagued by fear of driving businesses out of the state by tax increases. And politicians are naturally vulnerable if they become advocates of higher taxes. The only way state and local governments have been able to meet even partially the responsibilities placed upon them is by heavy resort to borrowing and to federal aid. In 1946, federal aid provided 7.3 per cent of state and local receipts; in 1954, 10 per cent; and in 1967, 17 per cent. In money terms, federal grants increased nearly sixfold between 1953 and 1967, from $2.7 billion in 1953 to $15.2 billion in 1967. As we have seen, federal aid brings disadvantages; so does borrowing. With large debts, state and local governments find interest payments constituting a rapidly growing component of their annual budgets. Many jurisdictions have already reached their constitutional or legal limitations on indebtedness and are having to employ even more costly devices, such as revenue bonds, to get around them. Thus borrowing becomes more expensive and legally more difficult as it is relied on more heavily. While popular, it does not offer either a permanent or a satisfactory solution to the revenue problem. Indeed, it would appear that the limits of its utility have about been reached. Both sound financial practice and the necessity of legal compliance should limit future expansion in that quarter.

"This persistent lag of revenues behind requirements accounts for the pressures that have become the bane of governors and mayors. It creates the need for periodic tax increases that have contributed so conspicuously to political mortality among state and [local] political executives." [30] And it provides the excuse to turn to Washington for further aid, which only compounds the overall problem. This brings us back to the central issue: how to find a way to divert some portion of the easy-come federal revenues to the hard-pressed state and local units of government. The urgent problem in terms of American federalism is finding a way to inject into the financial bloodstreams of the ailing state and local partners in the federal operation a stimulant sufficient to keep them operating and fulfilling their important roles until such time as broadscale reform may take place. It is first necessary to get the patients out of shock; when that is accomplished, thought can be given to their long-term recovery.

The solution currently receiving the most discussion is the development of some form of tax-sharing between the national government and the states and their local subdivisions. "After years of wandering in the wilderness," Walter W. Heller wrote recently, "Federal-state-local fiscal relations are at last on the threshold of a promised land created by vigorous economic growth and balanced political reapportionment. Growth is generating a flow of Federal revenues which will permit the study of major new fiscal coordination devices to move from the barren ground of hypothetical discussion—where it has languished for thirty or forty years—to the fertile ground of practical, fundable proposals. And reapportionment will strengthen the legislative base for new initiatives for revitalizing the states." [31]

If Heller's two premises are valid ones—that the national government will have so great a revenue escalation that it can afford to share the "take" with the other units in the federal system, and that reapportioned legislatures will in fact take a different tack as far as state and local abilities to spend are concerned—the case for

30. *Ibid.*
31. Walter W. Heller, *New Dimensions of Political Economy* (New York: Norton, 1967), p. 117. This book should be read in its entirety by students of intergovernmental fiscal relations. See also Walter W. Heller and Joseph A. Pechman, *Questions and Answers on Revenue Sharing*, The Brookings Institution Reprint 135 (Washington, 1969); "Revenue Sharing and Its Alternatives: What Future for Fiscal Federalism?" *Tax Review*, December, 1967, Vol. 28, No. 12, a publication of the Tax Foundation, Inc.; and Leonard Opperman, "Aid for the States: Is Revenue Sharing the Answer?" *The Review of Politics* 30:43-50 (January 1968).

a tax-sharing program seems strong. It should be noted at the outset, however, that these are two very large ifs; since Heller began to discuss the possibility, the war in Vietnam, inflation, and the drain on the American dollar have escalated to the point where economy and restrictions are now in order. It may already be a moot point whether a federal surplus—which is basic to the Heller scheme—is a real possibility any time in the immediate future. And whether reapportioned legislatures will provide improvements is equally problematical. William G. Colman has commented on the "shift of State . . . legislative control to the suburbs" as the first result of reapportionment. "There is a notorious lack of identification between the suburbs and most central cities, which may well mean the continued neglect of the latter, despite the primary urgency of their problems." It is not at all impossible that a suburb-central city conflict will replace the rural-urban conflict of yesteryear.[32] That the final outcome would be any improvement over the past is at least doubtful.

But assume that Heller's two premises can be relied upon. What are the "practical, fundable proposals" of which he speaks? A number of proposals have been made. The one offered by Heller himself, calling for "per capita revenue sharing," has received the most attention. He would go back to the early federal "fiscal dividends" to the states, only he would systematize them and establish them not as a matter of federal largesse but as a matter of right. "In capsule, the . . . plan would distribute a specified portion of the Federal individual income tax to the states each year on a per capita basis, with next to no strings attached. This distribution would be over and above existing and future conditional grants."[33] Heller visualizes an annual set-aside of one to two per cent of the federal income tax base (the amount reported on federal income tax forms as net taxable income). The sums to be given to the states would be automatically placed in a trust fund, from which periodic distributions would be made in a manner separate from the annual budget and appropriation process. Distribution would be strictly on the basis of population, although Heller sees the desirability of setting aside a small percentage of

32. Colman, "Creative Federalism," *op. cit.*, p. 23738.
33. Heller, *New Dimensions of Political Economy, op. cit.*, pp. 145-147.

the fund for supplements to states with low per capita income, a high incidence of poverty, or other specially severe economic deficiencies. Upon receipt of the monies, the states would be virtually free to use them as they wish. There would of course be auditing, accounting, and reporting requirements, and there would be no reneging on the application of Title VI of the Civil Rights Act of 1965 which requires that federal funds not be employed in racially segregated activities. Heller hopes that even broad program restrictions—to education, health, or community development, for example—would be foresworn, although he feels that a negative restriction barring expenditures for highways might be in order. Once set in motion, the system would presumably continue to operate into the indefinite future and so provide the states (and through them the local units of government) with a firm and increasing fiscal rock on which to base their own fiscal policies.

Much the same idea is embodied in other proposals for tax-sharing. One would be for a fund made up of a one per cent share of federal taxable income reported, from which portions would be distributed to the states on the dual basis of population and the individual state's tax effort, which would be revealed by the ratio of state and local revenues collected to total personal income in the state. A portion of the fund would be set aside for supplementing distribution to the poorer states, as measured by per capita income. Other variants are plans calling for the return of a fixed percentage (most commonly 3 per cent) of federal personal income tax collections in each state to that state, with an equalization factor to assist the poorer states and with no federal controls imposed; and the proposal that the federal government appropriate to the states a fixed sum annually for a period of years (say $5 billion a year) with no restrictions except that the states would have to develop and follow through on plans to reorganize and modernize their own governments and those of their local subdivisions. Control of the program might lie in the hands of regional groupings of governors who would have the power to approve or disapprove of a state government's modernization program. Their approval would be necessary to qualify a state for its share of the federal appropriation.

Such proposals are offered as ways of providing state and local governments with an additional revenue source which would grow as the economy develops and expands. It is argued that the adoption of one of them would help free states from undue competition with other states in the tax arena; would supply the less prosperous states with enough supplemental income to enable them to provide at least minimum standards of basic services to their people; and, finally, would facilitate long-range planning by the states, since the amount they received from the trust fund would not be subject to the vagaries of the appropriation process.

With the urging of such persuasive people as Walter Heller and the backing of many members of Congress and of the National Governors Conference, the tax-sharing proposals moved to the front of public discussion as feasible, if partial, remedies for the financial crisis of federalism; and quite possibly, were it not for the escalation of the war in Vietnam and rampaging inflation, one of them might be well down the policy-making ways of Congress toward launching as a law. *Might be*—for there has been a great deal of opposition to the tax-sharing idea on many grounds. It has been pointed out that "the pitfalls of unrestricted revenue allocation are many and are sufficiently complicated to warrant extensive examination. . . . In general, however, states vary so extensively in their attitudes and machinery for providing their own revenues, planning for their own needs, administering their programs, and ensuring the civil and economic rights of their citizens, that any kind of federal revenue sharing that ignores the uneven pace of efforts to modernize state and local tax, finance, planning, and administrative policies would provide windfalls to some states and inequities to others." [34] In summary form, the most frequent arguments against the plan are as follows:

1. There is the nagging fear that, constituted and governed as they are, the states cannot be trusted to spend the new income wisely. To give large sums to them would only be to pour federal funds down the proverbial rathole.

2. There is the danger that the states would use the new in-

34. Muskie, "The Challenge of Creative Federalism," *op. cit.,* p. 14.

come to fund existing state and local services rather than to finance new and/or improved services.

3. There is the feeling among representatives of urban areas in particular that to share tax revenues with the states would do little to relieve the most serious complex of state and local problems, which occurs in metropolitan centers. "Tax sharing is the most dangerous idea in America today," Mayor John F. Collins of Boston declared. A president of the National League of Cities echoed him, saying that "state governments [can] not be trusted to respond to urban needs." [35] To get around this complaint, some proponents of the tax-sharing idea have suggested either a channeling of specified funds to local governments or tax sharing with state and local governments separately.

4. There is opposition on the part of some state and local officials who fear that Congress might come to regard general revenue-sharing programs as a replacement for existing categorical grants-in-aid, to the greater eventual loss of the states. None of the proponents of tax sharing have advocated doing away with the existing grant-in-aid program, however. In Walter Heller's words, "Categorical and general-purpose grants have very different functions, and these cannot be satisfied if the federal system is limited to one or the other . . . Categorical grants are needed because the benefits of many public services 'spill over' from the community in which they are performed to other communities. Expenditures for such services would be too low if financed entirely by state-local sources, because each state or community would tend to pay only for the benefits likely to accrue to its own citizens." General-purpose grants, on the other hand, help equalize the capacity of the states to pay for their own set of services.[36]

5. State and local officials of the more affluent states object to the redistributive aspect of tax-sharing plans.

6. Economic purists raise the point that it is wrong to divorce the responsibility for collecting taxes from responsibility for their use. "In this view, the national government should either continue

35. Quoted in *The New York Times*, February 7, 1967, p. 1.
36. Walter W. Heller, quoted in *Congressional Record* 113: S10633 (August 2, 1967).

to tax and spend or else should reduce its tax take to afford lee-way for states and localities to increase theirs, which presumably they would do in that case.[37]

7. It is asserted that there are higher priorities for the use of federal tax monies than assistance to the states.

8. Some argue that if the national government acquires a sufficient excess of income over expenditures, it is *prima facie* evidence that tax rates are too high and that either the surplus should be applied to debt retirement or taxes should forthwith be reduced. Certainly, runs the argument, no other course in the event of surplus revenues is admissible.

9. Some insist that a system of revenue sharing would not in fact inspire state and local governments to an effort at strengthening their own revenue situation but instead would encourage them to relax and ride with the waves.

As a matter of practical fact, if not because of the weight of opposition arguments, it appears that the drive toward passage of any of the tax-sharing proposals will have hard going, despite the facts that President Nixon came out squarely with his own version of the plan early in his administration [38] and that the legislatures of a good many states have endorsed some variation of the idea.[39]

Tax sharing is not the only alternative which might be adopted in an effort to redress the fiscal mismatch of American federalism, however. A method which has received almost as much support is a system of tax credits. Under this system, individual taxpayers (and possibly corporate taxpayers as well) would be allowed to deduct the aggregate amount of taxes paid to state and local governments in any one year from their federal

37. *Morgan Guaranty Survey, op. cit.*

38. President Nixon's plan provided for 1) ⅓ to 1 per cent of personal taxable income to be appropriated on a rising scale between 1969 and 1976; 2) the funds to be distributed on the basis of each state's share of the nation's population, adjusted to the state's own revenue efforts; 3) a portion of the allocation to each state to be distributed to all general purpose local governments therein; and 4) the states and their local entities to be given virtually complete freedom in the use of such funds, except for auditing, accounting, and reporting requirements. (*Congressional* Record 115:S9957 [August 13, 1969].)

39. See *Congressional Record* 114: E9777–9799 (November 1, 1968).

tax liability. This is already in effect in a limited way: taxpayers may include certain state and local tax levies among their deductions in figuring out their yearly income tax.[40] The tax-credit device would permit a much broader—perhaps total—offset of state and local taxes. Presumably this would encourage state and local units to increase their own taxes, especially the income tax, since the fear of voter reprisal at tax increases would be largely removed, inasmuch as the total payment individuals would be required to make would not be altered. Only the balance between federal taxes paid and those paid to state and local governments would change. Tax credits have the disadvantage that they "could have a troublesomely disruptive effect on Washington's budget process since federal receipts would become acutely sensitive to the varying revenue actions of states and localities. Some limitation on the extent of the tax-credit device is therefore probably a practical necessity."[41] Nor does the tax credit make any provision for special help to the lower-income states. It could, however, be used in combination with a tax-sharing program to achieve that objective.

Still another approach, and one which could be taken independently of any other action, would be to simplify the existing federal grant-in-aid system, first by combining narrow categories into broader categories, and secondly by standardizing allocation formulas and matching ratios into a logical and consistent pattern. Under such an approach, single grants to the states for public assistance, for medical care to the aged, for the construction and operation of elementary and secondary schools, for higher education, and for other public purposes might be made. Then the number of separate grant programs could be brought down markedly.

The possibilities of greater tax coordination should not be overlooked. "Tax coordination means the assignment of sources and/or the allocation of the revenues derived therefrom in such a manner as to accomplish an equitable distribution of the yield and

40. The instructions accompanying the 1969 federal income tax forms state that real estate taxes, state and local gasoline taxes, general sales taxes, state and local income taxes, and personal property taxes could all be deducted if a tax-payer chose to itemize his deductions.
41. *Morgan Guaranty Survey, op. cit.*

to eliminate competition, overlapping, and duplication." [42] It offers the possibility of "designing an efficient and equitable tax system which would place ample sources of tax revenue within the reach of all but the poorest state and local governments. . . ." [43] Although a good deal has been achieved along these lines over the past twenty-five years as the result of a great many studies and recommendations, [44] the possibilities are still great. "The major obstacle to development of . . . a [coordinated] system is tax competition among the states." [45] But the national government has been reluctant to yield any of its tax sources, so that it too presents a barrier to action.

Whatever the outcome, the very fact that so much attention has been paid to solving the problems of fiscal federalism indicates their seriousness. William G. Colman concludes that "it is apparent that some major surgery is needed on our traditional Federal-State-local allocation of fiscal resources." [46] The Advisory Commission on Intergovernmental Relations has recently devoted much of its staff time and a number of reports to how that might be accomplished. [47] Both the National League of Cities and the National Association of Counties have devoted considerable attention to the same end. [48] And the Committee for Economic Development directed a large part of its two reports on state and local government to fiscal matters. The difficulty is thus not

42. Graves, *American Intergovernmental Relations, op. cit.,* p. 451.
43. *The Brookings Bulletin,* Vol. 5, No. 3 (Winter 1967), p. 3, reviewing Break, *op. cit.,* in which the author pays particular attention to tax coordination.
44. See Graves, *American Intergovernmental Relations, op. cit.,* for a detailed description of those studies and recommendations.
45. *The Brookings Bulletin, op. cit.*
46. Colman, "Creative Federalism," *op. cit.* See also D. S. Wright, *Federal Grants-in-Aid: Perspectives and Alternatives* (Washington, 1968).
47. The complete report is available from the Commission. It is summarized by Will S. Myers, Jr., in "Fiscal Balance in the American Federal System," *State Government* 41: 57–64 (Winter 1968).
48. See National League of Cities, *National Municipal Policy* (Washington, 1966), Chapter 18, and National Association of Counties, *The American County Platform* (Washington, 1965), section 9. See also the report of the National Conference on Local Government Fiscal Policy, held in Washington, D.C., November 16–19, 1966, reprinted in *Congressional Record* 113: S2075–2078 (February 16, 1967), for a concise list of recommendations to improve the financial status of local units of government.

a lack of remedial courses of action. It lies instead in transmitting the urgency of the problem to the public and then converting their awareness into appropriate constitutional, legal, and administrative actions through the many action centers in the American federal system. That is truly a formidable undertaking, slow in the accomplishment. Probably the best that can be hoped for is a number of minor adjustments within the system, many of which are already beginning to be made at all three levels, and continuing effort to see the financial difficulties as a part of the whole problem of federal government. In the long run, the fiscal problem may prove insoluble, one of the prices we pay for a dual system of government. Its worst effects can be relieved, however, and it may be necessary to settle for that.

IX

AMERICAN FEDERALISM
IN THE FUTURE

WE HAVE SEEN that the old federalism of disparate programs, policies, and administrative procedures has given way to a new federalism which stresses intergovernmentalism and administrative devolution. Further changes can be expected in the years ahead, especially as understanding of the nature of federalism and of its utility as an instrument of social change is developed and extended among both public and private policymakers and the public at large.

The future of American federalism is hard to predict with precision. There are a great many variables in the American equation to be taken into account, there is an unfortunate lack of information to draw upon, and the experiences of other federations provide only the most limited help, so unique is each federal system. A number of generalizations can nevertheless be made.

The future of American federalism depends first of all on the satisfaction the American people feel about its performance now and in the past. Although there is no hard data on the subject, it appears that a majority of Americans approve of it. Federalism has been described in these pages as neither the product of a carefully articulated theory nor a system designed for efficiency. It has been presented as the peculiar product of a peculiar people, who would rather work within its limitations and imperfections than sacrifice it for theoretical purity and administrative precision. Americans appear to be proud of their federalism and to expect that it will be maintained. And it probably will be, for it grew out of peculiarly American experiences and beliefs, no other tribal or national identities compete with it for our loyalties, and no cultural, historical, or basic psychological barriers separate most Americans from one another. Moreover, federalism appeals to the pragmatism that is so characteristic of Americans, and it has the virtue of having been tested in the crucible of civil war. Finally, it will likely endure because lately there are so many agencies working for its improvement and success.[1]

It goes without saying too that the future of American federalism is part and parcel of the future of the nation as a whole. The federalism we know was conceived in a spirit of compromise, developed with no definite guidelines to follow, and matured in a rapidly changing world. It still bears its original restrictive cast, as well as the scars of the many conflicts through which it has passed. Its future form will likely be determined more by external factors than by its past and present composition. The future of federalism hinges to some extent on the attention and perception the President brings to bear on the problems of an intergovernmental system. As with all aspects of American government, federalism responds to leadership. But it does not respond to presidential leadership alone. It also responds to the actions and beliefs of governors and members of Congress, to Supreme Court decisions, and to the force exerted by pressure groups and political parties, as well as to demands from the public at large. Thus every election, many Supreme Court cases, and virtually every important national issue open up wide possibilities of change.

The future of federalism in the United States depends as well on how the four problems described earlier in this book are attacked, not to say solved. Improved public administration re-

1. Although primary attention has been given in these pages to the role of the Advisory Commission on Intergovernmental Relations, the contributions at least of the Council of State Governments, the National Municipal League, and the state Commissions on Interstate Cooperation should also be recognized. See, re the latter, F. L. Zimmermann and Richard H. Leach, "The Commissions on Interstate Cooperation," *State Government* 33: 233–242 (Autumn 1960).

mains a "major intergovernmental hurdle" to be surmounted as federalism is developed.[2] In addition,

The future of American federalism—and our capacity as a nation to manage effectively a wide range of complex public programs—depends in large measure upon the solution we devise to one paramount problem, the urgent need for more and better qualified personnel at all levels of government.[3]

State and local governments continue to encounter "great difficulty in maintaining an acceptable position within the total political system in relation to the management and control of new and emerging functions of government." [4] The problem of metropolitan government remains largely untouched; and though the fiscal imbalance which has become increasingly characteristic of American federalism is getting to be more widely recognized, no satisfactory solutions have been devised for it to date. How to accomodate working federalism to the facts of American party politics remains unclear, as does how to resolve the clash of private interests in the federal process.

And the future of federalism will depend on developments on the international scene. Until the crises in Vietnam and the Middle East are settled, and the danger of a major confrontation developing from or independently of those conflicts alleviated, the major budgetary and planning efforts of the national government will be directed toward those quarters. Basic to thoughtful consideration of major internal redirection is long-term peace.

Federalism's future is also closely connected with the racial situation in the United States. No one can fail to perceive the centrality of the racial crisis to every aspect of American life. It is obviously the nation's most serious domestic problem. Issues of federalism are woven into virtually every strand of that problem and cannot be avoided when solutions to racial issues begin to be

2. David B. Walker, an assistant director of the Advisory Commission on Intergovernmental Relations, quoted in *Public Administration News* 17:3 (August 1967).
3. Representative John Brademas of Indiana, *Public Administration Review* 29:332 (March/April 1969).
4. H. Clyde Reeves, "Role of State Governments In Our Intergovernmental System," *ibid.*, p. 267 (May/June 1968).

developed. Indeed, in the face of black claims that their manhood and dignity do not permit extension of administration of blacks by whites, pressure to establish Negro communities as autonomous institutions—to redraw the traditional units of federalism, in other words—is growing. W. H. Ferry, vice president of the Center for the Study of Democratic Institutions in Santa Barbara, California, recently argued the case for "a New Federalism" based on "a new kind of coexistence between blacktown and whitetown," in which blacks would have virtual independence in their own communities to run their own affairs. Such a scheme, Ferry is sure, would involve many "transfers of authority to blacktown," a great deal of financial assistance from the national government, and "constant negotiation between the two communities." As Ferry sees it,

the vision of coexistence is not that of a New Jerusalem, nor is it that of a national community struggling with the untenable doctrines of integration. It is a vision of a new federalism that will give 10 per cent of our citizens the chance they are seeking to make whatever they want to make of themselves, their culture, and their community.[5]

If these pressures are victorious, the implications for the federal system as we have known it and as it has been described in this book are far-reaching. The failure of federalism in Nigeria and more recently in Malaysia point to the long-term incompatibility between racial conflict and federalism.

Federalism in the years ahead will depend on what the needs of the American people are and to what degree governments must help in meeting them. Senator Muskie has listed some of those needs as he sees them:

The need for educational facilities for pre-schoolers, basic and adult education, junior colleges, and higher education; the need for employment and manpower programs, vocational education, and rehabilitation facilities; the need to eliminate substandard housing, to provide for low-income families, and to develop welfare services; integrated transportation systems; hospitals, health clinics, diagnostic centers, sanitariums, and nursing homes; emergency services, such as adequate police and fire protection, air and water pollution control

5. W. H. Ferry, "The Case for a New Federalism," *Saturday Review,* June 15, 1968, pp. 14–17.

and abatement programs; better streets and highways; and open space for recreation and parking facilities, beautification, and land for industrial development and commercial offices.[6]

The list could certainly be expanded. In each area of need, a different situation exists and a different combination of governmental forces will be necessary. The flexibility of federalism will be put to its severest test in the process.

Finally, federalism will develop in the future in response to basic changes in American society. It is of course not possible to present in outline form what may befall the nation in the years ahead, but certain trends are clearly indicated, and their impact on federalism can be accepted as probabilities.

1. The nation will continue to expand economically as the population increases and further developments in science and technology occur. Both greater abundance and better distribution of the amenities of life are to be expected.

—The role of the national government in providing optimum conditions for economic growth and development will continue to be important, but increased participation can be expected from state and local governments.

2. Urban growth and consequent urbanism will continue to be the basic pattern of American life. There is no indication at all of a return to the land, of a revival of our rural past.[7] Living in cities in comfort and safety is already difficult, however, and promises to become even more so as pressure for better housing, more satisfactory mass transit, better crime control, improved schools and recreational facilities, and sufficient clean air and water continues to build up with increased population.

—Increased national support of state and local efforts to achieve better urban conditions will continue to be necessary.

3. A series of social crises may be expected in the nation as the demands of the younger generation are presented to and resisted by the older generation.

—Though the national government has a part to play in clos-

6. Opening Statement of Senator Edmund S. Muskie at Hearings on S. 3509 and S.J. Res. 187, 89th Congress, 1st Session, November 16, 1966. Mimeo copy, p. 1.
7. See "How Your City Will Grow by 1975, As Estimated by U.S. Census Bureau," *Congressional Record* 115: E3776 (May 8, 1969).

ing the generation gap—the 91st Congress was deluged with suggestions and proposals for federal action to that end—state and local governments, but in this case particularly, the private sector, have the largest responsibility to bear.

4. The pollution of the natural environment may be expected to continue as uncontrolled technological development consumes an ever larger proportion of the country's capital of land, water, and other resources.

—Witnesses before a Congressional committee testified in the spring of 1969 that nothing less than "a major change in the political and social system in the United States could save the country from destroying its natural environment." [8] Such a change would inevitably involve a radical reconstruction of the federal system. In the process, national power to protect the environment would undoubtedly be increased.

5. Further international crises are inevitable as the powers in world politics seek to work out a *modus vivendi* with one another.

—The national government's pre-eminence in foreign affairs and defense is unquestioned, but there is considerable spillover to all other aspects of American life.

6. The nation's orientation toward and dependence on the products and processes of science and technology promise to be maintained and to increase.

—Governmental assistance to science will be required, and the need to bring the advantages of science to every American will require the involvement of every level of government. Of special importance to federalism is the possible impact of systems analysis and Planning-Program Budgeting System (PPBS) as it comes to be more widely used in the operations of government in the United States.

Under PPBS, programs will be "project oriented," and if the old political units or established administrative agencies are found irrelevant or obsolete, they will be discarded. . . . Solutions to large social problems will be evolved through careful cost-benefit analysis. Their solution will be pursued pragmatically through whatever combination of public and private interests seems appropriate. The old concerns about "jurisdiction," by agency or by level of govern-

8. *The New York Times*, April 28, 1969, p. 26.

ment, will give way to a much more urgent concern for coordination.[9]

As these few illustrations make clear, intergovernmentalism in American life will inevitably develop in reaction to what is going on in the world around it. Obviously, the interlevel exercise of governmental power in the United States can be expected to continue, if not increase. These illustrations also make clear, however, the possibility of a growing dominance of the national government in the most important areas of national life, a dominance to be avoided if federalism is to continue to mean a sharing of power and responsibility. "Rich uncle's handouts to the children rarely help to build a happy family," one observer has declared. "Can the increasingly direct role of Central Government in the community life and local governments of America expect any better result?" [10] As already noted, it was this concern which led to the whole series of efforts in the 1950's and 1960's to examine federalism and find ways to maintain some kind of balance of power among the units involved in American intergovernmentalism. For by now the conviction is widely shared that the successful functioning of the federal system requires joint effort and mutual forebearance. It will not work if any of the partners either fails to pull his weight or pushes his own interests too hard. The national government for its part has to resist the temptation to act the part of the rich and overbearing uncle, and the states and local governments must resist the equally strong temptation to accept their uncle's provender and become his willing sycophants. Federalism works most effectively when governments at all levels are willing to work together for the national good and to respect the others' roles and jurisdictional claims, while at the same time the stronger help the weaker to meet their responsibilities. Federalism works best when it is understood that the national government will not enter the provinces of the other units of government without their willing

9. *The Condition of American Federalism: An Historical View. A Study Submitted by the Subcommittee on Intergovernmental Relations to the Committee on Government Operations, United States Senate. October 15, 1966*, Committee Print, p. 16.

10. Robert Taft, Jr., quoted in *Congressional Record* 112: A2257 (April 26, 1966).

consent and that where the several units share an area of jurisdiction, they do so in close cooperation. Federalism functions only when the parties to it accept compromise as a working principle. The difficulty is that actions based on compromise become easy targets for people who choose to ignore the real nature of the problems involved and claim that a general agreement to solve them must mean an individual surrender, if not capitulation, of rights and privileges. In sum, it is now understood that federalism is akin to a partnership, all the partners giving fully of their strengths and talents to the enterprise, all of them continually alert to their own roles in the governing process and to the need regularly to assess their own practices to assure that they are performing at the maximum level of possibility and with the minimum amount of conflict, overlap, and duplication. As the Advisory Commission on Intergovernmental Relations concluded,

our pluralistic, pragmatic system of government and politics has great intrinsic worth. Its traditional traits—mutual forebearance, compromise, and moderation—now are viewed as more relevant than ever . . . [As] the Nation continues its search for a New Federalism —dedicated to balance; designed to correct structural, functional, and fiscal weaknesses; and rooted in a vital partnership of strong localities, strong States, and a strong National Government. Federalism, after all, seeks to enhance national unity while sustaining social and political diversity. The partnership approach is the only viable formula for applying this constitutional doctrine to late Twentieth Century America. Yet, this approach can succeed only if all the partners are powerful, resourceful, and responsive to the needs of the people. The alternative is a further pulverizing of State and local power, and the consequent strengthening of the forces of centralization.[11]

The problem is how to convert the on-going system to this ideal; as suggested earlier, very little attention has been devoted to its attainment.[12] The major power forces in the federal system have been too busy working in an *ad hoc* way to solve parts of the problem, or too convinced of one or another theory of federalism, or diverted too often by side issues and minor skirmishes, to pay attention to practical proposals for general amelioration

11. Advisory Commission on Intergovernmental Relations, *Tenth Annual Report* (Washington, 1969), p. 10.

12. See Carl W. Stenberg and David B. Walker, "Federalism and the Academic Community," *Political Science* 2:155–167 (Spring 1969).

and adjustment.

By the late fifties and early sixties, as we have seen, even the *ad hoc* utility of federalism seemed to be affected by basic dislocations, and a number of people became seriously interested in devising ways to revitalize and energize the federal system to equip it to meet the push of public problems in the sixties and seventies. For perhaps the first time in American history, a great deal of thought was given to the operation of federalism, and as a result a number of changes were introduced. Some of them have been described in the foregoing pages; other changes seem likely in the future.

But changes do not come easily. The resistance of vested interests, the counter pull of inertia, and hesitation to embark on a course of trial and error all work against their introduction, especially at the state and local levels. What Leonard Opperman (as a member of the Indiana Senate) had to say about Indiana is generally true in the other states and even more so at the local level:

> In Indiana, while reform is not impossible, it is difficult. The limited attention of state government is largely taken up by lobbyists representing important interests. Underpaid public servants are no match for their highly paid counterparts in regulated industries. Because of the constitutional limitations upon gubernatorial succession in Indiana, continuity and expertise do not exist together in state government, and the vested interests are generally satisfied with maintaining things as they are. But no less an important impediment to reform is public apathy. Hoosiers do not appear especially dissatisfied with the status quo. The inevitable grumbles that one reads in "letters to the editor" columns in newspapers are about the outer limits of public dissatisfaction. This is the reality that one sees from the perspective of a state capitol. . . . Against a background of this kind of reality what then are the chances that . . . our federal system [can be revitalized]? They are not very promising.[13]

If the impetus for revitalization has not come from the junior partners of the federal system, can it be expected from the recently recognized private partners in the system? Probably not. Although the Committee for Economic Development, composed of eminent members of the private sector, has produced viable master plans for modernizing state and local government, and al-

13. Opperman, "Aid for the States," *op. cit.*, p. 49.

though there is evidence of increasing awareness elsewhere in that sector, such as the Urban Coalition movement to seek action in the urban crisis, there are not many signs that the initiative is being taken there. Thus, by default, it has been and will continue to be chiefly to the national government that those hoping for changes in the federal system must look for leadership. And recent years have seen a good deal of innovative action taken there. A number of "new style" intergovernmental programs have been instituted recently. In 1956 Sir Kenneth Wheare saw as one of the possibilities for change in the federal system "the future reorganization of American government along lines of functional regionalism such as T.V.A., or interstate organizations sponsored and coordinated by agencies and departments of the national government," [14] and in the years since he wrote that, regionalism has indeed developed. The T.V.A. example has not been followed, but departmental regionalism has occurred in some areas. One of the best examples is the regional organization of the national attack currently being mounted against heart disease, stroke, and cancer. The Regional Medical Programs Act, enacted by Congress in 1965, provides federal funding of the campaign against those major diseases on a regional program basis, each program to be drafted by the regions themselves to suit their own needs and circumstances. The U.S. Public Health Service reviews and approves the regional plans submitted to it. Other examples of the regional device are the interstate regional commissions for economic development. The first such commission was the Appalachian Regional Development Commission, created in 1965. Since then, the Ozarks Regional Development Commission, the Coastal Plains Regional Commission, the Upper Great Lakes Commission, the New England Regional Commission, and the Four Corners Commission (Utah, New Mexico, Arizona, and Colorado) have all been established, though under a different legislative mandate. All of them are dedicated to the development and execution of plans for the stimulation of economic growth in the region under their jurisdiction. Operating with co-equal national and state chairmen and including state governors as members, the commis-

14. Wheare, *Federal Government, op. cit.*, pp. 211–212.

sions were not, as Wheare thought such bodies might be, set up as protégés of particular federal departments or agencies. They were created as independent bodies empowered to conduct research and establish blueprints and guidelines for regional economic development, in the execution of which local, state, national, and private efforts and funds will all be involved. In late 1967, President Johnson ordered the Secretary of Commerce to pull the activities of the several commissions together. "Under the new White House order, the commerce secretary is required to 'co-ordinate' all commission activities, to lay down policy guidelines, and take a hand in the critical matter of budget making. . . ." "The order seemed designed," reporter Carroll Kirkpatrick wrote, "to head off a potentially chaotic situation in which semi-autonomous commissions, backed by regional political blocs in Congress, would one day confront the [national government] with conflicting economic growth plans and with impossible demands on the federal treasury." [15] The presidential order also created a supervisory council composed of assistant secretaries from the federal departments and agencies associated with the commissions and the federal co-chairmen of each commission. It is too early to tell how this over-structure will work. Its operation may well prevent the commissions from developing into anything new. They nevertheless bear watching as possible portents of the future.

Besides such federally created and supported programs, a good many interstate regional programs have been developed in recent years. The interstate compact began to be utilized as early as 1921 to create joint bodies in such program areas as transportation, water-pollution control, education, and port development, and a variety of less formal methods of interstate cooperation have been developed as well. In New England and the Rocky Mountain states, a broad approach to groups of interrelated problems through regional action has been taken,[16] and more recently

15. *International Herald Tribune*, December 30, 1967, p. 3.
16. See the detailed study by Edward W. Webber, "Regional Cooperation: A Modus Vivendi for New England," *State Government* 38:186–190 (Summer 1965); see also Robert A. Shanley, ed., *Intergovernmental Challenges in New England* (Amherst, Mass.: Bureau of Government Research, Univ. of Massachusetts, 1965)

metropolitan regionalism has been recognized as a broader way of attacking the metropolitan area problem.[17] Aside from program operation, regional consultation and discussion have come to be the accepted norm all across the country. Governors regularly consult with one another on a regional basis,[18] as do an increasing number of other state and local officials, and recourse is quite normally had to regional conferences as matters of special concern arise. Indeed, regionalism must be recognized as a major new development in modern American federalism.[19] It is hard to disagree with the conclusion of a recent study that "the promise of regionalism for the future development of [the] nation appears bright. Our national tendencies toward sectional rivalry and competition may never be completely erased, but the dominant thrust of regionalism will be positive and bold. If the interstate compact and other vehicles of regional intergovernmental cooperation continue to increase in effective usage, then regionalism . . . as a political device will enhance its already significant contribution" to American society and government.[20]

Regionalism, like federalism, "has emerged upon the American intergovernmental scene without the advantage of a sound theoretical underpinning." [21] It can be approached from social, cultural, geographic, economic, and political points of view, and as yet there is no agreement as to what constitutes a region, except that all regions encompass more than one governmental unit. Nor has a clear distinction been made between regionalism and sec-

17. See "Regional Appraisal Stressed in Connecticut," *National Civic Review* 45: 212–213 (April 1966).

18. See Jay A. Sigler, "Governors Confer on Regional Basis," *National Civic Review* 45: 512–513 (October 1966).

19. It is not, however, a peculiarly American phenomenon, nor has its development been isolated to federal states. Parliament has begun to make use of regional boards in England (see G. H. Jones, B. C. Smith, and H. V. Wiseman, "Regionalism and Parliament," *The Political Quarterly* 38:403–410 (October–December 1967); and in Italy, regional bodies with a large measure of local autonomy have existed for some time in Sicily, Sardinia, and three northern border areas, and the Chamber of Deputies enacted a bill late in 1967 to create four additional regional governments by 1969.

20. Irving Howards and Edwin A. Gore, Jr., *Some Notes on Regionalism with Particular Reference to New England* (Amherst, Mass.: Bureau of Government Research, Univ. of Massachusetts, 1966), p. 7.

21. *Ibid.*, p. 2.

tionalism, though "in a general sense . . . regionalism . . . is associated with increased national unity and the idea that the region is a component part of the whole, contributing to its total integration," [22] while sectionalism is seen as tending toward disunity and the strength of the parts. Although the literature on regionalism is sparse, more and more attention to this and other aspects of developing federalism can be expected in the future. Very likely, however, regionalism will come into use as federalism itself did, without first being clearly defined or wholly understood.

Different from the regional commission approach is that described by the U.S. Bureau of Outdoor Recreation in its report under Public Law 89–616, in which the 89th Congress directed it "to study the feasibility and desirability of a Connecticut River National Recreation Area, in the States of Connecticut, Massachusetts, Vermont, and New Hampshire. . . ." In recommending the establishment of such an area, the bureau provided "a regional format upon which [work can be begun] to restore the Connecticut River to its original beauty. . . ." [23] The recreation area proposed would consist of three separate units, each multijurisdictional, each with individual characteristics, and each providing diverse recreation opportunities. In the operation of each unit, there would be roles for all three levels of government and for private interests as well. The National Park Service of the federal government would administer the entire area, and the federal government would help the states acquire the necessary land and develop it on a coordinated basis. Local units of government would be asked to develop the scenic possibilities of their river fronts and to participate in recreational planning, and private industry in the area would be urged to develop some of its holdings for recreation purposes. The study's entire action plan is based on intergovernmental and governmental and private cooperation. "It creates no Federal juggernaut to steamroller over the area," Senator Abraham Ribicoff of Connecticut assured the Senate. Instead, it takes "into account the legitimate interests of the towns and

22. *Ibid.,* p. 7.
23. *Congressional Record* 114:S10544 (September 11, 1968). The entire report is printed at pp. S10545–10563.

municipalities in the affected areas" and enlists "the people and all levels of government in a joint venture to preserve the Connecticut River." [24] It remains to be seen what action is taken on the Bureau's report.

A third innovation in operational federalism made by the national government is the Demonstration Cities Program enacted by Congress in 1966. It features the concentration of resources from all quarters on problems of urban blight and decay, the coordination of governmental and private talent and assistance in deploying those resources, and the mobilization of local leadership and initiative to assure that the citizens affected by the action planned take part in the decisions leading up to it.[25] The basic relationship in this program, nicknamed the Model Cities Program, is between the federal government's Department of Housing and Urban Development and city demonstration agencies. The states are not directly involved. To date, some 150 model city projects have been approved by the Department of Housing and Urban Development. Early in the Nixon Administration, acting upon recommendations from the Council for Urban Affairs, Secretary of the Department George Romney made a number of revisions in the program. Local governments were asked to establish clear priorities among proposals for action in an effort to get at the most urgent civic problems first rather than dissipate resources trying to attack all of them at once; greater efforts were made to involve state governments; and the regional offices for the program were shifted to the same cities as the offices for the Department of Housing and Urban Development, the Office of Economic Opportunity, and the Department of Health, Education and Welfare. (The latter two are the other federal agencies chiefly involved in the development of model city projects.) The Nixon Administration has pledged to support the model cities program, but at a reduced level of financial assistance, so that it will be some time before it can demonstrate its merits or demerits.

A fourth kind of approach is that provided in the Delaware

24. *Congressional Record* 115:S3172 (April 15, 1969).
25. The Declaration of Purpose of the Demonstration Cities and Metropolitan Development Act, Public Law 89-754, Title I.

River Basin Compact of 1961. Although the states of Delaware, New Jersey, New York, and Pennsylvania joined the Congress of the United States as parties to the compact, the federal government was the prime mover in the original development of the concept. The compact recognizes that "the water and related resources of the Delaware River Basin [are] regional assets vested with local, State, and National interests, for which they have a joint responsibility"; that only a comprehensive multipurpose plan, involving all those interests, will "produce the most efficient service in the public welfare"; and that those resources "are presently subject to the duplicating, overlapping, and uncoordinated administration of some forty-three State agencies, fourteen interstate agencies, and nineteen Federal agencies, which exercise a multiplicity of powers and duties resulting in a splintering of authority and responsibilities." To remedy the situation, the compact created the Delaware River Basin Commission, representative of all five parties to the compact, to develop and effectuate plans, policies, and projects relating to the basin's water resources. In particular, the Commission is to adopt and promote uniform and coordinated policies for water conservation, use, control, and management and in accord with those policies, to encourage planning, development, and financing of water resources. Like the other new approaches, the Commission has not been operative long enough to permit a final judgment to be made on its effectiveness.

These innovations indicate recognition not only of the essential adaptability of federalism, but also of the important leadership role the federal government has in bringing adaptations into practice. The national government, indeed, has done more than provide such leadership. In recent years it has endeavored to preserve room for state action and to involve the states in decisionmaking. Professor Wheare, commenting in 1956 on the Supreme Court's apparent willingness to let Congress have a free hand in determining the boundaries of possible national action, concluded that "the survival of the states depends apparently upon the self-restraint of the national government." [26] Wheare wrote before the New Frontier and the Great Society gave clear evidence that

26. Wheare, *Federal Government, op. cit.*

the essential role of the states in carrying out national programs and policies was understood and appreciated. In recognition of that role, for a good number of years now, the national government has directed much of its energies to enhancing the power of the states, less from reasons of self-restraint than from administrative necessity. For example, Congress recently enacted meat- and poultry-inspection bills (the Wholesome Meat Act of 1967 and the Wholesome Poultry Products Act of 1968) which provided in part for *state* inspection of some plants selling meat and poultry for intrastate distribution only, with federal aid to bring state inspection systems up to national standards. The most significant part of the two acts, their principal author, Senator Joseph Montoya of New Mexico, declared, is that they "provided a foundation on which the individual States could establish and develop their own inspection programs to control the shipment of unsafe meat and poultry within their borders." [27] The states were given two years to act (with a possible one-year extension if progress is being made) or lose their jurisdiction to federal inspectors. "Under this bill," the *Washington Post* commented editorially,

consumers will have full assurance of clean meat in the marketplace . . . The extra cost of these higher standards will be cheerfully borne by taxpayers and consumers in the interests of health and a wholesome food supply.

It is also important, however, that this vital protection of the consumer is to be achieved with a minimum disturbance of federal-state relations. Congress could undoubtedly sweep all meat inspection into the federal realm on the ground that a unified system is essential to the protection of interstate commerce in meat. But there has been no showing that such a drastic remedy is essential to produce the desired results. We think Congress has wisely given the laggard states a chance to put their own houses in order and offered to help them do so. In our view, every state ought to respond to this challenge out of self-respect and concern for preservation of its authority even if it remains unconcerned about the health of its people. Here is a chance for the states that have been inexcusably negligent to demonstrate that they are not yet ready to throw in the towel. [28]

Moreover, in the last few years, both the Johnson and the Nixon administrations have done a great deal to involve the states

27. *Congressional Record* 115:S9938 (August 13, 1969).
28. Quoted in *International Herald Tribune*, December 9–10, 1967, p. 4.

in federal project planning and development. Since the fall of 1966, regular contact has been maintained with state governors. On a number of occasions, meetings have been held with state legislative leaders as well, and more recently, with local government leaders and their staffs. These have been at both the presidential and departmental levels and have resulted from Congressional direction as well as from executive leadership. The National Highway Safety Act of 1966, for example, requires that the Secretary of Transportation cooperate with the states in devising and promulgating standards for driver and pedestrian performance, and the result has been joint decision-making. Looking back on such developments, Senator Muskie observed,

A few years ago we heard protests that the Federal government was intruding its powers into local affairs so that State rights were somehow being minimized. And most recently we heard that States were not being consulted on the new Great Society reform programs which were moving forward in cities and rural areas across the Nation. . . . More and more, we hear a new voice. . . . It is the voice of cooperation. It is the voice of concerned interest. It is a voice which recognizes the common responsibility and partnership of the States and the Federal Government in a series of human and community renewal projects . . . The fact is that . . . the States now share more in . . . decisions in Washington than ever before in the history of the American Federal-State structure.[29]

The national government has also begun to make adjustments in grant-in-aid programs. Congress enacted the Partnership in Health Act in 1966 in a pioneering effort to provide states some leeway in using federal funds for other than specifically earmarked health purposes. In addition, ways are currently being devised to simplify the process of grant-in-aid applications, to avoid the delays caused by late Congressional appropriations, and to set uniform standards and formulas for determining allowable administrative costs and other program-related expenses.

Thus the national government has emerged since the mid-nineteen-fifties as the chief developer of modern American federalism. In its concern to perform its own role more adequately, it has recognized the necessity of modernizing the federal system as a whole. This is not to say that some of the states and local units

29. *Congressional Record* 113:S10400 (July 26, 1967).

of government have not seen the same necessity, or have remained inactive. But the record makes it clear that far from seeking to consolidate American government into a single national container, the national government has been, and continues to be, increasingly concerned to maintain and develop governmental efficacy at all levels.

The concern of the national government about the health of the federal system is not matched in equal amount by an informed concern on the part of the American people. Americans continue to hold a stereotyped image of federalism and are far from having a clear understanding of its nature and operation, perhaps because until recently there has not been sufficient data to make such an understanding possible.

But data is available today that never has been available before, and the procedures and facilities for using it are steadily growing sharper and more sophisticated. The availability of political data was first realized right after World War II, and a great many studies of voting, political behavior, and elections were made. V. O. Key's work, some of which has been cited here, is an outstanding example of such studies. By the 1960's, data was being collected which could be used to study policymaking, and studies of power and of decision centers began to appear. Thus a pattern for the use of data already exists. The problem is how to develop and test hypotheses about federalism.

Early in this book it was stated that federal*ism* is a misnomer because federalism is not systematic. Is there not now data enough to show that federalism is a dysfunctional arrangement, in which each subsystem (the federal government and its several parts, the states and their many subdivisions, and the multipartite private sector), considered individually, may be functional, but when taken all together is not?

What does the data now available about changes in population and in style of living, in race relations and in economic patterns, in the amount and type of crime and the availability of education, portend for federalism? Take population. Is it possible that a complicated multidimensional government system will no longer work in a nation of 300,000,000 people, a vast majority of them young people, which is the predicted condition of the

United States within a decade or so of the year 2000? How does federalism respond to massive population increase, to population concentration in metropolitan areas, to the shift westward of the population center of the United States? A careful examination of data on population change might show us what alterations in the federal system may be necessary to meet the challenge of the future.

Or take mobility. Modern Americans are constantly on the move, en route from farm to city (from 6,812,000 farmers in 1935, the number had shrunk by 1965 to fewer than 3.3 million, and population experts predict that people will continue to leave farms for cities at the rate of about 300,000 a year into the indefinite future), from city to suburb (urban population growth since 1960 has been almost wholly in suburban areas rather than in crowded and often deteriorating central city areas), and from one suburb to another. Aided and abetted by rapidly improved transporation facilities, nationalization of the job market, and a continually expanding economy, about one in five Americans now changes his residence every year. Within the advent of the mobile home, more and more Americans have eschewed permanent settlement altogether and simply live on the road. No other people has developed quite such a penchant for motion. What are the effects of this life style on federalism and on its viability in the future? What can the data reveal that will help us adjust to the facts of modern life?

Certainly federalism, like most aspects of American life, has developed over the years in reaction to events and personalities, rather than as a well-conceived plan based on conclusions derived from knowledge. As a result, governments have usually been late in responding to changing circumstances; witness their failure to meet the obviously urgent needs of American cities. Is such retroactive policy development necessary? Will it do in an age when development seems to be taking place at a geometric rather than an arithmetic rate of increase? Could not the use of new data and data-processing techniques bring about an era in federalism in which problems are diagnosed early and broadly and adjustments made more quickly and generally, and consequently with less damage than in the past?

Improvement through reliance on useful data will not alone justify the continuation of federalism in the United States. Justification will probably come from a reaffirmation of the connection between federalism and freedom. From the first, federalism has been regarded as one of the chief bulwarks of freedom in this country. A happy result of the federal system is that it prevents a majority from fully exercising its power arbitrarily and thereby preserves for the individual the possibility of a greater degree of self-government. The very existence of a large number of units of government, and the exercise of power by them, Governor Rockefeller has said, "stands as one of the principal barriers to the creation of a monolithic national bureaucracy that would stifle local initiative and regional creativity and threaten liberty and opportunity." [30]

There is more to it than that. Peter Odegard points out that the "freedom which federalism was designed to conserve has come to mean not merely freedom from monolithic arbitrary power but also freedom to take affirmative action to provide for the common defense, promote the general welfare and preserve the blessings of liberty to everyone regardless of race or class or creed." [31] The question is not simply one of freedom achieved negatively through decentralization—it can probably be demonstrated that decentralization by itself is no absolute protection against the arbitrary use of power—but one of freedom achieved positively, through combining the power forces necessary to each instance. A case in point is the recently enacted Safe Streets and Crime Control Act. The decentralist would assure us that freedom to walk the streets safely and to be secure from the effects of riots is best achieved by letting each local unit of government handle the problem at its own discretion. The realist understands that *in this instance* a combination of federal funds and local action is required to secure the safety of persons and property and so to make freedom in city streets meaningful.

There is no doubt that, as Professor Odegard argues, a free society requires as much individual participation in the decision-

30. Rockefeller, *The Future of Federalism, op. cit.,* p. 37.
31. Peter H. Odegard, "Freedom and Federalism," in Karl M. Schmidt, ed., *American State and Local Government in Action, op. cit.,* p. 10.

making process as possible. But it does not require either that individuals participate identically or that one governmental decision-making process always be used. Procedures can be differentiated by subject-matter, by time, by changing circumstances and altered conditions; indeed, as Odegard concludes, the individual's freedom may actually expand as the alternatives among which he may realistically choose are multiplied.[32] In short, as Representative Joe L. Evins of Tennessee observed in his book, *Understanding Congress*,[33] "the principal purpose of the Founders of our nation was that of perpetuating the liberties and freedoms . . . they had won in their successful War of Independence. To put it another way, our forefathers were more interested in guaranteeing the preservation of individual liberty and freedom than in efficiency in government." It was their concern to "discourage concentration of power through a limited government of divided powers and responsibilities" and to provide "enough obstructions" between the people and their use of power to assure "reflective delay" and the "preservation of the freedom and liberty of the citizens themselves."

But the problem in federalism is still the uneven sharing of power. Some segments of the population are excluded from the use of power, particularly in small units within the larger system. Farm migrant workers, Negroes, and the urban poor have not been afforded the representation that would secure for them the protection the framers intended for all citizens. If federalism is to survive and continue to make a contribution to American life, it must find a way to overcome this fundamental flaw.

From time to time it has seemed as if a balance of power in the federal system had been struck, as if the best possible safeguards of individual freedom had been devised. But always the balance has shifted, and further shifts are inevitable. The debate about power and the quality of freedom within the federal system will very likely continue for a long time to come. It is proper that it should. For, as Professor Mason has observed, "Distrust of power at all levels, of whatever orientation, is still the

32. *Ibid.*, pp. 8–9.
33. Joe L. Evins, *Understanding Congress* (New York: Potter, 1963), pp. 286–287.

American watchword. Eternal vigilance is still the price of liberty
. . . Jefferson declared that 'the jealousy of the subordinate governments is a precious reliance.' " A century and a half later,
Louis D. Brandeis thanked "God for the limitations inherent in
our federal system . . . Conflict between federal and state authority means 'vibrations of power,' and this, Hamilton said, is the
'genius of our government.' " [34] As long as the federal system
helps make these vibrations possible, free government in the
United States is secure—and so is federalism itself.

34. A. T. Mason, "Must We Continue the States Rights Debate?"
Rutgers Law Review 18:75 (Fall 1963).

INDEX